Combating Money Laundering in Africa

To Trinah, Shamiso and Simbi, with love
Not forgetting: Sam and family

Combating Money Laundering in Africa

Dealing with the Problem of PEPs

John Hatchard

Emeritus Professor of Law, University of Buckingham, UK, Visiting Professor, UN International Anti-Corruption Academy, Vienna and Vice-President, Commonwealth Legal Education Association

Edward Elgar PUBLISHING

Cheltenham, UK • Northampton, MA, USA

Published by
Edward Elgar Publishing Limited
The Lypiatts
15 Lansdown Road
Cheltenham
Glos GL50 2JA
UK

Edward Elgar Publishing, Inc.
William Pratt House
9 Dewey Court
Northampton
Massachusetts 01060
USA

A catalogue record for this book
is available from the British Library

Library of Congress Control Number: 2020944206

This book is available electronically in the **Elgar**online
Law subject collection
http://dx.doi.org/10.4337/9781789905304

Printed on elemental chlorine free (ECF)
recycled paper containing 30% Post-Consumer Waste

ISBN 978 1 78990 529 8 (cased)
ISBN 978 1 78990 530 4 (eBook)

Printed and bound in the USA

Contents

About the author

Professor John Hatchard is a Barrister and Emeritus Professor at the University of Buckingham, UK. He is also a Visiting Professor at the UN International Anti-Corruption Academy in Vienna.

He has held senior academic positions at universities in the UK, United States, Zambia and Zimbabwe. He has also served as the Chief Mutual Legal Assistance Officer at the Commonwealth Secretariat. He was also a Senior Fellow at the British Institute of International and Comparative Law and the Director of the University of Detroit-Mercy London Law Program. For many years he was Secretary-General of the Commonwealth Legal Education Association (CLEA) and now serves as a CLEA Vice-President.

He has published well over 100 books and articles in the areas of corruption and money laundering, criminal law, criminal justice and evidence, constitutional law, good governance and human rights, with particular reference to the Commonwealth and Anglophone Africa. He has undertaken consultancy work for a wide range of international organisations, particularly in the field of good governance, combating corruption and money laundering and human rights.

He is the author of, amongst other books, *Combating Corruption: Legal Approaches to Supporting Good Governance and Integrity in Africa* (Edward Elgar, 2014) and a co-author of *Corruption and Misuse Public Office* (Oxford University Press, 1st edn. 2005, 2nd edn. 2011, 3rd edn. 2017).

john.hatchard@buckingham.ac.uk

Preface – hope for the future?

I have an abiding interest in money laundering. I hasten to add that this is purely for professional, personal and academic reasons.

My professional interest arose from my time when I served as Chief Mutual Legal Assistance Officer (CMLAO) at the Commonwealth Secretariat (ComSec) in London. This gave me my first introduction to the Financial Action Task Force (FATF), to its meetings at the OECD in Paris and to the Forty Recommendations which have shaped and continue to shape the global anti-money laundering response.

A recognition of the need to support Commonwealth members to develop their international co-operation capacity had already led Commonwealth Heads of Government to agree to two Commonwealth schemes to assist member states with model legislation designed to facilitate extradition and mutual legal assistance arrangement inter se. These are the London Scheme for Extradition within the Commonwealth and the Harare Scheme on Mutual Assistance in Criminal Matters. Recognising the need to assist them to comply with their anti-money laundering (AML) obligations set out in the FATF Recommendations, part of my role as CMLAO was to help draft a 'model' money laundering law (or AML law – we could never agree on the title) for Commonwealth members. This work provided me with some vital insights into the development of practical and effective AML legislative provisions. The model law proved useful, with many Commonwealth members using it as a basis for introducing their first anti-money laundering legislation. The Commonwealth continues to do fine work in supporting members in technical assistance in the area of international cooperation.

Having lived and worked in Zambia and Zimbabwe and written on African issues for so long, I have witnessed the appalling impact of the abuse of power, corruption and money laundering by many political leaders on members of my extended family as well as on the lives of millions of ordinary people. Yet I also recognise that there are so many committed public officials who seek every day to carry out their responsibilities honestly and honourably and I take pride that so many of my former students from the University of Zambia and University of Zimbabwe are continuing to do so. The need for effective action is the catalyst for this book. In essence it takes the position that what is needed is not despair but the development of effective strategies both domestically and transnationally to bring hope for a better and more prosperous future for the victims of the greed of political leaders.

In 2011, I was appointed to a Chair in Law at the University of Buckingham. This gave me the opportunity to develop a new LLM course entitled 'Money Laundering, Off-shore Banking and Asset recovery'. My students came from a diverse range of jurisdictions and fell into three categories. There were those from the 'victim' states for whom the laundering of the proceeds of corruption by political leaders was a fact of life. For them, understanding how to combat money laundering was a priority. Several others came from off-shore jurisdictions such as the British Virgin Islands and the Cayman Islands whose economies have flourished thanks to the strong and vibrant financial sector facilitated by the secrecy that is maintained over bank accounts, companies and trusts. Their approach was very different: 'We are doing very nicely thank you very much and have no wish to alter the present arrangements.' The UK students often took the view that money laundering was not a local but a developing world problem. It was not until they realised that the UK is a money laundering centre as well as a 'safe-haven' state in which corrupt political leaders (amongst others) make use of the financial institutions for laundering purposes, as well as to use their proceeds of crime to purchase real estate and the like, that they understood the reality. I was able to emphasise this a few years later thanks to the words of President of Nigeria, Muhammadu Buhari. At a reception prior to a major international conference on corruption in London in 2016, the then UK Prime Minister, David Cameron, was overheard describing Nigeria as 'very corrupt'. At the Anti-Corruption conference the following day, I was sitting in the front row of the audience when President Buhari gave his keynote address. He was then asked about the Cameron comment. His response was simple: 'Give us back our money'.

In writing this book, I have encountered a few problems concerning terminology. Do I refer to 'states', 'countries' or 'jurisdictions'? The United Nations Convention against Corruption (UNCAC) and the African Union Convention on Preventing and Combating Corruption (AU Convention) both refer to 'State Parties' and 'states' whilst the FATF refers to 'countries'. Some of the most significant off-shore centres linked with facilitating money laundering such as the British Overseas Territories are neither but rank as separate 'jurisdictions', for example, for the purposes of international cooperation arrangements. I have therefore used the most appropriate term throughout the book.

A similar problem has arisen concerning references to private sector entities. Once again these are referred to using a range of terms. In the UNCAC the term 'legal persons' is adopted but without a definition. Article 1 of the AU Convention refers to the 'Private sector' as meaning the 'sector of a national economy under private ownership ... and other sectors of the economy not under the public sector or the government'. The FATF Recommendations use the term 'legal persons' to include 'companies, bodies corporate, foundations, anstalt, partnerships or associations and other relatively similar entities'. Given this choice, I have felt it safe to use whichever is the most useful term in the particular context.

I am well aware that seeking to adopt a pan-African approach to the subject is very ambitious. I make no apology for this. Money laundering by political leaders is a continent-wide problem and requires a continent-wide response. The FATF Recommendations provide the basis for doing so. Of course, it is not possible (or indeed necessary) to explore the position in every African country and whilst I have included a range of examples of good and bad practice, I realise that there are some I have overlooked. Hopefully, the book will also provide a catalyst for developing new and effective means of sharing good practice and experiences for all those dedicated to combating the money laundering evil.

I have sought to state the position as at 30 March 2020. Events move quickly in this area and I have endeavoured to include new developments that command inclusion, the Airbus affair and the impact from the publication of the Luanda Papers being just two prime examples.

As ever, my deepest love and thanks to my wife Trinah and to my children Shamiso and Simbi for all their support, assistance and patience.

Professor John Hatchard
Buckingham Law School
30 March 2020

Abbreviations

ADB	Asian Development Bank
African RB	African FATF-style regional body
AML	anti-money laundering
APRM	African Peer Review Mechanism
AU	African Union
AU Convention	African Union Convention on Preventing and Combating Corruption
BPI	Bribe Payers Index
CDD	customer due diligence
COE	Council of Europe
CoSP	Conference of States Parties
CSOs	civil society organisations
DNFBPs	designated non-financial businesses and professions
DoJ	Department of Justice (US)
DPA	deferred prosecution agreement
DPP	Director of Public Prosecutions
ECHR	European Court of Human Rights
ECOSOC	Economic and Social Council (UN)
ECOWAS	Economic Community of West African States
EDD	enhanced due diligence
EFCC	Economic and Financial Crimes Commission (Nigeria)
ESAAMLG	Eastern and Southern African Anti-Money Laundering Group
FATF	Financial Action Task Force
FCPA	Foreign Corrupt Practices Act (USA)
FIA	Financial Intelligence Authority
FIU	financial intelligence units
FOI	freedom of information

GIABA	Intergovernmental Action Group Against Money Laundering in West Africa
GRECO	Group of States against Corruption
ICC	International Chamber of Commerce
ICIJ	International Consortium of Investigative Journalists
IFFs	illicit financial flows
IGG	Inspector General of Government (Uganda)
JIT	Joint Investigation Team
KYC	know your customer
LPP	legal professional privilege
MENAFATF	Middle East and North Africa Financial Action Task Force
MLA	mutual legal assistance
MOU	Memorandum of Understanding
NCBAF	non-conviction based asset forfeiture
NGO	non-governmental organisation
OECD	Organisation for Economic Co-operation and Development
PEPs	politically exposed persons
PMLs	professional money launderers
PSC	Public Service Commission
SADC	Southern Africa Development Community
STRs	suspicious transaction reports
TCSPs	trust and company service providers
UNCAC	United Nations Convention Against Corruption
UWO	unexplained wealth order

Table of cases

Table of constitutions, legislation, conventions and related documents

CONSTITUTIONS AND LEGISLATION

Mauritania

Mauritius

Mozambique

Namibia

Nigeria

Rwanda

Vanuatu

Zambia

Zimbabwe

CONVENTIONS

OTHER DOCUMENTS

PART I

Setting the scene

1. Money laundering challenges in the African context: constitutions, law, politics and economics

1.1 THE PROBLEM OF PEPs

1.1.1 The Cashgate Case

Between 2009 and 2014 in Malawi, a number of government ministers and senior public officials manipulated the government payment control system, known as the Integrated Financial Management Information System (IFMIS). As a result, they were able to draw a series of fraudulent Government of Malawi cheques, the proceeds from which were either laundered through the purchase of real estate, expensive vehicles and other property in Malawi or paid in favour of numerous private contractors on the pretext that they had supplied goods and services to the government. In reality, none had been supplied. The transactions were then deleted from the IFMIS. Some US$365 million was stolen and laundered.[1] This became known as the Cashgate scandal.

The case is not an isolated one but neatly illustrates the manner in which huge sums of money can be looted from state coffers or acquired through other abuse of office and then laundered by politically exposed persons (PEPs).[2] These are individuals who are or have been entrusted domestically with prominent public functions, family members and close associates.[3] The term also includes members of ruling royal families.[4]

---

[1] Figure provided by Victor Chiwala of the Malawi Anti-Corruption Bureau in a presentation to the Global Expert Group Meeting on Corruption involving Vast Quantities of Assets, 2018.

[2] For a detailed account of such activity see Tom Burgess, *The Looting Machine*, William Collins, 2015.

[3] See FATF 2012 Recommendations, General Glossary. For a full discussion see Section 2.4 below.

[4] GIABA, *Corruption – Money laundering nexus: An analysis of risks and control measures in West Africa*, 2010 [54].

As the Financial Action Task Force (FATF) has explained 'PEPs pose a high risk of money laundering by the very nature of their position'.[5] This inevitably involves 'grand corruption' i.e. 'acts committed at a high level of government that distort policies or the central functioning of the state, enabling leaders to benefit at the expense of the public good'.[6]

Yet addressing the challenge effectively remains problematic and, as the Conference of States Parties (CoSP) to the UN Convention Against Corruption (UNCAC) has noted 'with regret' there is 'the risk that persons accused of crimes of corruption may escape justice and thus elude the consequences of their actions and may successfully hide their assets'.[7]

Combating the laundering of their proceeds of crime by PEPs demands a recognition that PEPs are a special case in that they are the most powerful political entities in any society with unique access to state assets and influence over state institutions. They are also in a position to control the anti-money laundering (AML) controls, for example by undermining the development and/or effectiveness of anti-corruption and anti-money laundering laws and institutions.[8] In addition they have the power to undermine key constitutional AML safeguards by constitutional means, for example, through their power to appoint and remove heads of key AML institutions.[9]

1.1.2 PEPs 'Don't Do It Alone'

So-called 'syndicate corruption' can exacerbate the problem. Here a number of PEPs in positions of authority in various government institutions or ministries conspire to circumvent anti-corruption and AML control mechanisms:[10] as in the Cashgate case. A further example comes from the East African Community (EAC) case in Uganda. Here PEPs located in the Ministry of the Public Service, the Office of the Administrator General, the Ministry of Finance and the Bank of Uganda combined to have billions of shillings paid as pensions and gratuities to 'ghost pensioners' and deceased pensioners of the defunct

---

5 FATF, *Laundering the Proceeds of Corruption*, Paris, 2011 [12].

6 Transparency International, 'How do you define corruption?' https://www.transparency.org/what-is-corruption#define (accessed 6 June 2020).

7 Resolution 7/2 'Preventing and combating corruption in all its forms more effectively, including, among others, when it involves vast quantities of assets, based on a comprehensive and multidisciplinary approach, in accordance with the United Nations Convention against Corruption', 2017, Preamble.

8 See Section 2.5 below.

9 See Section 8.7 below.

10 Inspectorate of Government (Uganda), *Bi Annual Report to Parliament, January–June 2017*, pp. xi and 13.

East African Community and Uganda protectorate. The PEPs then used the bank accounts of family members through which to launder the stolen funds.[11]

The syndicate may also include powerful individuals and families in the private sector through so-called 'state capture'. Thus in South Africa an allegedly corrupt relationship between PEPs, including the former President, Jacob Zuma and the Gupta family and their companies, led to state resources allegedly being diverted and laundered.[12]

The use of companies to assist in the laundering is also well established. Here PEPs use private companies they control to tender for government contracts without declaring their interest. Their power and influence over the process then facilitate the awarding of the contract to their company and the subsequent laundering of those assets, often to off-shore companies established for that purpose.[13]

1.1.3 PEPs 'Can't Do It Alone'

PEPs are often assisted by powerful individuals and institutions. For example, local as well as international financial institutions may facilitate the laundering of the dirty money. In the EAC case for example, the PEPs were assisted by senior managers at the Cairo Bank (U) Ltd, who facilitated the laundering of billions of Uganda shillings through opening fictitious bank accounts and filling in forged cash withdrawal slips purportedly signed by hundreds of 'pensioners' and then collected by a single individual posing as their agent. Professional money launderers, including lawyers and accountants may also facilitate the laundering.[14]

As regards the corporate sector, powerful multi-national corporate entities pay bribes (or are forced to pay bribes) to PEPs in order to obtain or retain business and are then often complicit in facilitating the laundering of the proceeds of corruption.[15]

---

[11] *Uganda v Lwamafa*, 2018, unreported. Available at https://ulii.org/ug/judgment/hc-anti-corruption-division-uganda/2018/11 (accessed 6 June 2020).

[12] See Ivor Chipkin and Mark Swilling, *Shadow State: The Politics of State Capture*, Wits University Press, 2018. See also the case of *Minister of Finance v Oakbay Investments (Pty) Ltd and Others* [2017] All SA 150 (GP) discussed at Section 5.4.3 below.

[13] See further the discussion in Chapter 12.

[14] A point noted in the Lima Statement on Corruption involving Vast Quantities of Assets (December 2018). See further the discussion in Section 2.6.1 below.

[15] See the Thiam case discussed in Section 2.1 below and generally Chapter 13.

1.2 THE ART OF PERSUASION AND THE THREE PRONG STRATEGY FOR COMBATING MONEY LAUNDERING BY PEPs IN AFRICAN STATES

Combating money laundering by PEPs is a major on-going challenge facing all African states. This is why it is entirely appropriate to explore AML issues and strategies as they relate to all African states. Given their diversity it is not realistic to expect a uniformity of constitutions or any change in the fundamental principles of their national legal systems. Rather the aim must be to ensure that there is 'functional equivalence' at the national level. Thus states must 'to the extent possible, develop and harmonise their policies and domestic legislation' to combat money laundering[16] 'according to their particular circumstances and constitutional frameworks'.[17]

This book therefore provides a critical analysis of the mechanisms and strategies required to combat the laundering of the proceeds of corruption by African PEPs and their operation in practice. Its aim is to provide ideas and strategies designed both to fight money laundering by PEPs and to facilitate the recovery of their proceeds of corruption.

Combating money laundering by PEPs requires a three prong approach i.e. effective action at the national, transnational and corporate levels.

1.2.1 National Level

Given the unique political, economic and financial power of those involved, combating money laundering by PEPs is not simply a matter of having in place constitutional safeguards and AML laws and institutions. These must be sufficiently 'persuasive' in order to make PEPs, financial institutions and other potential facilitators of money laundering comply with their AML obligations *whether they want to or not*. This means that all African states must adopt a multi-track approach as follows:

1. *To ensure that their constitutions (as the supreme law) and constitutional bodies fulfil their key AML roles and are robust enough to withstand efforts by PEPs to undermine them.*[18]

---

16 See Article 7(1) of the SADC Protocol Against Corruption.

17 Introduction to the FATF 2012 Recommendations.

18 See Section 6.2 below.

This requires persuading PEPs to uphold constitutional values and to exercise their powers appropriately to ensure that the Constitution performs its role as an effective AML instrument.[19]

2. *To have in place the necessary AML laws and institutions in line with their international obligations.*

This requires 'persuading' all states to have in place appropriate AML laws as well as introducing and maintaining effective AML institutions. Some AML obligations are found in the UN Convention Against Transnational Organised Crime; the UNCAC and the African Union (AU) Convention on Preventing and Combating Corruption.[20] However, through the work of the Financial Action Task Force and the African FATF-style regional bodies, all African states are part of the 'FATF family' and are subject to the AML requirements that are set out in the FATF Recommendations.[21]

3. *To ensure that all FATF AML requirements are complied with in practice.*

There is a need for effective mechanisms both to monitor the introduction and implementation of such laws and institutions and to hold individual states to account for non-compliance with their AML obligations. Whilst several international conventions contain useful monitoring provisions, the review process of the FATF and FATF-style African regional bodies provide a powerful and on-going persuasive function, including threats that a state which fails to comply will face serious adverse economic consequences.[22]

4. *To recognise that civil society organisations (CSOs) play a vital role in overseeing the operation of the AML safeguards.*

In particular, this includes what might be termed 'Constitution-watching'. CSOs have a key role in overseeing and protecting the operation of constitutional AML provisions and highlighting any attempt by PEPs to undermine them. 'Constitution-watching' is thus a potentially constructive and meaningful approach to preventing money laundering by PEPs.

---

19 This point is explored throughout the book.

20 See the discussion in Chapter 3.

21 See Chapter 4.

22 For example, the imposition of economic 'sanctions': see FATF Recommendation 19: see further Section 4.4 below.

1.2.2 Transnational Action

Given the transnational nature of money laundering by PEPs, national AML efforts require the active support and co-operation of other states.[23] The need to create the global political will to do so is essential through persuading all states to implement the appropriate legal, regulatory and operational AML measures.[24]

1.2.3 Corporate Action

Given the involvement of private sector entities in paying bribes to PEPs and assisting in laundering the proceeds of crime, effective mechanisms to persuade even the most powerful entities to commit to good corporate governance is essential.[25] These persuasive techniques consist of:

1. Gentle persuasion:

Here such entities are 'persuaded' to introduce effective codes of ethics that are designed to prevent both the payment of bribes to PEPs or involvement in laundering the proceeds of crime as well as a compliance regime designed to oversee its implementation.[26]

2. Forceful persuasion:

Here the bribe-paying company or the off-shore company used to launder the PEP's proceeds of crime is liable to criminal sanctions, whether in its 'home' jurisdiction or in the African victim state.[27]

3. Persuasive threats:

Debarment or the threat of debarment is a powerful economic weapon to 'persuade' the bribe-paying company to reveal all about its criminality. Debarment is the mechanism whereby a private legal entity or individual is prevented from tendering for, or participating in, projects funded, for example, by the African Development Bank, due to their involvement in corrupt practices. It is the fear

---

[23] See Section 8.5 below.

[24] This is the role of the FATF and the FATF-style regional bodies and is discussed throughout the book.

[25] See Chapter 13.

[26] See Section 13.5.2 below.

[27] Their 'home' jurisdiction may be the place where they are registered or where they have a corporate presence. See Sections 13.3.1 and 13.3.2 below.

Table 1.1 Framework for effective AML strategies against PEPs

NATIONAL LEVEL	TRANSNATIONAL LEVEL	CORPORATE LEVEL
AML CONSTITUTIONAL PROVISIONS AND BODIES	INTERNATIONAL CO-OPERATION MECHANISMS	CODES OF CONDUCT AND COMPLIANCE MECHANISMS
AML AND ASSET RECOVERY LAWS AND REGULATIONS	INTER-AML AGENCY CO-OPERATION	PROSECUTION OF BRIBE-PAYING COMPANIES
AML BODIES - FINANCIAL INTELLIGENCE UNITS - AML REGULATORS - ANTI-CORRUPTION AGENCIES	ASSET RECOVERY MECHANISMS	DEBARMENT AND THE THREAT OF DEBARMENT

of economic loss that motivates private sector entities not only to avoid bribe payments to PEPs but also to 'reveal all' to prosecutors.[28]

1.2.4 Persuasive AML Techniques

Persuasive techniques are therefore essential tools in developing the political will on the part of PEPs to combat money laundering and to exert economic and political pressure to deter both the bribe-payers and facilitators. It is the combination of effective constitutional AML provisions and laws coupled with the development of the political will and significant economic threats that offer the best prospect of combating money laundering by PEPs. The various strategies for achieving these AML goals are set out in Table 1.1.

1.3 RATIONALE FOR THE BOOK

In my book *Combating Corruption: Legal Approaches to Supporting Good Governance and Integrity in Africa*,[29] I argued the need for 'persuasive' techniques designed to develop the necessary political will on the part of PEPs to maintain good governance laws and institutions and combat corruption. The book therefore explored, for example, the key anti-corruption strategies for maintaining integrity in both the public service and the private sector and the challenges of investigating corruption-related offences.

This book is essentially a companion work taking as its focus the challenging issue of combating money laundering by PEPs. As the Report of the High

28 See Section 13.3.3 below.

29 Edward Elgar, 2014.

Level Panel on Illicit Financial Flows from Africa puts it: 'the nature of actors, the cross border character of the phenomenon and the effects of illicit financial flows on the state and society attest to the political importance of the topic'.[30]

In doing so, the book provides fresh insights into a number of vital issues:

- The relationship between constitutional rights and the AML requirements placed on countries by the FATF
- The potential role of national constitutions as AML instruments
- The strategies for challenging the power of PEPs to undermine constitutional AML safeguards
- The effectiveness of the FATF-style African regional bodies
- The effectiveness of financial intelligence units in African states
- The potential for developing a pan-African AML initiative
- The possibilities for introducing new AML techniques in African states.

There is considerable literature on money laundering particularly thanks to the numerous reports published by the FATF.[31] The disclosures from the Panama Papers and the Luanda Papers coupled with the outstanding work of the International Consortium of Investigative Journalists (ICIJ) have focused the spotlight as never before on the way in which PEPs make use of facilitating states in order to conceal their beneficial ownership of companies and trusts. Similarly, there is considerable literature on 'safe haven' states. For example, the studies by Transparency International and Global Witness on the use of off-shore companies owned by PEPs to purchase real estate in London.[32]

What is much less well documented is the challenge of dealing with money laundering by PEPs in the African context in practice and this demands its own specific study.[33] Somewhat surprisingly, there is also little literature or indeed discussion on the relationship between national constitutions and AML laws and institutions. This book seeks to address these deficiencies.

The book is largely the result of library research supplemented by discussions with a wide range of practitioners both in and from numerous African states. Much of the discussion is based on the work of FATF and the African FATF-style regional bodies. In those parts of the book dealing with preven-

---

[30] Report of the High Level Panel on Illicit Financial Flows from Africa *Illicit Financial Flows*, 2015, p. 65.

[31] The topic also enjoys its own journal, i.e. the *Journal of Money Laundering Law*.

[32] See Section 12.4 below.

[33] A recent book edited by Inge Amundsen, *Political Corruption in Africa: Extraction and Power Preservation*, Edward Elgar, 2019, provides a useful series of studies on the corruption and money laundering exploits of PEPs in several African countries. What it fails to do is provide any in-depth analysis of *how* to address these problems.

tive national strategies, a comparative constitutional analysis is appropriate, particularly between Anglophone African states. This is facilitated by the fact that virtually all have constitutions based on the Westminster export model.[34]

Numerous case studies are included in order to highlight both the challenges and possible strategies for addressing money laundering. Critical studies on the operation of key constitutional safeguards are also included with the important supportive case law being considered.[35]

This is an exciting time to be writing on this topic with significant developments taking place, both nationally and internationally, designed to address money laundering by PEPs and to facilitate asset recovery. The following chapters will assess their impact in practice.

1.4 ARRANGEMENT OF THE BOOK

The book is divided into four parts.

Part I 'Setting the Scene' focuses on the challenges of addressing the problem of money laundering by PEPs.

Part II then explores the international and Africa-specific strategies designed to combat money laundering. Chapter 3 reviews the AML provisions in the UNCAC, the AU Convention on Preventing and Combating Corruption and other international and regional AML-related instruments. Chapter 4 then explores the role of the FATF and the African FATF-style regional bodies and critically reviews the implementation of the FATF Recommendations in African states with particular reference to PEPs. This includes an analysis of the impact and effectiveness of the monitoring provisions of the FATF.

Part III considers strategies for developing and maintaining effective AML strategies in African states. Chapter 5 considers the role and effectiveness of financial intelligence units in detecting money laundering and that of financial regulators and supervisors in overseeing compliance with AML obligations by financial and non-financial businesses and professions as laid down in the FATF Recommendations. Chapter 6 considers the role of constitutions and constitutional institutions in the fight against money laundering by PEPs. Chapter 7 focuses on the role and effectiveness of the Auditor General in preventing money laundering through overseeing transparency and accountability in public finances. Chapter 8 considers the constitutional protections enjoyed by PEPs and their impact on the investigative powers of law enforcement authorities, with particular reference to the requirements laid down in the

---

[34] See Section 6.2 below.

[35] See the case study of the Office of the Auditor General in Chapter 7 and the discussion on the use and abuse of the presidential power of pardon in Chapter 11.

FATF Recommendations. Chapters 9 and 10 consider the constitutional rights of PEPs in relation to prosecution and asset recovery. Finally, Chapter 11 explores the use and abuse of the constitutional power of pardon especially when exercised in relation to PEPs.

Part IV then considers transnational AML initiatives in support of African states. Chapter 12 explores recent international developments on transparency in the beneficial ownership of companies whilst Chapter 13 assesses the developing mechanisms designed to persuade companies to 'reveal all' concerning their payment of bribes to PEPs to obtain or retain business and their assistance in laundering the proceeds of corruption. Chapter 14 examines the potential role of the African Court in combating money laundering by PEPs. Chapter 15 then provides an overview together with some final thoughts on further strengthening AML strategies in relation to African PEPs.

2. PEPs and the money laundering process in the African context

2.1 MAHMOUD THIAM: A CASE STUDY[1]

Between 2009 and 2010 Mahmoud Thiam was the Minister of Mines and Geology in Guinea. He was therefore a PEP. He was primarily responsible for negotiating directly with a Chinese conglomerate named CIF over the award of an important mining contract.[2] In 2008 a military government had seized power in Guinea and in a bid to attract foreign investors it was prepared to offer lucrative mining concessions. Thiam's position as Minister of Mines provided him with the power and influence to tout the benefits of such a deal with CIF. As the chief government negotiator, he oversaw the signing of a 'Shareholder's Agreement' with the conglomerate, which was given the right to be the 'first and strategic shareholder' in a national mining company. The effect of the deal was that CIF would possess practically all of Guinea's mining sector and the whole agreement was highly disadvantageous to the Republic of Guinea.[3]

Shortly before the signing of the Shareholder's Agreement, the Chief Executive Officer of CIF, one Sam Pa, transferred US$3 million into a Hong Kong bank account in Thiam's name which Thiam had opened the day before. A further $US5.5 million was later transferred to the same account via three executives of CIF. In order to conceal his status as a public official from the bank, Thiam listed his nationality as 'France', his job title as 'Consultant' and his monthly income as '200,000 or above'. Thiam then set about laundering some of the proceeds from his Hong Kong bank by making wire transfers to

---

1 The facts are drawn from *United States of America v Mahmoud Thiam* Government Sentencing Memorandum 4 August 2017, 17 Cr. 47 (DLC) https://globalinvestigationsreview.com/digital_assets/9d2c7d48-bf22-40bf-9573-a1cbb816cf0d/US-v-Thiam.pdf (accessed 6 June 2020).

2 It was also alleged that one of the companies was partially owned by a company based in Angola, ibid, p. 4.

3 The joint venture was via a private company, African Development Corporation Pte Ltd, incorporated in Singapore. CIF owned a total of 85% of the company with the Republic of Guinea owning the remaining 15%.

companies incorporated in Malaysia and Mozambique with the latter being used to purchase the Dutchess County Estate in New York for US$3.75 million. This enabled him to conceal the fact that he and his wife were the beneficial owners of the property. Some of the bribe proceeds were then used to make 'high-end renovations to the Dutchess County Estate'[4] as well as providing tuition for his childen at two private preparatory schools in Manhatten,[5] a ski vacation and skiing lessons and the purchase of a Steinway grand piano.[6]

Thiam also made large transfers from his Hong Kong bank account into a New York bank. He lied to the bank's compliance officer as to the source of the Hong Kong funds stating that they were derived from business transactions. This did not seem to satisfy the officer and shortly afterwards the account was closed. However, four days later, Thiam opened a new account at another New York bank. Again he concealed his status as a PEP claiming to be the chairman of a private company. He also failed to declare his income to the United States Inland Revenue Service.

The Thiam case neatly illustrates many of the issues and challenges in addressing money laundering by PEPs and these are discussed in this chapter. Section 2.2 reviews the money laundering process in the African context whilst Section 2.3 considers the impact of corruption and money laundering on national development. Section 2.4 considers who constitute PEPs whilst Section 2.5 explores their unique power to 'control the AML controls'.

Section 2.6 considers the 'you can't do it alone' principle and the issue of the facilitators i.e. those who assist PEPs in the laundering process whilst Section 2.7 considers the role of 'facilitating states' and 'safe haven states'. Whilst PEPs enjoy unique opportunities for corruption and money laundering, they also face unique vulnerabilities and these are considered in Section 2.8. The lessons from the Thiam case are then reviewed in Section 2.9.

2.2 HOW IS IT DONE? MONEY LAUNDERING IN THE AFRICAN CONTEXT

The FATF describes money laundering as 'the processing of criminal proceeds to disguise their illegal origin. This process is of critical importance, as it enables the criminal to enjoy these profits without jeopardising their source.'[7]

---

4 Costing approximately US$250,000.

5 Costing approximately US$88,767.

6 Costing approximately US$46,375. It was also reported that he had transferred some US$560,000 to a foreign minister of another (unnamed) West African state.

7 FATF, 'What is money laundering'. Available at www.fatf-gafi.org/faq/moneylaundering/ (accessed 4 June 2020).

A money laundering scheme is thus designed to 'take the raw proceeds of crime held by the offender, manoeuvre them through a process that will conceal their source and confuse or break the money trail, and then return them to the offender legitimised and ready for further safe use'.[8]

FATF Recommendation 3 requires countries to criminalise money laundering on the basis of the United Nations Convention Against Transnational Organised Crime (hereafter the Palermo Convention)[9] and the Vienna Convention.[10] Countries are required to apply the crime of money laundering to all serious offences with a view to including the widest range of predicate offences.[11]

Whilst the process may comprise a single act,[12] money laundering is often a highly sophisticated and complex transnational actitivity, especially when PEPs are involved. As the Thiam case demonstrates, this frequently involves a three-stage process: placement, layering and integration, and indeed this is now an established trend involving PEPs in African states.

Placement involves moving the proceeds from direct association with the crime. This is described in Article 6(1)(a)(i) of the Palermo Convention as follows:

> The conversion or transfer of property, knowing that such property is the proceeds of crime, for the purpose of concealing or disguising the illicit origin of the property; or helping any person who is involved in the commission of the predicate offence to evade the legal consequences of his or her action.

Here the 'Illicit money is disguised or misrepresented, then placed into circulation through financial institutions, casinos, shops, and other businesses, both domestically and transnationally. A variety of methods can be used for this purpose, including currency smuggling, bank transactions, currency exchanges, securities purchases and blending illicit with licit funds.'[13] Financial institutions and micro saving schemes remain particularly vulnerable[14] whilst

---

[8] National Crime Authority, *Taken to the Cleaners: Money Laundering in Australia*, Canberra, 1991, vol 1, at vii.

[9] See Section 3.1 below.

[10] I.e. the UN Convention Against Illicit Trade in Narcotic Drugs and Psychotropic Substances.

[11] Article 2(h) of the Palermo Convention defines 'predicate offences' as 'any offence as a result of which proceeds have been generated that may become the subject of an offence as defined in article 6 of this Convention'. Article 6 is discussed below.

[12] For example, see the *Katengeza* case, Section 8.1 below.

[13] US Department of State, *International Narcotics Control Strategy Report*, 2018, vol II, Introduction p. 11 (the US DoS report).

[14] Intergovernmental Action Group Against Money Laundering in West Africa (GIABA), *Money laundering relating to fraud in public procurement in West Africa: A case study of Nigeria*, 2014, at [47].

electronic money laundering or 'cyberlaundering' through the use of virtual currencies and mobile money[15] is now becoming increasingly prevalent.[16]

The placement is undertaken by either the PEP him/herself, by or with the assistance of family members or close associates, or via a professional money launderer(s). As the Thiam case highlights, representatives of the bribe-paying companies may themselves be involved in the placement stage.

The object of layering is to disguise the money laundering trail in order to foil pursuit. Article 6(1)(a)(ii) of the Palermo Convention describes this as:

> The concealment or disguise of the true nature, source, location, disposition, movement or ownership of or rights with respect to property, knowing that such property is the proceeds of crime.

Methods include converting cash into monetary instruments and wire transferring money between bank accounts.[17] Professional money launderers are especially active at this stage,[18] for example, by establishing off-shore companies in facilitating states (see below) through which to launder the proceeds of crime.

Article 6(1)(b)(i) of the Palermo Convention describes the integration stage as: 'The acquisition, possession or use of property, knowing at the time of receipt, that property is the proceeds of crime.' This is the final stage of the process in which 'the laundered money is introduced into the economy through methods that make it appear to be normal business activity'.[19]

In the African context in particular, the laundering of the proceeds of corruption by PEPs takes a number of different forms. An Eastern and Southern Africa Anti-Money Laundering Group (ESAAMLG) report notes that common methods for laundering are:

> through corporate vehicles (including shell companies), the use of off-shore jurisdictions, banks and other depository instruments and through the use of associates or nominees. These proceeds are used to finance and support lavish and expensive

---

15 For a helpful discussion on mobile money see James Whisker and Mark Lokanan, Anti-money laundering and counter-terrorist threats posed by mobile money, (2019) 22(1) *JMLC* 158–72.

16 See Section 8.2.2. See also A Irwin, J Slay, J Choo and L Lui, Money laundering and terrorist financing in virtual environments: A feasibility study, (2014) 17(1) *JMLC* 50–77.

17 US DoS report, 11.

18 These are defined as 'individuals, organisations and networks that are involved in third-party laundering for a commission or a fee': see Section 2.6.1 below.

19 US DoS report, 11.

> lifestyles. It is for this reason that most monies are invested in real estate by purchasing expensive properties and also for the purchase of expensive cars.[20]

In West Africa, PEPs reportedly launder their proceeds of crime either domestically or transnationally through financial institutions, microfinance, designated non-financial businesses and professions,[21] cross-border cash movements and the purchase of real estate.[22] There is particular concern over the real estate sector, which is subject to inadequate supervision coupled with the fact that many real estate purchases are made in cash.[23]

The mutual evaluation reports on African countries provides a full picture of the process and this is discussed in Section 4.6 below.

2.3 PEPs, CORRUPTION, MONEY LAUNDERING AND THE IMPACT ON NATIONAL DEVELOPMENT

2.3.1 Making the Link

The link between PEPs, corruption and money laundering is well established. The FATF has recognised that a significant amount of the proceeds of crime is generated from corruption offences,[24] whilst in the Preamble to the UNCAC, State Parties highlight the concern over this link and note that the 'illicit acquisition of personal wealth can be particularly damaging to democratic institutions, national economies and the rule of law'. Numerous African countries have reported that corruption remains a (or *the*) major predicate offence

---

20 ESAAMLG Report, *Procurement Corruption in the Public Sector and Associated Money Laundering in the ESAAMLG Region* (the ESAAMLG Procurement report), 2019, p. 8. Chapter 3 of the report provides a detailed analysis of the government procurement process and its vulnerabilities.

21 Defined by the FATF as (a) Casinos; (b) Real estate agents; (c) Dealers in precious metals and dealers in precious stones; (d) Lawyers, notaries, other independent legal professionals and accountants; (e) Trust and company service providers: See FATF Recommendation 22 and Section 4.2.2 below.

22 See for example, the country reports made to GIABA by Benin at [21], Burkino Faso at [27], Cape Verde at [34], Cote d'Ivoire [at 44], Ghana at [60], Liberia at [84], Mali at [95] and Sierra Leone at [132]: GIABA, *Annual Report 2017* (the GIABA report).

23 Businesses that are cash-intensive require enhanced CDD measures: IN to FATF Recommendation 10.

24 FATF, *Best Practices Paper: The Use of the FATF Recommendations to Combat Corruption*, Paris, 2013, at [82] (FATF Best Practices paper), at [1].

to money laundering.[25] This is highlighted in a 2019 report of the ESAAMLG, which demonstrates the strong link between PEPs, procurement corruption and money laundering.[26]

2.3.2 Corruption, Money Laundering and the Impact on Development

The laundering of the proceeds of corruption by PEPs inevitably leads to the lack of national development and acute economic hardship for the vast majority of the population. A particular area of vulnerability is the energy and related sectors. As the Inter-Governmental Action Group Against Money Laundering in West Africa (GIABA) has noted, 'For many African countries, the extraction and production of minerals constitutes significant parts of their economies, accounting for a high share of gross domestic product or total exports'.[27] Africa is home to about 30 per cent of the world's mineral reserves, 10 per cent of the world's oil, and 8 per cent of the world's natural gas[28] and the World Bank has emphasised, 'with good governance and transparent management, the revenues from extractive industries can have a transformational impact on reducing poverty and boosting shared prosperity, while respecting community needs and the environment'.[29] Yet the sector is highly vulnerable to the involvement of PEPs in corruption and money laundering activities and the impact is highlighted in the Thiam Sentencing Memorandum:

> While Guinea possesses vast natural resource wealth, including billions of dollars worth of bauxite, iron ore, gold and diamonds, about 60% of Guineans live below the poverty line, the average Guinean citizen lives on less than two dollars per day, and only about 7% of the Guinean population has access to plumbing and electricity.[30]

This point is emphasised in a report by Revenue Transparency Watch, which emphasises that the wealth from natural resources is often not translated into

---

25 See for example, the GIABA report, where corruption was identified as a major predicate offence by every one of the 18 member states.

26 ESAAMLG Procurement report 2019, pp. 33–6. See also Global Forum on Transparency and Exchange of Information for Tax Purposes *Tax Transparency in Africa 2020* (Addis Ababa, 2020).

27 GIABA, *Money Laundering and Terrorist Financing Linked to the Extractive Industry/Mining Sector in West Africa*, 2019 (the GIABA mining report).

28 See www.worldbank.org/en/topic/extractiveindustries/overview#1 (accessed 5 June 2020).

29 According to the World Bank, non-renewable mineral resources play a dominant role in 81 countries, which collectively account for a quarter of world GDP, half of the world's population, and nearly 70% of those in extreme poverty.

30 See note 1 above.

social and economic development in many of the resource-rich states due to the bribery of foreign PEPs by transnational corporations and assistance in the laundering of the proceeds of crime.[31]

The negative effect of laundering by PEPs is also highlighted in Malawi where the Cashgate case led to the withdrawal of donor aid by Norway, amongst others, and the witholding of a credit facility by the International Monetary Fund. This led to a government fiscal deficit worsening in one month from MK15 billion to MK40.4 billion[32] and the country being forced to adopt a 'zero aid' budget.[33]

It is surely no coincidence that the GIABA has highlighted the link between the political will to support and strengthen AML systems in some West African states, notably Benin, Cape Verde, Cote d'Ivoire, Ghana, Guinea Bissau and Sao Tome and Principe and their record of good governance and political stability.[34] Conversely an ESAAMLG report has noted that procurement corruption and money laundering is exacerbated by the lack of good governance standards and values.[35]

2.4 WHO ARE PEPs?

Corruption is found at all levels of public life. However, 'grand corruption' and 'syndicate corruption' are the preserve of PEPs.[36] These are 'individuals who are, or have been, entrusted with prominent public functions'.[37] Examples include Heads of State/government, senior politicians, senior government, judicial or military officials and important political party officials,[38] and members of a ruling royal family. In practice the term is open-ended and much

---

[31] Revenue Watch Institute/Transparency International, *Promoting Revenue Transparency: 2011 Report on Oil and Gas Companies*, 2011, 5.

[32] *R v Karonga*, [2018] MWHC 1 at 15.

[33] Noted in *R v Sengeza*, 2013, unreported, Malawi High Court.

[34] See GIABA report at [23], [38], [47], [64], [77] and [121] respectively.

[35] ESAAMLG Procurement report, above pp. 33–6.

[36] See generally: StAR Initiative, *Politically Exposed Persons: Preventive Measures for the Banking Sector*, Washington DC, 2012. Amundsen refers to this as 'political corruption': see Inge Amundsen, Extractive and power-preserving political corruption, in I Amundsen (ed.) *Political Corruption in Africa*, Edward Elgar, 2019, pp. 6–7.

[37] See FATF 2012 Recommendations, General Glossary. The UNCAC itself does not use the phrase 'politically exposed person' but this is widely used in other international fora and is meant to have the same meaning as the term 'persons with prominent public functions': FATF, *Guidance: Politically Exposed Persons*, Paris, 2013, at [1] (hereafter FATF PEPs paper).

[38] This definition is not intended to cover middle ranking or more junior individuals in these categories.

depends upon the size of the state, its structure (unitary, federal etc.) and the powers and responsibilities of the office-holder. The FATF Recommendations exclude middle ranking or more junior categories from the definition of a PEP, although such individuals may be used by PEPs to assist in money laundering activities.[39]

The term also applies to family members of PEPs and close associates. The former are individuals who are related to a PEP 'either directly (consanguinity) or through marriage or similar (civil) forms of partnership'.[40] Who constitutes a 'family member' depends upon the circumstances but given the nature of the extended family in many African societies, such individuals may be difficult to identify. A further problem can arise in smaller African countries. For example, during the mutual evaluation exercise in Cape Verde, the GIABA assessment team were told that 'all citizens and residents are related to each [other], thus it is almost impossible to have a Cabo Verdean national [who] is not considered a PEP, in the light of the FATF and the AML Act [Law 61/VIII/2014 and Law 62/VIII/2014] definition'.[41] This may well make AML investigations more difficult given that such cohesive networks often bring with them a strong degree of trust.[42]

'Close associates' are individuals who are closely connected to a PEP, either socially or professionally.[43] Their potential importance in assisting in money laundering is highlighted in South Africa where the Financial Intelligence Centre Act 2001 (as amended) refers to Prominent Influential Persons (PIPs) instead of PEPs, a term that is designed at the domestic level to include private sector officials who have business dealings with public sector officials and elected officials in the public services.[44] This is particularly relevant to the notion of state capture as highlighted in the Gupta case in South Africa.[45]

Being designated a PEP does not, in itself, carry any negative connotation and thus 'should not be so construed as to discourage or prohibit financial

---

[39] FATF PEPs paper, at [37].

[40] FATF PEPs paper, at [11].

[41] See GIABA, *Anti-money laundering and counter-terrorist financing measures – Cabo Verde, Second Round Mutual Evaluation Report*, 2019, at [224].

[42] See generally, G Bruinsma and W Bernasco, Criminal groups and transnational illegal markets, [2004] *Crime, Law and Social Change* 79–94.

[43] FATF PEPs paper, at [11]. Persons who are or have been entrusted with a prominent function by an international organisation are also included in the FATF definition. These are 'members of senior management i.e. directors, deputy directors and members of the board or equivalent functions'.

[44] See Schedule 3A.

[45] See Section 1.1.2 above.

institutions from doing business with any legitimate customer'.[46] However, financial institutions must adopt a 'risk-based' approach in every case.[47] As Unterhalter J rightly pointed out in *Kassel v Thomson Reuters (Markets) S.A.*: 'It is the office that gives rise to the risk because of the influence that attaches to it'[48] and thus the higher ranking the person's position, power or authority is, the higher the risks of this person being involved in money laundering crimes. Doing business with PEPs therefore requires, amongst other things, enhanced due diligence.[49]

Whether a person ceases to be a PEP upon leaving office is unclear. Whilst their opportunities for corruption and money laundering are often diminished, maintaining a check on the legitimacy of their source of wealth and that of their family is arguably necessary to ensure that there is no abuse of any remaining influence they may enjoy. Whilst this may require a 'once a PEP always a PEP' approach, as the FATF helpfully suggests, the handling of such a person should be 'based on an assessment of risk and not on prescribed time limits'.[50]

In practice, problems in identifying PEPs in African states abound. In some countries there is no enforceable obligation on financial institutions to identify PEPs whilst in others financial institutions fail to update information as to whether a customer is a PEP.[51] Further the task of actually identifying a customer as a PEP is often difficult given that in a single country the list can run into hundreds of individuals and never remain static as a result of promotions, elections, removal from office or marriage.[52] As the Thiam case highlights, a PEP may also deliberately provide insufficient, misleading and/or false information or details to the financial institution or seek to conceal their beneficial ownership of property.

---

[46] See UNCAC Article 52. See further United Nations, *Legislative Guide for the Implementation of the United Nations Convention Against Corruption*, 2nd revised edition, 2012, Vienna at [678].

[47] FATF Recommendation 1 and Interpretive Note.

[48] 2019 (1) SA 251 (GJ) [16].

[49] See Section 4.3 below.

[50] FATF PEPs paper, at [44].

[51] See Middle East and North Africa Financial Action Task Force report (MENAFATF), *Money Laundering and Terrorist Financing Trends and Indicators in the Middle East and North Africa Region – Update*, 2013, at [3.3].

[52] See the MENAFATF report *Politically Exposed Persons in Relation to AML/ CFT*, 2008, p. 5 and MENAFATF, *Typologies Report on Money Laundering and Corruption*, 2017, p. 32.

2.5 PEPs AND THE FUNDAMENTAL CONTROLS OVER MONEY LAUNDERING

The FATF has noted that due to their position and influence, many PEPs 'are in positions that can be abused for the purposes of committing money laundering offences and related predicate offences, including corruption and bribery'.[53] It means that combating money laundering by PEPs is a unique challenge for they possess the ability to 'control the AML controls'. These controls are considered in this section.

1. *Control over the Constitution*

The national constitution is the supreme law. Its fundamental role is to support just and honest government and articulate 'the values binding its people and disciplining its government'.[54] Given that 'corruption and maladministration are inconsistent with those values'[55] it plays a potentially key role in combating corruption and money laundering by PEPs.

However, as constitutional office-holders and/or holders of other senior government, military and political party positions, PEPs are in a unique position to 'control the constitutional controls', for example power over appointments to AML bodies. Thus undermining the Constitution by constitutional means becomes a key mechanism for facilitating corruption and money laundering by PEPs and as a result the document itself becomes an obstacle to effective investigation and prosecution of money laundering in African states.[56]

2. *Control over the economy*

PEPs inevitably enjoy considerable power over the national economy and access to government funds. As the Cashgate case highlights,[57] where this power is abused, corruption and money laundering may well result. Control over government procurement provides another opportunity for such criminality.[58] Indeed according to the findings of a 2019 ESAAMLG study, the evi-

---

[53] FATF PEPs paper, at [1].

[54] Per Mohammed JA in *S v Acheson* 1991 (2) SA 805 (Nm) at 813 A-B. See also the comments of the Supreme Court of Ghana in *Taffour v Attorney General* (1980) GLR 637 at 647–8 and the views of Aguda JA in *Unity Dow v Attorney General* [1992] LRC Const 623 at 668.

[55] Chaskalson, P in *South African Association of Personal Injury Lawyers v Heath* [2000] ZACC 22; 2001 (1) BCLR 77 at [4] (Constitutional Court of South Africa).

[56] See Chapter 6.

[57] See Section 1.1 above.

[58] For a useful diagram on corruption leakages in the public sector see International Monetary Fund *Fiscal Monitoring: Curbing Corruption*, 2019, Figure 2.3.

dence presented by member states indicated that corruption existed at all stages of the procurement process.[59] In the Thiam case, for example, as Minister of Mines he had the power to influence the award of lucrative government mining contracts to the Chinese conglomerate. This was facilitated by the lack of a strong procurement review mechanism.

3. *Control over financial institutions*

PEPs may use their power and influence to gain control over domestic banks and other financial institutions. For example, Carter asserts that doubts arose about the integrity of the Gabonese and French International Bank (BGFI), which was allegedly used by PEPs in Congo-Brazzaville, the Democratic Republic of Congo (DRC) and Gabon through which to launder huge sums of money.[60] Similarly, in Uganda, PEPs were able to launder billions of shillings from the EAC pensions scam through the Cairo Bank (U) Ltd thanks to the connivance of senior bank officials.[61]

As the Abacha case also vividly demonstrates (see below), control over the Central Bank of Nigeria provided almost unlimited opportunities for the theft of state assets and their global laundering. Again, in Kenya the Report of the Judicial Commission of Enquiry into the Goldenberg Affair alleged that the Governor of the Central Bank of Kenya had permitted the fraudulent movement out of the country by PEPs of KShs3.5 billion.[62]

4. *Control over the AML legislative and regulatory framework*

Combating money laundering requires a state to have in place an effective legal and regulatory framework designed to combat money laundering and facilitate asset recovery. Political control over the law-making process can ensure that the necessary AML legislation and/or regulations is delayed or that 'strategic deficiencies' will reduce the effectiveness of the AML regime.[63]

5. *Control over domestic investigations into corruption and money laundering*

---

59 See also the GIABA mining report, at [72].

60 Brett L Carter, The rise of kleptocracy: autocrats versus activists in Africa, (2018) 29(1) *Journal of Democracy* 54, at 63–4.

61 See *Uganda v Lwamafa*, 2018, unreported, High Court of Uganda. See also *Uganda v Byandala*, 2018, unreported, High Court of Uganda.

62 But see the judgment on the findings of the Commission by Nyamu J in the High Court of Kenya in *Kotut v Bosire* [2008] eKLR. See further John Hatchard, *Combating Corruption: Legal Approaches to Supporting Good Governance and Integrity in Africa*, Edward Elgar, 2014, pp. 224–7.

63 See further Section 4.5.

PEPs enjoy unique influence and control over the criminal justice system. They can ensure that corruption and money laundering-related investigations and/or prosecutions do not proceed, at least without their approval. For example, in Equatorial Guinea and despite his well chronicled money laundering from corrupt activities, Teodorin Obiang the son of the President has never faced any criminal charges in his home country. In addition, control over the appointment and removal of the Attorney General and other senior prosecutors, and the creation of separate investigative/prosecutorial agencies which have little interaction and co-operation *inter se* can also undermine investigations and prosecutions. This is often exacerbated by PEPs having control over the resources allocated to such agencies.[64]

6. *Control over national security*

Issues of national security are invariably the responsibility of the Head of State/government supported by security, intelligence and military chiefs. The secrecy inevitably surrounding it provides PEPs with unique opportunities for both looting state assets and facilitating their laundering abroad. This is epitomised by the case of Sani Abacha, who usurped power in Nigeria in 1993 following a military coup and until his death in 1998 reportedly looted over US$2 billion directly from the Central Bank of Nigeria. As Nicholls explains:

> This was done by issuing demands for funds to meet completely spurious 'national security' needs. Letters from Abacha's national security adviser, countersigned by Abacha and then presented to the Central Bank were about all that was required.[65]

Much of this money was then laundered through the City of London and went to bank accounts in Switzerland, Luxembourg and Liechtenstein. Indeed the Abacha family later admitted to receiving US$750 million in cash, which was paid into Nigerian bank accounts and then laundered through European bank accounts controlled by them. Remarkably, they then contended that the funds were being held for 'State and security purposes'.[66] A similar 'national security' excuse was used by former President Frederick Chiluba to loot millions of

---

[64] See Sections 5.6.4 and 8.7 below.

[65] Colin Nicholls et al., *Corruption and Misuse of Public Office*, 2nd edn., Oxford University Press 2011, at [8.122].

[66] See *Abacha v The Secretary of State for the Home Department* [2001] EWHC Admin 787 [1].

pounds from Zambia and launder them through the so-called Zamtrop account held in a London bank.[67]

7. *Control over international co-operation mechanisms*

The ability of PEPs to control or prevent investigations by other states into their corruption/money laundering activities is limited. Even so, the decision whether or not to provide assistance requested by foreign investigators seeking information or evidence in a money laundering case is ultimately a political one and a refusal to co-operate may seriously jeopardise those investigations.[68]

2.6 WHO ASSISTS PEPs? THE FACILITATORS

Whatever their political power, PEPs cannot undertake money laundering alone. As the Commission for Africa has put it:

> It is not only the politicians and public officials who create the problem: it is also the corporations, [the] bankers, the lawyers and the accountants, and the engineers working on public contracts.[69]

2.6.1 Professional Money Launderers

Professional money launderers (PMLs) are 'individuals, organisations and networks that are involved in third-party laundering for a commission or a fee'.[70] They are key facilitators, for without their assistance PEPs would find it extremely difficult to complete the laundering process. For example, Mwale J in *Katengeza* noted that the PEPs in the Cashgate case would have been unable to carry out their scheme without the active assistance of participants outside of government: in this particular instance the provision by Mrs Katengeza of business registration licences and bank accounts through which PEPs were able to launder the proceeds of crime.[71]

---

67 The money laundering scheme is set out in detail in *Attorney-General for Zambia v Meer, Care and Desai* [2007] EWHC 952.

68 For example, mutual legal assistance requests from the UK to Nigeria in connection with the investigation into money laundering by James Ibori, a former Governor of Delta State, were allegedly blocked during the presidency of Umaru Yar'Adua. It was only following the swearing in of a new President, Goodluck Jonathan, that effective cooperation was resumed: see John Hatchard, *Combating Corruption*, above, pp. 31 and 271.

69 Commission for Africa, *Our Common Interest*, 2005, p. 150.

70 FATF *Professional Money Laundering*, Paris, 2018, p. 6.

71 See Section 8.1 below.

The Panama Papers and Luanda Papers revelations also highlight how PMLs such as accountants, bankers and legal professionals assist PEPs, particularly through the use of the off-shore world. Along with other trust and company service providers (TCSPs), they register shell and shelf companies and trusts in off-shore jurisdictions which are designed to enable PEPs to conceal their beneficial ownership.[72] Such entities can then be used to purchase real estate and other valuable assets in 'safe haven' or 'beneficiary' states.[73]

The case of Bhadresh Gohil is a classic example of the involvement of lawyers in facilitating money laundering. Gohil was a solicitor and a partner in a London firm of solicitors. From 2005 the firm acted for James Ibori who was the Governor of the Delta State in Nigeria between 1999–2007, during which time he allegedly defrauded the state of some US$89 million.[74] Gohil provided a client account through which Ibori laundered large sums of money via off-shore companies, accounts and trust funds. As the firm's money laundering reporting officer, Gohil was able to ensure that no AML safeguards were implemented. He was later convicted of a series of money laundering offences and in 2011 was sentenced by a court in London to a total of ten years' imprisonment.[75]

The Luanda Papers provide another stark illustration of the point. These concern the activities of Isabel dos Santos, the daughter of the former President of Angola and her husband. Here a leaked database of some 715,000 documents allegedly reveal that European and American management consultants, accountants and lawyers assisted Dos Santos and her husband to move huge sums of public money from Angola through global financial institutions and into off-shore bank jurisdictions via 400 companies and subsidiaries in 41 countries including 94 in Malta, Mauritius and Hong Kong.[76]

2.6.2 Financial Institutions

Almost inevitably, at some stage in the laundering process the proceeds of corruption will pass through financial institutions. A startling feature of the

---

[72] It must be emphasised that establishing a company or trust in an off-shore jurisdiction is perfectly legitimate and a common business practice: it is the intended use of that vehicle for money laundering purposes that raises the problem.

[73] See 'Vulnerabilities of Professional Intermediaries' in FATF/Egmont Group, *Concealment of Beneficial Ownership*, Paris, 2018, pp. 46 et seq.

[74] In 2012 at the Southwark Crown Court, London, he pleaded to 10 counts of fraud and money laundering and was sentenced to a total of 13 years' imprisonment.

[75] The facts appear in *R v Gohil* [2018] EWCA Crim 140.

[76] Details are found on the ICIJ website: www.icij.org/investigations/luanda-leaks/read-the-luanda-leaks-documents/ (accessed 3 June 2020).

Thiam case was his ability to open and utilise bank accounts with several major international banks through which to launder his proceeds of corruption. He did so by constantly lying to bank officials as to the source of the funds. The history is instructive.

- Hong Kong bank (not identified): When opening the account, Thiam claimed to be a 'consultant' with an income of US$200,000 per month. Whether his claim was checked is not apparent. He concealed his status as a PEP by producing a French passport. The fact that millions of US dollars were transferred to his account in a short space of time seemingly did not raise any suspicions of money laundering on the part of the bank.
- JPMorgan Chase Bank (USA): Thiam transferred funds from his Hong Kong account to an account in his name in the United States. He falsely claimed that the funds were from business transactions with a close associate named Baker Al-Sadi.[77] He made no mention of his status as a PEP. Thiam was interviewed by the bank's compliance officer where again he gave a false account of the source of the funds. The bank then closed the account.
- HSBC Bank (USA): When Thiam opened a new account at this bank he falsely told a bank employee that he was employed by a natural resources company. By an extraordinary chance, his status as the Guinean Minister of Mines came to light when an HSBC Bank employee happened to see Thiam being interviewed on television. At a subsequent interview with the bank, he admitted his status as a PEP but this time he falsely claimed that the funds were from savings and proceeds of land sales in Africa.

No efforts were seemingly made by any of the banks to carry out an effective check as to the veracity of Thiam's statements, especially when, in the case of HSBC, it became known that he was a PEP and his various explanations must have raised suspicions as to their truthfulness. Further, none of the banks seemingly made a suspicious transaction report to their national financial intelligence unit as required by AML regulations.[78]

This certainly suggests that the banks were more interested in Thiam's custom than the source of his funds. As a result, key AML safeguards were undermined. There is no record of any criminal or administrative action being taken against the banks or the bankers involved.

---

[77] Who told Thiam that this was a viable arrangement but who added 'Let's hope they don't dig too deep'. See note 1 above at [7].

[78] The United States FIU is the Financial Crimes Enforcement Network (FinCEN). In Hong Kong it is the Joint Financial Intelligence Unit. For a discussion on FIUs see Chapter 5.

2.6.3 Corporate Bribe-payers and Facilitators

Corporate entities may be involved in both bribe-paying as well as in assisting PEPs in laundering their proceeds of corruption. Here the role of the CIF consortium in the Thiam case is instructive. Having obtained the lucrative mining contract through bribery, the Chief Executive Officer of CIF, Sam Pa, transferred US$3 million into Thiam's newly opened bank account in Hong Kong with a further US$5.5 million later being transferred by three other high-ranking CIF officials. There is no record of any action being taken against any of them, whether in Guinea, Hong Kong, China or the United States.

2.7 WHERE IS IT DONE?

Whilst the laundering of at least some of the proceeds of corruption may take place domestically, PEPs often choose to launder their proceeds transnationally through facilitating states and into safe haven states.

2.7.1 Facilitating States[79]

Obscuring the money trail for PEPs often involves PMLs establishing companies, trusts and bank accounts located in a variety of off-shore jurisdictions. These are the 'facilitating states' which offer the secrecy and anonymity which PEPs demand in order to further their money laundering schemes. In exchange facilitating states enjoy significant economic benefits. This has long resulted in a lack of the political will to address the need for transparency in the off-shore sector.

In Thiam's case, for example, his purchase of the Dutchess County Estate in New York[80] was undertaken by wiring the proceeds of corruption to a company in Malaysia in exchange for a wire transfer for the same amount from a different company registered in Mozambique to the United States. As the Department of Justice (DoJ) Sentencing Memorandum puts it: 'This complex set of transactions, which served no legitimate purpose, was intended to conceal Thiam's use of the bribe proceeds to purchase the Dutchess County Estate.'[81]

---

[79] In this context, 'states' also includes jurisdictions such as the British Overseas Territories and Crown Dependencies: see the discussion at Section 12.5.1.

[80] The Sentencing Memorandum states the amount as US$350,000 but a later DOJ Press Release states that the correct figure was $US3.75 million.

[81] Ibid, at p. 12.

2.7.2 Beneficiary/Safe Haven States

A safe haven state enables PEPs to enjoy their laundered proceeds of corruption. For example, the purchase of real estate by an off-shore company enables them to conceal their beneficial ownership of the property. According to the CSO, Global Witness, 'over 87,000 properties in England and Wales are owned by anonymous companies registered in tax havens. The value of these properties is at least £56 billion according to Land Registry data - and likely to be in excess of £100 billion when accounting for inflation and missing price data.'[82] Transparency International has also reported that 40,725 London properties are owned by overseas companies with the main jurisdictions of registration being the British Virgin Islands (BVI), Jersey, the Isle of Man, and Guernsey.[83]

2.7.2.1 'Corrupt' and 'clean' states

These figures also raise a vital point concerning so-called 'corrupt' and 'clean' states. The FATF has asserted that there is a:

> strong correlation between corruption and income (GDP per capita). Richer countries have lower levels of corruption. Countries with the highest levels of corruption are developing and transition countries.[84]

The 2019 Transparency International *Corruption Perceptions Index* also categorises African states as being the most 'corrupt' with Western states being the 'cleanest'. This is a highly questionable and indeed damaging analysis. In reality, corruption in so-called 'clean countries' is of a different nature, albeit no less serious. This is emphasised by the litany of cases of Western-based companies paying bribes to African PEPs in order to obtain or retain business and assisting in the laundering process.[85] As Cassim points out, companies from the ten 'cleanest' countries have paid fines of over US$5.43 billion in penalties since the enforcement of the US Foreign Corrupt Practices Act

---

[82] See Press Release '£100bn of property in England and Wales is secretly owned, estimates show', 17 March 2019. Of course this does not imply that these were purchased by PEPs using the proceeds of crime.

[83] See Transparency International report, *Corruption on Your Doorstep: How Corrupt Capital is Used to Buy property in the UK*, London, 2016, p. 15. All are linked with the United Kingdom: the BVI is a British Overseas Territory whilst the others are all Crown Dependencies: see further Section 12.4.

[84] FATF, *Laundering the Proceeds of Corruption*, Paris, 2011, at [17].

[85] See Chapter 12 below.

(FCPA) began.[86] Since 1980, companies headquartered in the 'clean' countries have paid US$17.24 billion in 239 FCPA enforcement actions.[87] Similarly, as noted earlier, facilitating states and safe haven states are directly and actively involved in the money laundering process and without their assistance it would be almost impossible for PEPs to launder and enjoy their proceeds of corruption.

In practice, unless effective action is taken against the facilitating states and safe haven states, African PEPs will continue to enjoy their proceeds of crime.[88]

2.8 THE VULNERABILITY OF PEPs

Whilst PEPs enjoy a range of unique money laundering opportunities, they are also subject to risks of detection that other criminals do not face and which makes them particularly vulnerable if AML safeguards are utilised effectively. This vulnerability is considered throughout the book, but it is useful to note them here.

2.8.1 The National Level

2.8.1.1 Constitutional provisions

There are a series of constitutional provisions that are designed to ensure transparency and ethics in government. For example, several African Constitutions require PEPs to make regular asset and income declarations and the CoSP has recognised the potential effectiveness of such schemes in preventing corruption and money laundering.[89] In fact, a failure to comply with the constitutional requirement can itself have significant consequences. For example in 2019 the Code of Conduct Tribunal[90] banned the then Chief Justice of Nigeria, Walter Onnoghen, from office for 10 years and ordered him to forfeit any assets he could not account for to the state. This followed allegations that he had failed

---

[86] Denmark, Finland, Germany, Luxembourg, Netherlands, New Zealand, Norway, Singapore, Sweden and Switzerland: Transparency International, *Corruption Perceptions Index 2019*, London, 2019.

[87] Harry Cassim, 'Is the CPI upside down?', FCPA blog, 24 January 2020.

[88] Strategies for doing so are considered in Chapters 12 and 13 below.

[89] UNCAC CoSP resolution 7/5 'Promoting preventive measures against corruption', 2017, at [3].

[90] Established in the Constitution of Nigeria, Fifth Schedule.

to divulge cash in five foreign bank accounts in contravention of rules governing the declaration of assets by public officials.[91]

In addition, the actions (or omissions) of PEPs regarding public spending, including procurement contracts, are scrutinised by a range of constitutional bodies, including the Auditor General and the Public Accounts Committee of the legislature.[92]

2.8.1.2 External oversight

Many African states are the recipients of donor aid. Development partners often require an external audit of government expenditure which may disclose or at least suggest criminality by PEPs and require further investigation.

2.8.1.3 Enhanced due diligence

FATF Recommendation 12 requires enhanced due diligence (EDD) obligations on financial institutions and designated non-financial businesses and professions when undertaking business relationships with PEPs.[93]

2.8.1.4 CSOs and enhanced media interest

The activities of PEPs inevitably attract the attention of CSOs, political opponents and the media at the domestic level. This means that 'constitution-watching' and scrutinising the exercise of governmental powers and operation AML institutions are potentially invaluable AML supporting strategies.

These are enhanced by publications by international non-governmental organisations (NGOs), such as the ICIJ, of information concerning the alleged laundering activities of PEPs, for example, via the Panama Papers and Luanda Papers.

2.8.1.5 Shifting political will

The political will in a state may vary from time to time depending upon the policies of the current regime or following regime change. Under one regime, corrupt PEPs may feel (or be) protected but they become vulnerable to investigation and prosecution when they fall out of favour or when there is a change of government and they lose office. The 'state capture' saga being played out in South Africa provides a classic example where the government of President of South Africa, Cyril Ramaphosa, set up the Judicial Commission of Inquiry

---

91 'CCT Axes Onnoghen, To Forfeit Money, Barred for Ten Years' *Vanguard* 19 April 2019 https://www.vanguardngr.com/2019/04/cct-axes-onnoghen-to-forfeit-money-barred-for-10-years/ (accessed 4 June 2020).

92 See Chapter 7 below.

93 See Section 4.3 below.

into Allegations of State Capture (the Zondo Commission) to investigate the alleged corruption and money laundering activities of former President Jacob Zuma and his associates.

Similarly, Joao Lourenco, the hand-picked successor to the former President of Angola, Jose Eduardo dos Santos, has taken action against Isabel dos Santos following the leak of the Luanda Papers, with her assets in the country being frozen and she now faces prosecution on money laundering charges in Angola.

2.8.1.6 Whistleblowers and plea bargains

PEPs 'cannot do it alone' and almost inevitably other public officials will have some knowledge of their activities. Domestic whistleblowers therefore play a potentially vital way through which to break through the secrecy surrounding corruption and money laundering. Placing an obligation on public officials to report[94] or providing a financial incentive are potentially useful approaches.[95] In the case of individuals, the need to provide effective anonymity for themselves and members of their families remains essential.[96]

An exciting development is the rise of 'super-whistleblowers'. These may make use of the anonymity of social media to disclose information on money laundering, the Panama Papers disclosures being a prime example.[97] Information concerning the payment of huge bribes by Rolls Royce to PEPs in Africa and indeed globally was also disclosed by a social media leak in Hong Kong.[98] CSOs may also be dedicated to such activity. For example, in 2020 the 'Luanda Leaks' concerning the alleged corruption and money laundering activities of Isabel dos Santos was provided by the CSO Platform to Protect Whistleblowers in Africa.

In addition, an effective plea bargaining system between prosecutors and a corrupt PEP or an accomplice can provide significant evidence as to the

---

[94] See for example, section 9 Good Governance and Integrity Reporting Act 2015 (Mauritius).

[95] For example, in Mauritius the Integrity Reporting Board may reward an individual (or company) who has disclosed malpractices leading to the confiscation of unexplained wealth: see section 10(d) Good Governance and Integrity Reporting Act 2015. A 'reward' includes payment to compensate victims of fraud, white collar crimes or retaliation, or such other payment as may be prescribed: ibid, section 2. For a discussion on the meaning of 'unexplained wealth' see Section 10.3 below.

[96] See further discussion regarding the protection of such whistleblowers in Section 9.4.1 below.

[97] For a detailed account see Bastien Obermeyer and Frederik Obermaier, *The Panama Papers*, OneWorld, London, 2016.

[98] For the background to the case see *Serious Fraud Office v Rolls-Royce*, 2017, High Court of England and Wales. The judgment is available at www.judiciary.uk/judgments/serious-fraud-office-v-rolls-royce/ (accessed 4 June 2020).

scope and manner of money laundering activities by other PEPs. The development of appropriate principles found in the Cashgate case of *R v Karonga* provides an excellent model for other African states.[99]

2.8.2 The Transnational Level

Whilst PEPs can seek to undermine the AML controls at the domestic level, they are much less able to do so at the transnational level and this makes them especially vulnerable.

Firstly, all countries have criminalised money laundering in line with FATF Recommendation 3 and a money laundering offence is committed in whichever jurisdiction the proceeds of crime are located or through which they travel. Thus unless a PEP is able to claim immunity from prosecution,[100] they are liable to both prosecution and the forfeiture of their proceeds of crime in other jurisdictions.[101]

Secondly, external pressures have brought about a 'shifting political will' scenario in which facilitating states are moving towards publishing the records of the beneficial ownership of off-shore companies, thus facilitating investigations into their use by PEPs for money laundering purposes.[102]

Thirdly, there is a developing use of deferred prosecution agreements and non-prosecution agreements under which bribe-paying companies can avoid prosecution (or prosecution for a corruption-related offence) in exchange for disclosing to investigators details of their corrupt payments to foreign PEPs and providing details of the money laundering trail.[103]

Fourthly, co-operation between financial intelligence units can lead to the provision of financial information from an overseas financial intelligence unit (FIU) regarding the money laundering activities of domestic PEPs and their use of financial institutions. The FBME Bank case from Tanzania provides an excellent example.[104]

---

[99] [2018] MWHC 1. See Section 9.2.2 below.

[100] See Section 9.3 below.

[101] A prosecution may be impractical when the PEP is not in the jurisdiction, but this does not prevent the imposition of non-conviction based asset forfeiture orders or unexplained wealth orders against the proceeds of crime: see Sections 10.2 and 10.3 below.

[102] See Section 12.5 below.

[103] See the discussion on the Alstom and Airbus cases at Sections 13.2 and 13.4.

[104] See Section 5.5 below.

2.9 THE THIAM CASE: OUTCOME AND LESSONS

Unfortunately for Mr Thiam his 'safe haven' state turned out to be one which was prepared to prosecute him. In May 2017 he was convicted in a United States District Court on one count of transacting in criminally derived property and one count of money laundering.[105] He was sentenced to seven years in prison and three years of supervised release for laundering the bribes paid to him by the Chinese consortium. Crucially, the court also ordered the forfeiture of US$8.5 million to the United States.[106] It is not clear as to whether any of this money was returned to the people of Guinea.

Overall, combating money laundering by African PEPs presents unique challenges. It involves taking on the most powerful groups in any society: political leaders, domestic and international financial institutions, as well as multi-national corporate entities. This criminality is supported by PMLs. It involves jurisdictions worldwide where there is often no political will to address the problem because of the economic benefits it brings. Meanwhile it is the people of the victim African states who suffer.

Yet PEPs are uniquely vulnerable if there is the political will to utilise the AML safeguards effectively both domestically and transnationally. Whilst this is work in progress, the fight against money laundering by African PEPs is producing remarkable results. This fight is the focus of the following chapters.

---

[105] In contravention of Title 18, United States Code, section 1957 and 1956 respectively.

[106] *United States of America v Thiam* Case number 1:17CR00047-01 (DLC), Judgment dated 25 August 2017.

PART II

The global and Africa-specific strategies designed to combat money laundering

3. The international and Africa-specific AML-related instruments

3.1 UN TRANSNATIONAL ORGANISED CRIME CONVENTION (THE PALERMO CONVENTION)

The Palermo Convention entered into force on 29 September 2003. As at 1 June 2020, there are 190 States Parties to the Convention including all African states with the exception of Somalia and South Sudan. The Convention contains provisions relating to the main AML pillars i.e. criminalisation, prevention, international co-operation and asset recovery.[1]

3.1.1 'Criminalisation of the Laundering of Proceeds of Crime'

Article 6 focuses on the need for 'functional equivalence' in the criminalisation of money laundering. It requires each State Party to adopt, 'in accordance with fundamental principles of its domestic law, such legislative and other measures as may be necessary to establish' a series of money laundering offences when committed intentionally. These address the placement, layering and integration stages which were discussed in the previous chapter.[2] These are particularly significant in that the FATF Recommendations require countries to criminalise money laundering on the basis of the Palermo Convention (and the Vienna Convention).[3]

---

[1] The Preamble states that the UN General Assembly is 'Strongly Convinced' that the Convention 'will constitute an effective tool and the necessary legal framework for international cooperation in combating, inter alia, ... money-laundering [and] corruption ...'.

[2] Article 6 is discussed in Section 2.2 above.

[3] FATF Recommendation 3. The reference to the Vienna Convention is to the UN Convention Against Illicit Trade in Narcotic Drugs and Psychotropic Substances. This Convention is wholly concerned with addressing international drug trafficking.

3.1.2 Prevention of Money Laundering

Article 7 of the Palermo Convention requires each State Party to introduce a series of measures to prevent money laundering. These include:

> instituting a comprehensive domestic regulatory and supervisory regime for banks and non-bank financial institutions and, where appropriate, other bodies particularly susceptible to money-laundering, within its competence, in order to deter and detect all forms of money-laundering.

This requires the introduction of provisions relating to customer identification, record-keeping and the reporting of suspicious transactions.[4] States Parties are also to consider 'implementing feasible measures to detect and monitor the movement of cash and appropriate negotiable instruments across their borders'.[5]

3.1.3 International Co-operation and Asset Recovery

The Convention emphasises the importance of co-operation between AML bodies both at the national and transnational levels, including measures to undertake joint investigations for the purpose of confiscating the proceeds of crime.[6] States Parties must also consider establishing a FIU 'to serve as a national centre for the collection, analysis and dissemination of information regarding potential money-laundering'.[7]

To facilitate international co-operation, States Parties are required to (1) 'afford one another the widest measure of mutual legal assistance in investigation, prosecutions and judicial proceedings' in relation to Convention offences;[8] and (2) 'adopt, to the greatest extent possible within their domestic legal systems, such measures as may be necessary to enable confiscation of ... the proceeds of crime ... and ... instrumentalities used in, or destined for use in offences covered by this Convention'.[9] Article 14 requires a State Party to dispose of the confiscated proceeds of crime 'in accordance with its domestic law and administrative procedures'.

---

4 Article 7(1)(a).

5 Article 7(2). See also FATF Recommendation 14.

6 Articles 19 and 13 respectively.

7 Article 7(1)(b). See also Article 7(4). For a discussion on the role of FIUs with particular reference to African states see Chapter 5 below.

8 Article 18(1). See further Section 4.3 below.

9 Article 12.

3.2 UN CONVENTION AGAINST CORRUPTION

The UNCAC is the 'only globally accepted framework for action by states in relation to the issue of corruption'.[10] It entered into force on 14 December 2005 and as at 1 June 2020 has 187 State Parties including all African states with the exception of Eritrea and Somalia. The Convention has three purposes:

(a) to promote and strengthen measures to prevent and combat corruption more efficiently and effectively;
(b) to promote, facilitate, and support international co-operation and technical assistance in the prevention of, and fight against, corruption, including asset recovery; and
(c) to promote integrity, accountability, and proper management of public affairs and public property.[11]

Combating money laundering through prevention, criminalisation, international co-operation and asset recovery is an integral part of the Convention.

3.2.1 UNCAC and PEPs

The Convention defines a 'public official' as including 'any person holding a legislative, executive, administrative or judicial office of a State Party, whether appointed or elected, whether permanent or temporary, whether paid of unpaid, irrespective of that person's seniority'. The concluding words indicate that the term is somewhat wider than the FATF definition of a PEP.[12] However, the requirement to prevent and detect the transfer of the proceeds of crime enshrined in Article 52 (see below) is limited to 'individuals who are, or have been, entrusted with prominent public functions and their family members and close associates'.

There are several PEPs-specific provisions. In particular, Article 52(1) requires EDD as regards PEPs. Thus domestic financial institutions are required 'to verify the identity of customers, to take reasonable steps to determine the identity of beneficial owners of funds deposited into high-value accounts and to conduct enhanced scrutiny of accounts sought or maintained by or on behalf of individuals who are or have been, entrusted with prominent public functions and their family members and close associates'.

---

[10] CTOC Secretariat briefing note 'Five years of UNCAC Reviews: What have we learned?', 16 September 2015, CTOC/COP/WG.8/2015/CRP.3, at [1].

[11] Article 1.

[12] See Section 2.4 above.

3.2.2 Preventing Money Laundering

Article 14(1)(a) UNCAC requires States Parties to:

> institute a comprehensive domestic regulatory and supervisory regime for banks, non-bank financial institutions including natural or legal persons that provide formal or informal services for the transmission of money or value and, where appropriate, other bodies particularly susceptible to money-laundering, within its competence, in order to deter and detect all forms of money-laundering.

According to a Note by the Inter-Governmental Working Group on the Prevention of Corruption (the IWG), the Article 14 measures are intended to 'ensure that States Parties have in place a legal and administrative framework to deter and detect money laundering'.[13] In doing so, Article 14(4) calls on States Parties to use as a guideline the 'relevant initiatives and standards of regional, interregional and multilateral organizations against money-laundering'. During the Convention negotiations, this was understood to refer in particular to the FATF Recommendations.[14]

The drafters recognised that to deter and detect money laundering requires an AML regime that goes beyond merely addressing financial institutions. Thus Article 14(1) applies to both banks and to 'non-bank financial institutions'. The FATF Recommendations extend this requirement to 'designated non-financial businesses and professions' (DNFBPs).[15]

Article 14(1) also requires State Parties to institute requirements for know your customer (KYC) and, where appropriate, beneficial owner identification, record-keeping and the reporting of suspicious transactions (STRs). According to the Interpretive Notes to the UNCAC, 'the words "suspicious transactions" may be understood to include unusual transactions that, by reason of their amount, characteristics and frequency, are inconsistent with the customer's business activity, exceed the normally accepted parameters of the market or have no clear legal basis and could constitute or be connected with unlawful activities in general'. Article 40 states that each State Party must ensure that the investigation of convention offences is not obstructed by bank secrecy laws.

---

[13] Working Group on the Prevention of Corruption, 'Measures to prevent money laundering (Article 14 of the United Nations Convention against Corruption): Note to the Secretariat' 2015, CAC/COSP/WG.4/2015/2 (WG Note).

[14] WG Note p. 4. These are considered in Section 4.2 below.

[15] FATF Recommendation 22. These cover: Casinos; Real estate agents; Dealers in precious metals and dealers in precious stones; Lawyers, notaries, other independent legal professionals and accountants; and Trust and company service providers. These are discussed in Section 4.2.2 below.

3.2.2.1 Co-operation between AML agencies

The need for effective co-operation between AML agencies is emphasised in Article 14(1)(b) UNCAC, which requires each State Party to:

> ensure that administrative, regulatory, law enforcement and other authorities dedicated to combating money-laundering (including, where appropriate under domestic law, judicial authorities) have the ability to cooperate and exchange information at the national and international levels within the conditions prescribed by its domestic law and, to that end, shall consider the establishment of a financial intelligence unit to serve as a national centre for the collection, analysis and dissemination of information regarding potential money-laundering.

A major feature of AML work in recent years is the development of FIUs in African states (and indeed globally). Their role is considered in Chapter 5.

3.2.2.2 Article 14 in practice

In 2015 States Parties were invited to provide information to the UNCAC Implementation Review Group (IRG) on the implementation of Article 14 and information was provided by 28 states.[16] The process is notable for two reasons: firstly, the full text of the submissions by all States Parties has been published and secondly, the IWG analysis identifies states by name. According to the WG Note, all States Parties reported they had a system in place requiring institutions to make STRs to their national FIU or other designated body.[17] In addition most states had basic AML provisions in place. Whilst useful, in practice similar, albeit more detailed, provisions are found in the FATF Recommendations and all FATF members are subject to a mutual evaluation process to ensure their compliance with such requirements.[18]

3.2.3 Money Laundering Offences

Article 23(1) requires each State Party to take the necessary steps 'in accordance with fundamental principles of its domestic law' to establish a series of money laundering offences. These are identical to those in the Palermo Convention.[19]

'Proceeds of crime' means 'any property derived from or obtained, directly or indirectly, through the commission of an offence'[20] and most States Parties

---

16 Algeria and Egypt were the only African states to provide any information.

17 WG Note at [48].

18 See Section 4.2 below for a discussion on the FATF requirements.

19 See Section 2.2 above.

20 Article 2(e).

have adopted similar or equivalent definitions.[21] The UNCAC CoSP continues to encourage States Parties to interpret the term in a manner consistent with the Convention.[22]

Money laundering requires the commission of a 'predicate offence'. For the purposes of the UNCAC this means 'any offence as a result of which proceeds have been generated that may become the subject of an offence as defined in Article 23'.[23] Each State Party 'shall seek to apply' Article 23 to the widest range of predicate offences and must include as a minimum 'a comprehensive range of criminal offences established in accordance with this Convention'.[24] The Convention offences comprise:

- bribery of national public officials;
- bribery of foreign public officials and officials of public international organisations; and
- embezzlement, misappropriation or other diversion of property by a public official.

Optional offences include:

- trading in influence;
- abuse of functions; and
- illicit enrichment.

In practice, the majority of States Parties have adopted an 'all-crimes' approach and this is recognised as the one which best serves the purposes of Article 23.[25]

3.2.4 International Co-operation

In the Preamble to the UNCAC, States Parties recognise that 'corruption is no longer a local matter but a transnational phenomenon that affects all societies and economies, making international co-operation to control and prevent it essential'. Article 46 therefore requires States Parties to afford each other the

[21] WG Note at [63].

[22] CAC/CoSP Resolution 6/2; 'Facilitating international cooperation in asset recovery and the return of proceeds of crime', 2015, at [8]. The CoSP is discussed in Section 3.2.6.

[23] Article 2(h).

[24] Article 23(2)(a) and (b).

[25] WG Note at [64]. Curiously, whilst money laundering is one of the fourteen crimes within the jurisdiction of the African Court of Justice and Human and Peoples' Rights, corruption is the only predicate offence: See Chapter 14 for a full discussion on the Court.

widest measure of mutual legal assistance in investigations, prosecutions and judicial proceedings in relation to Convention offences.

This is reinforced in Resolution 6/4, in which the CoSP 'urges States Parties to provide each other with the widest possible assistance in investigations of and proceedings in civil and administrative matters relating to corruption offences'.[26] The importance of the UNCAC provisions on international co-operation is emphasised in FATF Recommendation 36, which requires countries to take 'immediate steps' to implement fully the UNCAC and Palermo Convention provisions on international co-operation.

3.2.5 Asset Recovery

In recognition of the fact that cases of corruption 'involve vast quantities of assets, which may constitute a significant proportion of the resources of States, and that threaten the political stability and sustainable development of those States',[27] the return of assets acquired through corruption is a fundamental principle of the UNCAC. Article 51 requires States Parties to 'afford each other the widest measure of co-operation and assistance in this regard', whilst Chapter V is entirely devoted to asset recovery provisions. A particular feature of the Convention is that it also provides for non-conviction-based asset forfeiture.[28]

3.2.6 Implementing and Monitoring the Convention

Chapter VII contains the 'Mechanisms for Implementation'. Article 63 establishes the CoSP to the Convention with the mandate 'to improve the capacity of and co-operation between States Parties to achieve the objectives set forth in this Convention and to promote and review its implementation'. The CoSP convened for the first time in 2006 but it was not until its third session in Doha in 2009 that it adopted the terms of reference for the Mechanism for the Review of Implementation of the Convention (IRM) and also established the IRG whose task is to oversee the review process.[29] This process is designed, amongst other things, to be transparent, efficient, non-intrusive, inclusive and impartial and not produce any form of ranking.[30] The IRG is supported

---

26 CAC/CoSP Resolution 6/4, 'Enhancing the use of civil and administrative proceedings against corruption, including through international cooperation, in the framework of the United Nations Convention against Corruption', 2015, at [1].

27 Preamble to the UNCAC.

28 See Article 54 and the discussion in Section 10.2 below.

29 CAC/CoSP Resolution 3/1: 'Review Mechanism', 2009.

30 Compare this to the FATF review process discussed at Section 4.4 below.

by the Open-ended Inter-Governmental Working Group on the Prevention of Corruption and the Open-ended Inter-Governmental Working Group on Asset Recovery. As noted above, the CoSP has paid particular attention to the AML aspects of the Convention.

Given the range of other review mechanisms, the terms of reference emphasise that the IRM is intended to 'complement existing international and regional review mechanisms in order that the Conference may, as appropriate, cooperate with those mechanisms and avoid duplication of effort'.[31]

3.3 AFRICAN UNION CONVENTION ON PREVENTING AND COMBATING CORRUPTION (AU CONVENTION)

The AU Convention was adopted in July 2003 by member states of the African Union and entered into force on 5 August 2006. As at 1 January 2020, 40 of the 55 members of the AU have ratified the Convention.

In structure, the Convention contains the four anti-corruption pillars with sections dealing with Prevention, Criminalisation, International co-operation and Asset recovery. Unlike the UNCAC, all the substantive provisions of the AU Convention are mandatory.

There are several provisions which have AML implications.

3.3.1 Prevention

The Convention contains strong good governance measures in the public sector. States Parties 'commit themselves', amongst other things to:

(i) Require all or designated public officials to declare their assets;[32]
(ii) Establish a code of conduct and to monitor its implementation; and
(iii) Ensure transparency, equity and efficiency in public procurement.[33]

In recognition of the problem of PEPs, Article 7 provides that 'any immunity granted to public officials shall not be an obstacle to the investigations against and the prosecution of such officials'. This is an important and difficult provision. Constitutions almost invariably provide for presidential immunity from

---

31 Ibid, at [3(j)].

32 Such information is potentially of considerable importance in AML investigations, particularly as regards FIUs: see Section 5.4.3 below. The term 'public official' means 'any official or employee of the State or its agents including those who have been selected, appointed or elected to perform activities or functions in the name of the State or in the service of the State at any level of its hierarchy': see Article 1.

33 See Article 7. See further Section 7.1 below.

prosecution whilst in office and some extend this to other senior PEPs.[34] The presidential power to grant a pardon to PEPs post-conviction (and, on occasions, in pre-trial situations) also provides a means to protect corrupt PEPs.[35]

3.3.2 Criminalisation

Article 6 requires State Parties to adopt such legislative and other measures as may be necessary to establish an offence of laundering the proceeds of corruption. These largely follow the approach in the Palermo Convention and the UNCAC.

3.3.3 International Co-operation

States Parties are required to provide mutual legal assistance in respect of corruption and related offences.[36] In response to the problem of foreign bribery, States Parties are required to 'collaborate with countries of origin of multi-nations to criminalise and punish the practice of secret commissions and other forms of corrupt practices during international trade transactions'.[37]

3.3.4 Asset Recovery

State Parties are required to adopt the necessary legislative and other measures to enable its competent authorities to find, freeze and confiscate the proceeds of corruption.[38]

States Parties must also 'encourage all countries to take legislative measures to prevent corrupt public officials from enjoying ill-acquired assets by freezing their foreign accounts and facilitating the repatriation of stolen or illegally acquired monies to their countries of origin'.[39]

3.3.5 The Future

2018 was designated by the AU as the African Anti-Corruption Year. Amongst other things, agreement was reached on the need to review the AU Convention and to review the challenges of member states in putting it into practice. In

---

34 See Section 9.3 below.

35 See Chapter 11.

36 Article 18(1).

37 Article 19(1). On dealing with the bribe-payers, see further the discussion in Chapter 13.

38 Article 16(1).

39 See the discussion in Section 10.1 below.

addition, the AU Advisory Board on Corruption is developing a common African position on asset recovery: see further Section 10.8.[40]

3.4 ARAB ANTI-CORRUPTION CONVENTION

The Arab Anti-Corruption Convention was drawn up in 2010. It is thus the only international anti-corruption convention that post-dates the UNCAC. States Parties to the Convention include Algeria, Comoros, Libya and Morocco. The Convention aims to:

- foster measures to prevent, fight and uncover all forms of corruption and other offences related to its commission, and the prosecution of its perpetrators;
- foster integrity, transparency, accountability and the rule of law; and
- encourage individuals and CSOs to take an active part in preventing and fighting corruption.[41]

The Convention addresses the four key anti-corruption pillars found in the UNCAC and AU Convention, including requiring States Parties to criminalise money laundering.[42]

3.4.1 Prevention of Corruption

Article 10 provides that each State Party shall, in accordance with its laws, 'lay down, implement and consolidate effective and coordinated policies to prevent and fight corruption'. These shall include 'the strengthening of community participation and the application of the principles of the rule of law, good administration of public affairs and property, integrity, transparency and accountability'.

The important contribution that civil society can make is reflected in the Preamble which notes that 'fighting corruption is not limited to Government authorities but also includes individuals and civil society organizations which shall play an effective role in this regard'. Article 11 then requires each State Party to 'take appropriate measures to encourage civil society organizations to participate effectively in preventing and combating corruption'.

---

40 See AU Advisory Board on Corruption *Concept note on the 3rd Edition of the African Anti-Corruption Dialogue on the theme 'Towards a Common African Position on Asset Recovery'*, 2019 and the *Report of H.E. Muhammadu Buhari to the Assembly of the African Union*, 2019, Assembly/AU/19(XXXII) at [27–28].

41 Article 2.

42 Article 4.

3.4.2 Criminalisation

The 'laundering of proceeds of crime'[43] is a convention offence with the predicate offences covering a similar range to those in the UNCAC.

In an unusual but welcome provision, victims of corruption offences must be given the opportunity to 'air their views' at the appropriate stages of the criminal process and be provided 'with the means to obtain compensation and remedy'.[44]

3.4.3 Inter-agency Co-operation

The Convention has detailed provisions requiring close co-operation between investigative agencies both domestically and transnationally, with Article 20 following closely the provisions of the UNCAC.

3.4.4 Asset Recovery

Each State Party is required to have legislation designed to assist in the finding, freezing and confiscation of the proceeds of corruption. A particular feature of the Convention is the duty of each State Party in cases of embezzlement or laundering of public funds, to return any confiscated property upon request to the 'victim' state.[45]

3.5 THE MALABO PROTOCOL

In 2014 the Malabo Protocol was adopted by AU Heads of State and Government.[46] This provides for the establishment of the African Court of Justice and Human and Peoples' Rights, the first ever pan-African court with jurisdiction to hear and determine cases (amongst others) of corruption and money laundering against PEPs. The Court is discussed in Chapter 14.

---

43 Article 4.
44 Article 15.
45 Article 30.3.
46 Protocol on Amendments to the Protocol on the Statute of the African Court of Justice, Human and Peoples' Rights.

3.6 THE AFRICAN PEER REVIEW MECHANISM (APRM) AND HIGH LEVEL PANEL ON ILLICIT FLOWS FROM AFRICA

3.6.1 The APRM

The APRM was initiated in 2002 and established as part of the New Partnership for Africa's Development (NEPAD) initiative and is seen as a part of the development of 'South-South co-operation in the fight against corruption'.[47] It is a specialised agency of the AU with a mandate that includes 'tracking the implementation, and overseeing the monitoring and evaluation, of the Continent's key governance areas'. The economic management area specifically refers to fighting money laundering.

The primary purpose of the APRM is:

> To foster the adoption of policies, standards and practices that lead to political stability, high economic growth, sustainable development and accelerated sub-regional and continental economic integration through sharing of experiences and reinforcement of successful and best practice, including identifying deficiencies and assessing the needs of capacity building.[48]

Several country reports have been published. These are lengthy and detailed documents which provide a wealth of information about good governance and corruption challenges in individual African states. The High Level Panel on Illicit Financial Flows from Africa has noted that the APRM is a good instrument for the continuous monitoring of illicit financial flows (IFFs) from Africa and recommended that steps be taken to include IFFs in areas covered by the Mechanism.[49]

Participation is voluntary and only a limited number of African states have joined the process and been involved in the monitoring process.[50]

---

[47] See background paper prepared by the Secretariat of the Conference of State Parties to UNCAC 'South-South cooperation in the fight against corruption', 2009, CAC/COSP/2009/CRP.6.

[48] APRM Self-Assessment Questionnaire.

[49] Ibid, p. 52.

[50] As at 30 June 2020 the following are member states of the APRM: Algeria, Angola, Benin, Burkina Faso, Cameroon, Djibouti, Egypt, Ethiopia, Gabon, Ghana, Kenya, Lesotho, Malawi, Mali, Mauritania, Mauritius, Mozambique, Nigeria, Republic of Congo, Rwanda, Sao Tome and Principe, Senegal, Sierra Leone, South Africa, Sudan, Tanzania, Togo, Uganda, and Zambia.

3.6.2 High Level Panel on Illicit Flows from Africa

In 2011, Resolution 886 (XLIV) was adopted in 2011 at the 4th Joint Annual Meeting of the AU/Economic Commission for Africa Conference of Ministers of Finance, Planning and Economic Development. This mandated the Economic Commission to establish a High Level Panel on Illicit Financial Flows from Africa. Chaired by the former South African President, Thabo Mbeki, in February 2015 the High Level Panel launched its final report entitled *Illicit Financial Flows*.[51]

Its Recommendations found in Chapter V include:

- Transparency of ownership and control of companies, partnerships and trusts is essential: beneficial ownership declarations should be required of all parties entering into government contracts;[52]
- African governments should ensure investigators and prosecutors are trained and empowered to investigate financial-related crimes;[53]
- African states should ensure that the public can access budget information and that processes and procedures for budget development and auditing are open and transparent to the public;
- African governments can greatly help in the fight against money laundering by publishing lists of PEPs and information as to whether the country's laws prohibit or restrict the ability of their PEPs to hold financial accounts abroad;
- 'Given the vital and positive role of civil organizations' in efforts to curb IFFs, 'it is essential that they should be given the operating space and legal freedoms required for advocacy, activism and research in this area'.[54]

The Panel also calls for stronger collaboration and consistent engagement between Africa and global players such as the G20 and International Monetary Fund to help ensure greater transparency in the international banking system. Its findings and recommendations for action by African countries were then endorsed by the AU Assembly Special Declaration on Illicit Financial Flows.[55]

---

[51] Global Financial Integrity (GFI) defines IFFs as 'money that is illegally earned, used or moved and which crosses an international border' *GFI Illicit Financial Flows to and from 148 Developing Countries: 2006–2015*, 2019.

[52] On developing transparency in beneficial ownership, see Chapter12 below.

[53] See further Section 9.2 below.

[54] *Illicit Financial Flows*, p. 84.

[55] Assembly/AU/Decl.5.(XXIV), 2015. See also the work of the Global Forum on Transparency and Exchange of Information for Tax Purposes.

3.7 OECD CONVENTION ON COMBATING BRIBERY OF FOREIGN PUBLIC OFFICIALS IN INTERNATIONAL BUSINESS TRANSACTIONS (OECD ANTI-BRIBERY CONVENTION)

3.7.1 Scope of the Convention

The inclusion of the OECD Anti-Bribery Convention as an 'AML instrument' needs little explanation. The Thiam case is just one of the many examples where the proceeds of crime are derived from bribes paid by foreign corporate entities to PEPs in exchange for obtaining or retaining business and which may then assist them in the laundering of those funds. To address this activity, the Commission for Africa has rightly demanded that: 'rich nations should put in place a series of measures to ... deter their own companies from paying bribes in the first place'.[56]

If such measures are to be effective, there is the need to persuade even the most powerful foreign corporate entities to desist from paying bribes to African PEPs. The OECD Anti-Bribery Convention is the key.[57]

The Convention came into force on 15 February 1999. It is concerned wholly with 'active corruption' i.e. bribery on the supply side. Its significance is emphasised by the fact that the 41 parties to the Convention are involved in some two-thirds of world exports and almost 90 per cent of total foreign direct investment outflows.[58]

Article 1(1) states that:

> Each Party shall take such measures as may be necessary to establish that it is a criminal offence under its law for any person intentionally to offer, promise or give any undue pecuniary or other advantage, whether directly or through intermediaries, to a foreign public official, for that official or for a third party, in order that the official act or refrain from acting in relation to the performance of official duties, in order to obtain or retain business or other improper advantage in the conduct of international business.

For the purposes of the Convention, a foreign public official means 'any person holding a legislative, administrative or judicial office of a foreign

---

56 Commission for Africa, *Our Common Interest*, 2005, p. 31.

57 For a detailed review of the Convention, see Mark Pieth, Lucinda Low and Nicola Bonucci, *The OECD Convention on Bribery: A Commentary*, 2nd edn., Cambridge University Press, 2014.

58 These comprise the 35 OECD member states plus Argentina, Brazil, Bulgaria, Colombia, Russian Federation and South Africa. China remains a conspicuous absentee.

country, whether appointed or elected; any person exercising a public function for a foreign country, including for a public agency or public enterprise; and any official or agent of a public international organization'.[59] Indeed, this definition is wider than that for a PEP.

In view of the economic interests and/or political pressure that might affect prosecutions, Article 5 makes it clear that investigations and prosecutions:

> shall not be influenced by considerations of national economic interest, the potential effect upon relations with another state or the identity of the national or legal person involved.

Article 5 is supported by paragraph 6 of the Annex to the 1997 Revised Recommendations of the OECD Ministerial Council, which stresses that 'public prosecutors should exercise their discretion independently, based on professional motives'.[60]

3.7.2 A Note on China

Whilst China continues to foster a close economic relationship with numerous African countries, Chinese companies have faced numerous accusations of involvement in bribing African PEPs in order to obtain lucrative contracts as well as assisting in the laundering of the proceeds of crime. For example, the Thiam case arose following a bribe paid to the Minister of Mines in Guinea by a Chinese consortium. Even though the OECD has called upon China as well as other emerging economies[61] to join the Convention,[62] it has not done so. In addition, there are no known bribery related cases being brought by the Chinese government.[63] Clearly the OECD must continue its efforts to persuade China to become a party to the Convention.

---

[59] Article 1(4)(a).

[60] Commentary 27 to the OECD Anti-Bribery Convention makes it clear that the decision must not be subject to improper influence by concerns of a political nature. Prosecutorial discretion may include the application of a public interest test but this is to be determined by the prosecutor.

[61] Singapore, India, Hong Kong SAR and South Korea in particular.

[62] For example, see OECD, *Working Group on Bribery Annual Report*, Paris, 2011, at p. 3.

[63] For a useful discussion see Transparency International, *Exporting Corruption: Progress Report 2018*, London, 2018, pp. 93–5. On combating the bribery of African PEPs see Chapter 13 below.

3.7.3 Debarment Threats

The influence of the Convention is greatly enhanced by the threat of debarment of a corporate entity for involvement in foreign bribery by the African Development Bank, World Bank or other multilateral development agencies following a foreign bribery conviction. This has 'persuaded' even the most powerful corporate entities to make agreements with prosecutors which include identifying those PEPs who received or demanded the bribes and how the proceeds of crime were laundered.[64]

3.8 OVERVIEW

This chapter has highlighted the fact that African states are not short of AML obligations. However, given the power of PEPs to 'control the controls' the real question is how effective these instruments are in practice. To a limited extent the International Review Mechanism has explored state compliance with the UNCAC AML provisions. However, it has no 'teeth' and its most useful contribution is to support states in implementing the Convention especially through providing training and technical assistance. It follows that more forceful persuasion is needed for African states both to put in place AML laws and institutions and to make them effective in practice. This is the role of the FATF and African FATF-style regional bodies and is considered in the following chapter.

---

[64] See Chapter 13 for a full discussion. Interestingly, the African Development Bank has debarred a number of Chinese companies for involvement in the bribery of African PEPs based on information provided by other rival Chinese companies: information provided by a confidential source.

4. PEPs, FATF and the African FATF-style regional bodies

INTRODUCTION

This chapter considers the work of the FATF and the development of the FATF Recommendations with particular reference to PEPs. It also explores the implementation of the FATF Recommendations in African states, focusing on the role and work of the four FATF-style African regional bodies[1] (African RBs).

4.1 THE ROLE AND GLOBAL INFLUENCE OF THE FATF

The FATF describes itself as an inter-governmental policy-making body whose objectives are to 'set standards and promote effective implementation of legal, regulatory and operational measures for combating money laundering'.[2] Its origins stem from international concern over drug trafficking and the resultant vast profits being made by organised crime groups. This issue was discussed in July 1989 at a meeting of the G7 in Paris[3] at which it was concluded that there was an 'urgent need for decisive action, both on a national and international basis' to counter drug production, consumption and trafficking as well as the 'laundering of its proceeds'.[4] The result was the establishment of the FATF with the mandate to:

> assess the results of co-operation already undertaken in order to prevent the utilisation of the banking system and financial institutions for the purpose of money laundering, and to consider additional preventive efforts in this field, including the

---

1 See Section 4.5 below.

2 Introduction to the FATF Recommendations 2012.

3 These comprise Canada, France, Germany, Italy, Japan, United Kingdom and the United States of America.

4 William Gilmore, *Dirty Money: The Evolution of Money Laundering Countermeasures*, 2nd edn., Council of Europe Publishing, 1999, p. 79.

adaptation of the legal and regulatory systems so as to enhance multilateral judicial assistance.[5]

As well as the G7 members (and the European Commission), eight other states became members of FATF.[6] No African state participated in the discussions.

Work then commenced on developing an AML plan of action and in 1990 a report was published containing 40 separate Recommendations. The '40 Recommendations' were born and despite several re-draftings and a considerable expansion of their detail and scope, the number has remained constant.

The FATF is not underpinned by a legally binding treaty nor is it a permanent body. Thus at the outset it was agreed to continue the FATF for five years and then to review progress after three years. This review recognised the need to continue with the Task Force. Since then, its mandate has been extended on several occasions with the latest extension being until 2020. The intention now is to transform the FATF into a legal body in recognition of the fact that it has 'evolved from a temporary forum to a sustained public and political commitment to tackle anti-money laundering'.[7]

Whilst the original FATF members took steps to implement the Recommendations at the national level, it was recognised that as other countries posed a money laundering risk, unilateral AML measures themselves were not sufficient. It was therefore imperative that there was a global response and outreach. Thus FATF membership has expanded to 37 states and two regional organisations, which represent most of the major global financial centres.[8] South Africa is the only African member of FATF. To complete the global 'family' the FATF has developed a series of FATF-style regional bodies which perform similar tasks to the main body. In the African context, there are currently four such regional bodies.[9] The result is that over 200 jurisdictions

---

5 Ibid.

6 Australia, Austria, Belgium, Luxembourg, the Netherlands, Spain, Sweden and Switzerland.

7 FATF, *Report to G20 Finance Ministers and Central Bank Governors*, Paris, 2018, at [1]. See also at [6].

8 The full membership list is: Argentina, Australia, Austria, Belgium, Brazil, Canada, China, Denmark, European Commission, Finland, France, Germany, Greece, Gulf Co-operation Council, Hong Kong (China), Iceland, Ireland, Italy, Japan, Luxembourg, Mexico, Kingdom of the Netherlands, New Zealand, Norway, Portugal, Russian Federation, Singapore, South Africa, South Korea, Spain, Sweden, Switzerland, Turkey, United Kingdom, United States (as at 1 June 2020).

9 See Section 4.5 below.

have become members of the FATF and/or of a FATF-style regional body and have committed to implementing the FATF Recommendations.[10]

4.2 DEVELOPMENT OF THE FATF RECOMMENDATIONS

4.2.1 The Pre-2012 FATF Recommendations

The 1990 set of FATF Recommendations stated that countries[11] should implement the following multi-faceted approach to combating money laundering:

(i) improve national legal systems to combat money laundering, including criminalising 'drug money laundering';
(ii) require the active involvement of financial institutions in the identification and reporting of suspicious transactions to a designated authority. This in recognition of the vulnerabilities of the financial sector and the need to preserve its integrity;
(iii) have in place mechanisms to enhance international co-operation both as regards mutual legal assistance and extradition. This in recognition of the transnational nature of money laundering; and
(iv) have in place provisions enabling countries to confiscate the proceeds of crime.

These requirements remain the basic pillars for global AML action. Each of the Recommendations provided that countries 'should' undertake some specified action, thus suggesting that compliance was not obligatory. In order to clarify and give practical guidance on the application of specific recommendations, between 1990 and 1995 the FATF developed a series of 'Interpretive Notes'. These remain a key part of the Recommendations.

The 1996 Revised Recommendations were wider in scope and designed to be of universal application. Here 'functional equivalence' was the aim as they were said to be 'principles for action ... for countries to implement according to their particular circumstances and constitutional frameworks', and which all countries were encouraged to adopt. Further, that they were not 'particularly complex or difficult, *provided that there is the political will to act*' (emphasis added).[12] This again highlights one of the key challenges raised in this book:

---

10 See FATF website 'Country members': http://www.fatf-gafi.org/countries/ (accessed 5 June 2020).

11 'All references in the FATF Recommendations to *country* or *countries* apply equally to territories or jurisdictions': FATF Recommendations 2012, General Glossary.

12 Introduction to the 1996 FATF Recommendations.

i.e. how to develop and maintain the political will to deal effectively with money laundering by PEPs.

Another feature of the 1996 Recommendations was their extension to include 'non-bank financial institutions' such as money transmission services and bureaux de change. Attention was also paid to preventing the use of life insurance policies to facilitate money laundering. Customer identification requirements were enhanced but there were no specific provisions relating to PEPs. Following the 2001 attack on the World Trade Center, the FATF extended its mandate by creating eight (and later) nine Special Recommendations on Terrorist Financing.

In 2003, a fresh set of 40 Recommendations were published which were designed to provide 'a new comprehensive framework for combating money laundering and terrorist financing'. Countries were called upon to take the necessary steps to comply with them although in recognition of their diverse legal and financial systems, the Recommendations set minimum standards with countries free to implement 'the detail according to their particular circumstances and constitutional frameworks'.[13] In addition to the general KYC requirement, for the first time the issue of PEPs was specifically addressed. Recommendation 6 required financial institutions to perform EDD when doing business with foreign PEPs, although countries were encouraged to extend the requirements to domestic PEPs.

4.2.2 The 2012 FATF Recommendations

In 2012 the FATF published a fresh set of Recommendations entitled *The International Standards on Combating Money Laundering and the Financing of Terrorism and Proliferation* (the 2012 Recommendations). These comprise a much expanded set of 40 Recommendations together with detailed Interpretive Notes and a General Glossary. Significantly, the due diligence and reporting requirements in the 2012 Recommendations also apply to 'DNFBPs'. These cover certain activities of casinos, real estate agents, dealers in precious metals and precious stones, lawyers, notaries, other independent legal professionals[14] and accountants, and TCSPs.

The 2012 Recommendations 'set out the essential measures that countries must have in place to:

- identify the risks, and develop policies and domestic coordination;

---

13 Ibid.

14 The Interpretive Note to FATF Recommendation 23 states: 'It is for each country to determine the matters that would fall under legal professional privilege or professional secrecy'. See further the discussion in Section 8.3 below.

- pursue money laundering …;
- apply preventive measures for the financial sector and other designated sectors;
- establish powers and responsibilities for the competent authorities … and other institutional measures;
- enhance the transparency and availability of beneficial ownership information of legal persons and arrangements; and
- facilitate international co-operation'.[15]

Countries must adopt a risk-based approach 'to ensure that the measures to prevent and mitigate money laundering ... are commensurate with the risks identified'.[16] This has resulted in countries undertaking National Risk Assessments (NRAs) to fulfil this requirement.[17] Where countries identify higher risks 'they should ensure that their [anti-money laundering] regime adequately addresses such risks'. PEPs clearly fall into this higher risk category with the mandatory EDD requirements now being extended to both foreign and domestic PEPs and PEPs who are members of international organisations.[18]

Money laundering methods are constantly evolving: for example, the use of new technologies and products such as virtual currencies prepaid cards and mobile-payments or virtual assets and virtual asset service providers.[19] In response, a revised set of Recommendations were issued in 2018 with further updates appearing as and when required.[20]

4.3 PEPs AND THE FATF RECOMMENDATIONS

The FATF Recommendations require countries to ensure that 'financial institution secrecy laws do not inhibit implementation of the FATF Recommendations' and that financial institutions keep and retain the records of financial transactions, both domestic and international, for at least five years.[21] In addition, each country must have in place a legislative/regulatory framework requiring financial institutions and DNFBPs to implement cus-

---

15 Introduction to the 2012 FATF Recommendations.

16 FATF Recommendation 1.

17 See further Section 4.5.3 below.

18 FATF Recommendation 12.

19 A point noted in the Preamble to UN Security Council Resolution 2462 (2019).

20 For example, in June 2019 the FATF adopted an Interpretive Note to Recommendation 15 to clarify how the FATF requirements should apply to virtual assets and virtual asset service providers: see further FATF, *Guidance for a Risk-Based Approach: Virtual Assets and Virtual Asset Service Providers*, 2019.

21 FATF Recommendations 9 and 11 respectively. References to financial institutions include DNFBPs.

tomer due diligence (CDD) and 'KYC' measures when either establishing business relations or carrying out occasional large financial transactions, where there is a suspicion of money laundering or where the financial institution has doubts about the veracity or adequacy of previously obtained customer identification data.[22]

As PEPs pose a higher risk of money laundering,[23] the FATF has identified a number of 'red flags' which financial institutions and DNFBPs must take into account when considering their business relationships with PEPs. Here the Thiam case provides an excellent illustration:[24]

- PEPs attempting to shield their identify through the use of corporate vehicles.[25] In Thiam's case these were located in Malaysia and Mozambique.
- The involvement of PEPs with a high risk industry: for example, the arms trade and defence industry, construction infrastructure, mining and extractive industries. In the Thiam case it was the mining industry.
- The higher ranking the person's position, power or authority is, the higher the risks of this person being involved in money laundering crimes. As Minister of Mines, Thiam had effective control of the contractual process.
- PEPs from a higher risk country or region: for example, countries identified by credible sources as having a higher risk of corruption or countries that have not or insufficiently implemented relevant anti-corruption conventions such as the UNCAC or OECD Anti-Bribery Convention. Identifying such a person is not always easy especially where the PEP is able to conceal their nationality, for example through the use of a second passport. Thiam concealed his identity as a PEP by using his French passport to open a bank account.
- PEPs from countries with political systems that are based on personal rule, autocratic regimes or countries where a major objective is to enrich those in power.[26] In the Thiam case, Guinea was under a military regime during part of the period in question.

The result is that in addition to performing the normal CDD measures, in relation to both foreign and domestic PEPs (whether as customer or beneficial owner), financial institutions and DNFBPs must:

---

[22] FATF Recommendation 10. The applicable threshold is US$/EUR15,000.

[23] See FATF PEPs paper.

[24] See Section 2.1 above.

[25] See generally StAR (Stolen Assets Recovery) Initiative, *The Puppet Masters: How the Corrupt Use Legal Structures to Hide Stolen Assets and What to Do About It*, Washington DC, 2011.

[26] See FATF PEPs paper, at [27–32].

(a) have appropriate risk-management systems to determine whether the customer or the beneficial owner is a politically exposed person;
(b) obtain senior management approval for establishing (or continuing, for existing customers) such business relationships;
(c) take reasonable measures to establish the source of wealth and source of funds; and
(d) conduct enhanced on-going monitoring of the business relationship.[27]

The requirements for all types of PEPs also apply to family members or close associates of PEPs.

To ensure compliance with the Recommendations, countries are required to ensure that financial institutions are subject to adequate regulation and supervision and to establish a FIU.[28]

4.4 GLOBAL INFLUENCE OF THE FATF AND ITS 'TEETH'

As the FATF is a policy-making body the FATF Recommendations have never had binding force as a matter of international law.[29] Yet given the political, economic and financial power of PEPs it is essential that the Recommendations are sufficiently 'persuasive' to ensure countries globally implement them effectively and in total. Several factors give the FATF the 'teeth' with which to do so.

Firstly, FATF members comprise the majority of global financial centres. Their economic and political power and influence enable the FATF to impose its will by ensuring that countries globally become members of the 'FATF family' via the regional FATF-style regional bodies.

Secondly, the Recommendations almost invariably provide that some AML action 'should' be undertaken. On the face of it, this is a non-mandatory requirement and provides an option for FATF members as to whether or not to implement the particular action or strategy. Indeed the very title

[27] The Interpretive Note to FATF Recommendation 12 requires financial institutions 'to take reasonable measures to determine whether the beneficiaries of a life insurance policy and/or, where required, the beneficial owner of the beneficiary are politically exposed persons'. In such circumstances financial institutions must conduct 'enhanced scrutiny on the whole business relationship with the policyholder and consider making a suspicious transaction report'. See also FATF Recommendations 17 and 18 as regards foreign-based financial institutions.

[28] See Chapter 5.

[29] The UN Security Council Resolution 2462 (2019) strongly urges all States to implement the 'comprehensive international standards embodied in the FATF Recommendations ... and its interpretive notes', at [4].

'Recommendations' implies the same thing. However, hidden in the General Glossary to the 2012 Recommendations is the following:

> For the purposes of assessing compliance with the FATF Recommendations, the word *should* has the same meaning as *must.* (emphasis in the original)

In other words, 'Recommendations' is FATF-speak for 'Requirements'.

Thirdly, all members of the FATF 'family' are subject to regular and on-going mutual evaluation reviews, a process which gives it real 'teeth'.[30] As the FATF has noted:

> In order to protect the international financial system from money laundering and financing of terrorism (money laundering/CFT) risks and to encourage greater compliance with the AML/CFT standards, the FATF identifies jurisdictions that have strategic deficiencies and works with them to address those deficiencies that pose a risk to the international financial system.[31]

This includes an on-going follow-up process. In the African context, this is discussed at Section 4.5 below. To support states in their efforts to comply with their AML obligations, the FATF produces regular Guidance and Best Practice Papers.

Fourthly, countries with 'strategic deficiencies' are publicly identified, with the FATF and African RBs then working with them to implement action plans designed to address those deficiencies.[32] Thus Ethiopia, Kenya, and Sao Tome and Principe [33] were identified as having strategic weaknesses, with the FATF calling on its members to 'consider the risks arising from the deficiencies associated with each jurisdiction'. Such pressure had a dramatic effect on the political will to address the deficiencies. In 2013 Ethiopia enacted a new AML law[34] whilst Kenya enacted the Proceeds of Crime and Anti-Money

---

[30] Noted by the then President of the FATF, Bjorn Aamo, in an address to the ESAAMLG in Maputo, Mozambique, 31 August 2012.

[31] FATF 'High-risk and other monitored jurisdictions': http://www.fatf-gafi.org/publications/high-risk-and-other-monitored-jurisdictions/more/more-on-high-risk-and-non-cooperative-jurisdictions.html (accessed 4 June 2020).

[32] 'Jurisdictions with strategic AML/CFT deficiencies that have not made sufficient progress in addressing the deficiencies or have not committed to an action plan developed with the FATF to address the deficiencies. The FATF calls on its members to consider the risks arising from the deficiencies associated with each jurisdiction'.

[33] See FATF Public Statement of 22 February 2013. Available at http://www.fatf-gafi.org/topics/high-riskandnon-cooperativejurisdictions/documents/fatfpublicstatement22february2013.html (accessed 4 June 2020).

[34] Proc. No. 780/2013 (Prevention and Suppression of Money Laundering and Financing of Terrorism).

Laundering (Amendment) Act, which the FATF noted addressed deficiencies in the criminalisation of money laundering and asset recovery. The FATF also noted that Sao Tome and Principe had addressed a key deficiency by providing for the enforcement of its AML/CFT law in the new Penal Code.[35] The challenge continues for, as of March 2020, Botswana, Ghana, Mauritius, Uganda and Zimbabwe are on the FATF list of jurisdictions having strategic AML deficiencies.[36]

Failure to comply with the identified weaknesses can lead to the implementation of 'forceful persuasion' techniques through calling on all countries to apply 'EDD' measures against them. FATF Recommendation 19 states as follows:

> Financial institutions should [must] be required to apply enhanced due diligence measures to business relationships and transactions with natural and legal persons, and financial institutions, from countries for which this is called for by the FATF. The type of enhanced due diligence measures applied should be effective and proportionate to the risks.
>
> Countries should [must] be able to apply appropriate countermeasures when called upon to do so by the FATF. Countries should [must] also be able to apply countermeasures independently of any call by the FATF to do so. Such countermeasures should [must] be effective and proportionate to the risks.

The Interpretive Note to FATF Recommendation 19 contains a series of examples of countermeasures that countries may take in mitigating risks. These include limiting business relationships or financial transactions with the identified country or persons in that country and requiring financial institutions to review and amend, and if necessary terminate, correspondent relationships with financial institutions in the country concerned.[37]

Overall, the 'teeth' are designed to 'persuade' countries to take their AML obligations seriously, for otherwise the ability of their financial institutions and individuals to participate in the global financial system is potentially seriously

---

35 The three states also had other strategic deficiencies which necessitated their remaining on the FATF list.

36 As regards Ghana, Mauritius and Uganda see Section 4.7 below. In the case of Botswana and Zimbabwe, action is still required for improving transparency in beneficial ownership information and improving supervision of DNFBPs. In the case of Zimbabwe, see the Money Laundering and Proceeds of Crime (Amendment) Act 2019 which is designed to address these deficiencies.

37 'Correspondent banking is the provision of banking services by one bank (the correspondent bank) to another bank (the respondent bank). Respondent banks may be provided with a wide range of services including ... cheque clearing, payable through accounts and foreign exchange services': FATF Recommendations 2012, General Glossary.

impaired. Thus it is the *economic* weapon that is the key feature in developing and maintaining the *political* will to comply with the FATF Recommendations and hence to combat money laundering by PEPs.

4.5 THE ROLE OF THE AFRICAN RBs

4.5.1 Background

The need to address drug-related money laundering through jurisdictions in the Caribbean and Central America resulted in the establishment in 1990 of the first FATF-style regional body, the Caribbean Financial Action Task Force (CFATF). For similar reasons, this was followed by the creation of the Asia/Pacific Group on Money Laundering (APG). The four African FATF-style regional bodies date from 1999 with the establishment of the ESAAMLG.

A key feature of the work of African RBs is the mutual evaluation process which all member countries are required to undergo. This is characterised by a very detailed review procedure leading to the production of a mutual evaluation report (MER) on each country that critically assesses technical compliance with each of the individual FATF Recommendations and their implementation in practice.

There are a number of general principles governing such evaluations undertaken by all the African RBs. Amongst other things, these should:

- produce objective and accurate reports of a high standard in a timely way;
- ensure MERs are consistent, especially with respect to the findings, recommendations and ratings;
- encourage the implementation of higher AML standards;
- identify and promote good and effective practices; and
- alert governments and the private sector on areas that need strengthening.

The MERs provide a unique opportunity to understand the challenges facing individual African countries in complying with their AML obligations, including dealing with PEPs and also identifying money laundering typologies.

4.5.2 ESAAMLG

4.5.2.1 Background

The Group was launched in August 1999 at a meeting of southern African ministers and high-level representatives in Arusha, Tanzania. In June 2010 it became an associate member of the FATF. Its mission is to consolidate and sustain the combined efforts to combat money laundering in the Eastern and Southern Africa region.[38] From the original membership of nine African states,[39] the Group has expanded to 18 members,[40] all of which are signatories to a Memorandum of Understanding (MoU)[41] in which they commit to the adoption and implementation of the FATF Recommendations and agree amongst other things: (1) to apply AML measures to all serious crimes; and (2) to 'implement any other measures contained in multilateral agreements and initiatives to which they subscribe for the prevention and control of the laundering of the proceeds [of all serious crimes]'.[42]

4.5.2.2 Structure and work

The key decision-making body of the ESAAMLG is the Council of Ministers, which consists of at least one ministerial representative from each member country. The presidency of the Council rotates amongst members of the Group with the incumbent holding office for one year.[43] The Council is responsible, amongst other things, for approving and developing a Strategic Plan setting out the Group's on-going AML goals and objectives. It is also responsible for approving the mutual evaluation procedures and adopting the MER on each member country. The current Strategic Plan for 2017–2020 again[44] focuses on strengthening the evaluation and monitoring of state compliance with the FATF Recommendations, expanding the membership of the Group and strengthening international co-operation.[45]

The ESAAMLG Task Force consisting of senior officials from each member country meets twice a year and, amongst other things, considers the country reports and makes recommendations for any further action. It

---

[38] ESAAMLG, *Annual Report 2016–2017*, Dar es Salaam, 2017, p. iii.

[39] Botswana, Kenya, Mauritius, Mozambique, South Africa, Tanzania, Uganda, Zambia and Zimbabwe. For a helpful history see ESAAMLG, *20 Years: From Arusha to Ezulwini: Looking Back and Looking Ahead*, Dar es Salaam, 2019, pp. 14–17 (hereafter the ESAAMLG report).

[40] The additional members are Angola, Ethiopia, Lesotho, Madagascar, Malawi, Namibia, Rwanda, Seychelles and Swaziland (Eswatini). Comoros was formerly a member of the Group but later withdrew. Eritrea has observer status with a view to joining the Group in 2020. There are also 30 regional and international observers including the Africa Development Bank, the Egmont Group of Financial Intelligence Units, the FATF, the International Monetary Fund and the World Bank.

[41] *Memorandum of Understanding among Member Countries of the Eastern and Southern Africa Anti-Money Laundering Group (ESAAMLG)*. This has been amended on six occasions at the Council of Ministers, the latest being in 2018.

[42] Article I.

[43] To avoid any disputes, this is based on an alphabetical order. In 2019–2020 the Presidency was held by Eswatini (formerly Swaziland).

[44] This is the fourth such plan.

[45] ESAAMLG report, pp. 16–17.

is assisted by a Steering Committee which plays an advisory role on policy matters. The Secretariat is based in Arusha, Tanzania, and performs technical and administrative functions.[46]

4.5.2.3 The mutual evaluation process

To ensure compliance with their AML obligations, each ESAAMLG member agrees to participate in an on-going self-assessment programme as well as a mutual evaluation process designed to monitor state compliance with the FATF Recommendations.[47] The First Round took place between 2007 and 2012 whilst the second round started in 2015 and is due for completion by 2023.

The mutual evaluation process consists of an on-site visit to a member country conducted by a team of experts[48] from other member counties (and, on occasions, from international organisations) with the aim of assessing compliance with each of the FATF Recommendations.[49] A comprehensive draft report is then produced which highlights any AML 'deficiencies' and makes recommendations for action. In doing so the member country is categorised on each FATF Recommendation as either 'compliant', 'largely compliant', 'partially compliant', or 'non-compliant'. The country report is reviewed by the Task Force and then adopted by the Council of Ministers. Thereafter the report is published.[50]

There is then a follow-up process. Once a member country has made sufficient progress in addressing the deficiencies highlighted in the MER it exits the follow-up process. Where the evaluation reveals strategic deficiencies, there is provision for the drawing up of an 'Implementation Action Plan' setting out a time-frame to address them[51] as well as follow-up visits to review progress. Where a member country is found to have significant shortcomings

---

[46] For details see ESAAMLG report, pp. 29–30.

[47] Articles XIII and XIV.

[48] The team normally consists of 5–7 experts from the legal, financial and law enforcement sectors.

[49] ESAAMLG members may be assessed in one of three ways: by an ESAAMLG Mutual Evaluation; by an IMF or World Bank-led assessment; or for the members of the ESAAMLG who are also members of the FATF or the Off-Shore Group of Banking Supervisors (OGBS), jointly by the FATF or the OGBS and ESAAMLG: See ESAAMLG, *Mutual Evaluation Procedures*, 2008.

[50] A state may object and in this case this fact is publicly noted. The 1st round of mutual evaluations was completed in 2012 and all reports and follow-up reports are publicly available. The reports generally refer to 'states' rather than 'countries'.

[51] See 'Procedures for the ESAAMLG 1st Round of AML/CFT Mutual Evaluations and Follow-Up Process'.

in its technical compliance[52] or effectiveness systems,[53] there is 'enhanced follow-up' which involves a more intense follow-up process. Countries may request a re-rating of their technical compliance and this is undertaken as part of the follow-up process.[54] For example, in their MER on Zimbabwe, reviewers found that the definition of a foreign PEP in the Money Laundering and Proceeds of Crime Act did not comply with the FATF Recommendations and the country was rated partially compliant (PC) on the issue. This was rapidly addressed in an amendment Act which led to the ESAAMLG re-rating the country as compliant with the Recommendation.

The AML challenges identified in the MERs and the impact of the reviews in practice, particularly as regards PEPs, are discussed below.

4.5.3 Inter-governmental Action Group Against Money Laundering in West Africa (GIABA)

4.5.3.1 Background

The Group is a specialised institution of the ECOWAS and was established in 2000 by the ECOWAS[55] Authority of Heads of State and government. It comprises 16 state members.[56] Its role is to provide 'a focus for co-operative AML and anti-terrorism financing efforts' in the West African region. Its link with the FATF is highlighted in Article 2 of the Revised Statutes of the GIABA, which states that:

> the Group shall do everything possible to ensure that Member States recognise, adopt and implement ... the FATF norms including Recommendations especially [the 2012 Recommendations] adopted by the FATF members.

Article 2 also sets out the objectives of the Group which include: (1) combating the laundering of proceeds from crime and the financing of terrorism; (2) ensuring harmonised and concerted adoption of appropriate measures to combat money laundering and the financing of terrorism; and (3) evaluating, through self-evaluation and mutual evaluation according to the FATF procedure, progress and the efficacy of measures.

---

52 This addresses the specific requirements of the FATF Recommendations.

53 This focuses on analysing the extent to which the legal and institutional AML framework is producing the expected results: see ESAAMLG report, p. 35.

54 For example, Botswana, Ethiopia, Mauritius, Uganda and Zimbabwe have all asked for a re-rating.

55 Economic Community of West African States.

56 Benin, Burkina Faso, Cape Verde, Cote d'Ivoire, The Gambia, Ghana, Guinea, Guinea Bissau, Liberia, Mali, Niger, Nigeria, Sao Tome and Principe, Senegal, Sierra Leone and Togo.

4.5.3.2 Structure and work

The GIABA is headed by a Director General and comprises the Plenary, Evaluation and Compliance Group. Their role is discussed below. The Secretariat is based in Dakar, Senegal.

4.5.3.3 The mutual evaluation process[57]

The Secretariat liaises with individual countries concerning arrangements for the evaluation. A key practical issues is the language in which it will be undertaken.[58] Given the fact that the assessors come from different countries, this may involve the need to provide translation during the visit. Further, the process is often delayed by the need to have all documentation translated into several languages.[59]

Prior to the on-site visit, the country being reviewed is sent a standard questionnaire which it is required to complete. It has the onus of demonstrating that its AML regime is effective. The assessors, who are formally appointed by the Director General of GIABA, then conduct the mutual evaluation and produce a report assessing the country's compliance with the FATF standards both in terms of technical compliance and effectiveness. Given the importance of international co-operation in combating money laundering, GIABA member states, the FATF and other African RBs are invited to provide information on their experience of international co-operation with the country under review. This information is available to the assessors at the time of the on-site visit.

The draft MER is discussed with the reviewed country and considered at a meeting of the Evaluation and Compliance Group, which determines the key issues for discussion at the Plenary. The final report is then agreed by the Plenary and is then published on the GIABA website. As with the ESAAMLG process, the country is categorised on each FATF Recommendation as being either 'compliant' (C) 'largely compliant' (LC), 'partially compliant' (PC) or 'non-compliant' (NC).

---

[57] The detailed methodology can be found in GIABA, *Process and Procedures: Mutual Evaluations*, 2014, pp. 2–15.

[58] The official languages of the GIABA are English, French and Portuguese.

[59] The African RBs all face practical issues regarding the translation of documents. This may also extend to translating FATF documentation, which is frequently only available in English. For example, the GIABA assisted in the translation of the FATF report *Concealment of Beneficial Ownership* into French and Portuguese: see *Report of the GIABA Seminar on Transparency of Beneficial Ownership for Francophone African Countries*, GIABA *Annual Report 2018* (GIABA 2018 report), at [299].

4.5.3.4 The follow-up process

The process is intended to apply 'sufficient peer pressure and accountability' on member countries to implement the FATF standards in full. This is done by way of regular monitoring of their compliance. Following the adoption of the MERs, a country is placed on either the regular or an enhanced follow-up process. The regular process is the default mechanism and involves an on-going monitoring system, with each country being required to report back to the Plenary every two years as to the steps taken to address any AML deficiencies identified in its MER.

The enhanced follow-up process applies to any country where its MER has identified significant technical compliance or effectiveness deficiencies.[60] It is then required to report back to the Plenary on an annual basis as to the steps taken to address the deficiencies. In addition, the Plenary may take further enhanced measures to ensure compliance. These include bringing political pressure on the country, suspending or terminating its membership of GIABA or applying FATF Recommendation 19. In this case, a public statement is issued on the GIABA website stating that the country is insufficiently in compliance with the FATF Recommendations and recommending 'appropriate action' and whether additional countermeasures are required.

There is also provision for follow-up assessment(s) to assess improvements and this may lead to a re-rating on compliance. The follow-up reports may be published. Such follow-up may involve a series of visits. For example, in the case of The Gambia, the initial MER in 2008 highlighted a range of failures to comply with the FATF Recommendations. This was followed by no less than eight follow-up reports, each of which highlighted continuing concerns over the failure to comply with all the FATF Recommendations.[61]

4.5.3.5 The mutual evaluation rounds

The Group has undertaken two rounds of mutual evaluations based on the FATF Recommendations and the Interpretive Notes. An analysis of the First Round of mutual evaluations amongst members of the GIABA revealed an overall low level of compliance with the FATF Recommendations in numerous countries. It also highlighted that even with the necessary political support for AML measures, economic constraints limited the ability of many countries to comply fully with their obligations. Alarmingly, a key finding of the GIABA report was that the overwhelming majority of target-respondents were

---

[60] For example, where a country is rated NC or PC on eight or more of the FATF Recommendations for technical compliance: for a full listing see GIABA *Process and Procedures*, at [766]–[780].

[61] In the case of Liberia, seven follow-up visits have taken place.

unaware of the existence of the FATF Recommendations 'even though most of them are high-echelon functionaries of agencies and bodies responsible for the prevention and control of money-laundering'.[62]

Prior to the commencement of the second round in 2016, the GIABA directed all member countries to undertake and complete their respective NRAs in line with FATF Recommendation 1. The process is notable for the involvement of a broad range of participants from both the public and private sector and the detailed analysis carried out.[63] The GIABA has helpfully used the NRAs as well as country MERs to identify money laundering typologies and these are discussed below.

As noted earlier, the failure of individual states to comply with their AML obligations can lead to their being publicly identified as having 'strategic deficiencies' that requires remedial action or face the prospect of other countries taking countermeasures in line with FATF Recommendation 19.

4.5.4 Middle East and North Africa FATF (MENAFATF)

4.5.4.1 Background

At a ministerial meeting in November 2004, the governments of 14 states, including Algeria, Egypt, Libya, Mauritania, Morocco, Somalia, Sudan and Tunisia, signed a MoU establishing the MENAFATF.[64] The Preamble notes that countries in the region 'should work jointly to comply with [FATF] standards in order to establish an effective system which countries need to implement in a way that does not contradict their cultural values, constitutional frameworks and legal systems'.

The MENAFATF is voluntary and co-operative in nature and does not derive from any international treaty,[65] sets its own rules and procedures but cooperates with the FATF and other international bodies to achieve its objects. As with the other African RBs, these include adopting and implementing the FATF Recommendations; ensuring compliance with these standards and measures within the Middle East and North African region; and working with other international organisations to raise AML compliance worldwide.[66]

---

[62] At p. 84. This reached 80% and 90% of functionaries in Benin and Liberia respectively.

[63] See for example, Republic of Ghana, *National Anti-Money Laundering and Countering the Financing of Terrorism (AML/CFT) Risk Assessment of Ghana*, Accra, 2018.

[64] The Memorandum was amended in November 2013.

[65] Article 2.

[66] Article 1.

4.5.4.2 Structure and work

The MENAFATF consists of two bodies. The Plenary is the decision and policy-making body that meets twice a year. It is headed by a President[67] and comprises delegates appointed by member countries. It is a policy-making body as well as being responsible for approving the MERs of member countries and identifying their technical assistance needs.[68] The Secretariat is based in Bahrain and provides support for the country reviews and oversees the mutual evaluation exercises. Arabic is the official language although English and French may be used when required.[69]

4.5.4.3 The mutual evaluation process

All member countries are required to participate in the mutual evaluation programme. The first round of evaluations took place between 2006 and 2012 and was designed to assess conformity of member countries with the FATF standards. The second round of evaluations is now taking place. As with the other African RBs, each member country is assessed as to its compliance with each of the FATF Recommendations.

Where there are significant AML deficiencies identified, a follow-up process is conducted.[70] The Plenary is then informed on a regular basis of the measures being taken by the country to address the deficiencies identified in the MER. The aim is to motivate and encourage member countries to address the identified deficiencies in order to enhance the level of compliance and the effectiveness of AML/CFT systems and to exit the follow-up process within a reasonable time-frame. In practice this has proved a lengthy process with African member countries, amongst others requiring numerous follow-up visits and follow-up reports.[71]

4.5.4.4 Corruption and money laundering

The MENAFATF has also focused on the relationship between corruption and money laundering in the region as this is seen as a problem in many countries.

---

[67] The President and Vice-President/Next President remain in office for one year: Article 8.2.

[68] Article 8.3.8.

[69] Article 6. Note the potential problems surrounding the need for translation noted in Section 4.5.3.3 above.

[70] For a country to have taken sufficient action to be considered for removal from the process, it must have an effective AML/CFT system in force, under which it has implemented the core and key recommendations at a level essentially equivalent to C or LC.

[71] The number of follow-up reports for the African members were Egypt: five; Sudan: three; Algeria: seven; Tunisia: six; and Morocco: eight.

This led to a typologies exercise with the results published in 2017 and these are noted in the discussion below.[72]

4.5.5 Task Force on Money Laundering in Central Africa (GABAC)[73]

The Task Force on Money Laundering in Central Africa (GABAC) is a body of the Economic and Monetary Community of Central Africa. Established in 2015 its members comprise Cameroon, Central African Republic, Chad, Republic of the Congo, DRC, Equatorial Guinea and Gabon.

In essence it functions in the same manner as the other African RBs.

4.5.6 Co-operation between the African RBs

The sharing of information and networking between African RBs is now well established and is an example of good AML practice. It is potentially of great significance given that countries in each of the four regions face similar money laundering challenges. This includes the development of a series of workshops that are jointly organised by the four African RBs designed to address specific AML issues. For example, a joint workshop in 2018 focused on addressing money laundering risks and trends and professional money laundering networks.[74]

4.5.7 MERs and the Role of Civil Society

The weakness of CSOs and the media in raising public awareness of corruption and money laundering risks is noted in reports from the ESAAMLG, MENAFATF and GIABA. Two strategies are needed. Firstly, to ensure that individual country reports are widely circulated. This will enhance awareness of national AML deficiencies and provide an opportunity for parliamentarians, political opponents, CSOs and the media to raise public awareness of the process and to hold the government to account. Secondly, to provide appropriate training for CSOs and the media on AML trends.[75]

---

[72] MENAFATF, *Typologies Report on Money Laundering and Corruption*, 2017 (the MENAFATF 2017 report).

[73] Groupe d'Action contre le blanchiment d'Argent en Afrique Centrale.

[74] For details see GIABA 2018 report, at [414]. See also the work of the Committee on Strengthening Anti-Money Laundering Capacities in West Africa (the SAMWA project).

[75] See for example, the role of the Zambia Financial Intelligence Centre discussed in Section 4.6.2 below.

4.6 HOW IS IT DONE: MERs AND MONEY LAUNDERING TYPOLOGIES

All the African RBs report that combating money laundering by PEPs remains a common challenge for African countries. In order to effectively address this situation in practice, it is important to identify the sectors that display the greatest money laundering vulnerabilities. Conducting typologies exercises is a feature of both the FATF itself and the African RBs.

4.6.1 Money Laundering Typologies

The MERs themselves identify a consistent trend in money laundering typologies:

1. *Cash*: With most adults having no formal bank accounts,[76] most countries still have largely cash-based economics. This provides a ready vehicle for money laundering.[77] This includes cross-border cash movements, a problem identified in numerous countries.[78]
2. *Financial sector*: Not surprisingly this sector is much used for money laundering purposes with many financial institutions still failing to take reasonable measures to determine whether a customer or beneficial owner or beneficiary of a life insurance policy is a PEP.[79]
   Indeed, in order to facilitate money laundering PEPs may own or exercise considerable control over financial institutions, both domestically and in off-shore locations. This perhaps reflects the maxim that 'The best way to launder money is to own a bank'. This is a particular threat in weakly regulated jurisdictions that offer international banking services. For example, in February 2020, Cape Verde announced the closure of banks that only provided services to non-resident customers. This was the result of revelations from the Luanda Leaks investigation in which it was alleged that Isabel

[76] According to the GIABA Research Report, *The Vulnerabilities of Designated Non-Financial Businesses and Professions to Money Laundering and Terrorist Financing and the Adequacy of Control Measures in West Africa*, 2015 at [18], with the exception of Nigeria and Ghana, less than 23% of West African adults possess formal bank accounts: at [18].

[77] See for example, the MENAFATF 2017 report, p. 32.

[78] For example, Benin, Burkina Faso, Cape Verde, Comoros, Cote d'Ivoire, Guinea, Guinea-Bissau, Liberia, Niger, Sierra Leone and Togo: see GIABA Research Report.

[79] As required by FATF Recommendation 12. This has led to the de-risking of many people in the ESAAMLG region: see ESAAMLG, *Survey Report on De-risking in the ESAAMLG Region*, 2016.

dos Santos held 42.5% of the shares in an off-shore bank, the 'Banco Bic Cabo Verde', registered in the country. The bank was said to be an increasingly important part of her payments system as concern grew from other financial institutions over her financial dealings.[80] The case also highlights the significance of FATF Recommendation 13 which requires financial institutions, in relation to cross-border correspondent banking or similar relationships, to have in place enhanced customer due diligence measures and to be prohibited from having such a relationship with shell banks.[81] Whilst financial institutions remain vulnerable, there are increasing concerns over microfinance with the development of mobile banking and associated products and the use of virtual currencies.[82]

3. *Insurance and micro-insurance sectors:* Several countries have reported that these sectors are vulnerable to money laundering.[83]
4. *TCSPs*: These provide another important means for PEPs to launder proceeds of crime, especially through their assistance in establishing off-shore companies and trusts.
5. *Lawyers* The role of lawyers and other legal professionals in assisting money laundering also figures prominently in the MERs.[84]
6. *Other DNFBPs:* A constant theme found in the MERs is the lack of knowledge or understanding by DNFBPs as to their AML and EDD obligations. The real estate sector is widely seen as particularly vulnerable, especially in that many transactions still involve cash payments. The lack of regulation of dealers in precious metals and stones also makes this area of especial interest to money launderers. Other areas of vulnerability include car dealerships, casinos and related gaming establishments.

In an effort to address these issues, the ESAAMLG has established a Risk, Trends and Methods Group comprising experts from member countries. Its

---

[80] Ms dos Santos reportedly co-founded the bank in Angola in 2005. The bank later opened offices in Mozambique, Namibia and Portugal, as well as in Cape Verde: see Max de Haldevang 'How Africa's richest woman bought her way out of scrutiny from Western banks' QuartzAfrica, news report, 19 January 2020.

[81] According to the IN to FATF Recommendation 13, a shell bank means 'a bank that has no physical presence in the country in which it is incorporated and licensed, and which is unaffiliated with a regulated financial group that is subject to effective consolidated supervision'. See also the discussion in Section 4.5 above.

[82] Zimbabwe highlights the dramatic increase in mobile banking. Here financial inclusion figures have risen from 60% in 2011 to almost 80% as of 2018, largely driven by mobile money services.

[83] For example, Ethiopia and Cote d'Ivoire.

[84] Addressing the issue of lawyers raises constitutional issues: see the discussion in Section 8.3.

mandate is to carry out on-going typologies studies designed to identify new money laundering trends and methods and to provide training for investigators, prosecutors and law enforcement agents on addressing these challenges.[85] The ESAAMLG Public–Private Sector Dialogue was launchéd in 2013 with a view to engaging key policy officials and business stakeholders in emerging African markets in implementing effective AML regimes.[86] Regular meetings include addressing the problems of de-risking in the region, correspondent banking arrangements and new technologies.[87]

4.6.2 Money Laundering Typologies: A Case Study from Zambia

Section 5(2)(e) of the Financial Intelligence Centre Act 2010 mandates the Zambia Financial Intelligence Centre (ZFIC) to provide the public with information concerning money laundering trends. In doing, it is required to publish a regular 'Trends' report. The 2018 report[88] provides a wealth of information on money laundering typologies including highlighting the involvement of PEPs and making some important practical suggestions for addressing the problems. In doing so, it demonstrates the vulnerability of the public procurement process to corruption and money laundering by PEPs, both individually and as part of a syndicate. Of particular interest is the analysis of the specific methods by which the laundering of the proceeds of crime by PEPs takes place.

1. *The use of shell corporate vehicles*

The use of shell companies was identified as a key laundering mechanism, i.e. the use of 'registered companies that are non-operational and do not have any known physical address ... to conceal the identity of the beneficial owner'. The ZFIC notes that they were used both to obtain government contracts with, in some cases the contracts being awarded prior to the formation of the company, as well as for the laundering of the proceeds of crime. The report also notes the 'continuing trend' of using family members or associates of PEPs to hide the beneficial ownership of corporate vehicles and to own property.

---

85 For details of the RTM Group see ESAAMLG report, pp. 39–44.

86 The key attendees from the private sector are from financial institutions, money remitters, mobile money transfer companies, banking associations and DNFBPs (confidential source).

87 See further the ESAAMLG report, pp. 52–3.

88 Zambia Financial Intelligence Centre, *5th Money Laundering and Terrorist Financing Trends Report 2018*, Lusaka, 2018 (the ZFIC report).

2. *The vulnerability of lawyers*

The report notes the 'high usage of gatekeepers such as law firms and accounting/audit firms to facilitate the corrupt activities'. A particular feature was the assistance lawyers provided to PEPs via the use of client accounts through which to move proceeds abroad, purchase real estate and motor vehicles and distribute cash to beneficial owners. Alarmingly, in some cases, the PEPs involved were the AML regulators themselves.[89]

The report notes the need for effective supervision by professional bodies to 'ensure criminal elements do not hijack the operation of the supervisory bodies'.[90]

3. *Use of domestic financial institutions*

These included banks, microfinance institutions, pension funds and insurance companies. In a number of cases, these were used to transfer the proceeds abroad. The failure of the AML safeguards was highlighted in that there were instances of 'wilful blindness' on the part of reporting institutions in failing to make appropriate STRs. Here the ZFIC calls for additional powers in such cases to impose administrative sanctions, including financial penalties.[91]

The emergence of crypto-currencies such as Bitcoin, Litecoin and Ripple, as a ready mechanism for money laundering is also highlighted and the consequent need noted for regulation of users and financial institutions and DNFBPs that send, receive and store crypto-currencies.[92]

4. *Lack of regulation over real estate sector*

The use of laundered funds by PEPs to purchase real estate was also highlighted as a common money laundering typology. In addition, the ZFIC noted that, '[c]onstruction provides an easy and undetectable avenue for criminals to launder funds. The placement and layering of the illegal proceeds occur during the construction of the property. The integration of the proceeds of crime occurs when either the property is sold or leased for rental income.'[93] The report provides a useful example of syndicate corruption in the sector. Here PEP A, with the assistance of PEPs B and C, influenced the awarding of a lucrative government contract to a foreign construction company. In return

[89] This is another useful illustration of the power of PEPs to undermine AML controls: see further the discussion in Section 2.5 above.

[90] ZFIC report, p. 13.

[91] Ibid, p. 13.

[92] ZFIC report, p. 17.

[93] Ibid, p. 15.

the company constructed 49 residential properties for PEP A and purchased four properties for PEPs B and C.[94] Here the need for a regulator to oversee the property development in the real estate was highlighted.

The annual publication of a 'Trends' report is an invaluable contribution to national AML action and is an excellent supplement to the MERs. By providing a regular update on money laundering vulnerabilities, especially as regards PEPs, it provides a vehicle for highlighting, both for government and civil society, the areas for additional AML action. Other African countries should take steps to introduce a requirement for the publication of such reports by AML agencies.

4.7 THE IMPACT OF THE MUTUAL EVALUATION PROCESS: SELECTED COUNTRY CASE STUDIES

The impact of the mutual evaluation process and the MERs is best illustrated through a series of country case studies. These are drawn from countries from different African regions and with different constitutional and legal systems and traditions, again emphasising that all African countries are obliged to implement the FATF standards and are held to account if they do not do so. A common thread in each report is the attention to detail undertaken by reviewers in assessing compliance with those standards.

4.7.1 Uganda

Uganda is a member of the ESAAMLG with a common law system. Its Second Round MER was adopted by the Council of Ministers in 2016. The country was rated as non-compliant (NC) or partially compliant (PC) with 35 of the 40 FATF Recommendations. As regards FATF Recommendation 12 in relation to PEPs, the country was rated NC. As regards PEPs, they found major deficiencies in that:

- There were no legal obligations for financial institutions to take reasonable measures to determine whether beneficiaries were PEPs.
- There was no clarity on the application of the Anti-Money Laundering Act requirements on domestic PEPs.
- There was no requirement for enhanced on-going monitoring of PEPs.

[94] The properties were valued at ZMK70 million and ZMK 61 million respectively: ZFIC report, p. 19.

- The measures provided in relation to PEPs did not extend to beneficial owners of the PEPs as well as the beneficiaries of insurance policies.
- The EDD did not extend to domestic PEPs.

As a result, the country was placed in enhanced follow-up. This resulted in significant action being taken to address the deficiencies. In 2018 the reviewers returned to undertake a 'Detailed Analysis of Progress'.[95] This found that Uganda had made progress in addressing some of the compliance deficiencies identified in its MER and several were re-rated as Compliant (C). However, there remained deficiencies as regards others, including FATF Recommendation 12.

The reviewers recognised that Uganda had responded positively to the report but took the view that deficiencies remained as regards applying enhanced on-going monitoring of business relationships and obtaining the approval of senior management before establishing or continuing a business relationship with domestic PEPs.[96] As a result, Uganda was re-rated only PC with FATF Recommendation 12.

A further follow-up report will review further progress.

4.7.2 Ghana

Ghana is a member of the GIABA and has a common law system. Its 2009 MER identified 'strategic deficiencies' in 16 key FATF Recommendations including a failure to (1) adequately criminalise money laundering; (2) establish and implement adequate measures for the confiscation of funds related to money laundering; (3) establish effective CDD measures; and (4) establish a fully operational and effectively functioning FIU.[97] An Action Plan to address the deficiencies was produced and in October 2010, Ghana publicly made a political commitment to implement this within one year. However, in October 2011 FATF announced that Ghana had not made sufficient progress in addressing its deficiencies[98] and later issued a public statement calling on its members 'to consider the risks arising from the deficiencies in Ghana's

---

95 ESAAMLG, *Uganda: Second Follow-Up Report*, 2018, p. 10.

96 Ibid, at [27].

97 FATF press release dated 22 October 2010. Available at http://www.fatf-gafi.org/countries/d-i/ghana/documents/improvingglobalamlcftcomplianceupdateon-goingprocess-october2010.html (accessed 5 June 2020).

98 FATF press release dated 28 October 2011. Available at http://www.fatf-gafi.org/countries/d-i/ghana/documents/improvingglobalamlcftcomplianceon-goingprocess-28october2011.html#Ghana (accessed 5 June 2020).

AML/CT regime'.[99] This pressure produced a swift reaction. The Anti-Money Laundering Regulations 2011[100] were introduced which comprehensively addressed the CDD issue whilst the Economic and Organised Crime Office Act 2010 provided for the confiscation of proceeds of crime. In addition, the Ghana FIU, known as the Financial Intelligence Centre, became fully operational.

The GIABA then issued a second follow-up progress report which highlighted those areas where further action was still necessary.[101] Finally in January 2013, following an on-site visit to Ghana, the FATF International Co-operation Review Group (ICRG) announced that it was satisfied that the main action plan items had been substantially completed, and that there were political commitment and institutional capacity to implement appropriate AML reforms in Ghana. They concluded that Ghana was therefore no longer subject to FATF's monitoring process but that it would work with the GIABA so as to address the full range of AML issues identified in its MER.[102]

In 2017 the 2nd round MER on Ghana was adopted by the GIABA. Significant deficiencies in its technical compliance with the FATF Recommendations were noted and accordingly GIABA placed Ghana in 'enhanced follow-up'. One key deficiency in relation to PEPs was the lack of an express requirement for financial institutions to obtain and maintain beneficiary information and to include such information on cross-border wire transfers. This led to swift action with guidelines being issued in January 2018 which largely addressed the deficiency[103] and led to a re-rating by Ghana from partially compliant to largely compliant.[104]

---

99 FATF Public Statement dated 16 February 2012. Available at http://www.fatf-gafi.org/countries/d-i/ghana/documents/fatfpublicstatement-16february2012.html (accessed 5 June 2020).

100 LI 1987 of 2011.

101 http://www.giaba.org/media/f/267_2nd%20FUR%20ME%20-%20Ghana%20-%20dev011812%20-%20English.pd (accessed 5 June 2020).

102 See GIABA press release dated 22 February 2013.

103 See Bank of Ghana/Financial Intelligence Centre, *AML/CFT&P Guidelines for Banks and Non-Bank Financial Institutions*, issued in January 2018. A sanctions regime for breaches of the Guidelines was established by the Bank of Ghana in May 2018.

104 This is an interesting example of the detail with which reviews are undertaken. The reviewers noted that the new Guidelines did not ensure that all cross-border wire transfers were accompanied by the beneficiary's account number. This led to the re-rating of Largely Compliant. See GIABA, *Ghana: First Enhanced Follow-Up Report and Technical Compliance Re-Rating*, 2018, at [9].

However, as at March 2020, Ghana remains on the FATF list of 'Jurisdictions with strategic deficiencies'. These include the need to:

1. implement a comprehensive national AML policy based on deficiencies identified in the NRA, including measures to mitigate money laundering risks associated with the legal persons;
2. improve risk-based supervision, by enhancing the capacity of the regulators and the awareness of the private sector;
3. ensure the timely access to adequate, accurate and current basic and beneficial ownership information;
4. ensure that the FIU is focusing its activities on the risks identified in the NRA, and is adequately resourced; and
5. apply a risk-based approach for monitoring non-profit organisations. The FATF has noted that Ghana has made a high-level political commitment to work with the FATF and GIABA to address these concerns and to strengthen the effectiveness of its AML regime.[105]

4.7.3 Mauritius

Mauritius is a member of the ESAAMLG. It has a hybrid legal system being a mixture of French civil law and the English common law. In the African context it is unusual in that it is a financial services centre offering both banking and non-banking services. As was noted in its 2018 MER:

> the country generates a huge volume of business from outside the country through the global business sector in the form of deposits and investments. Most of the customers and investors are non-residents, corporates with sophisticated/ complex structures, *politically exposed persons* and high net worth individuals' (emphasis added).[106]

As a 'facilitating state', the assessors noted that Mauritius was therefore exposed 'to a substantial risk of attracting cross-border illicit financial flows for laundering purposes'.[107]

In fact the 2018 MER revealed that Mauritius was compliant with just two of the FATF Recommendations. As regards Recommendation 12 Mauritius was rated partially compliant. The main technical deficiencies included the fact

---

[105] See http://www.fatf-gafi.org/publications/high-risk-and-other-monitored-jurisdictions/documents/increased-monitoring-february-2020.html#ghana (accessed 7 June 2020).

[106] ESAAMLG, *Mauritius: Mutual Evaluation Report*, 2018, at [41].

[107] Ibid, at [213].

that not all financial institutions were covered; there was no requirement for senior management approval for persons who become PEPs after commencement of relationship; financial institutions did not apply the same standards to family members and close associates of PEPs; and there was no requirement to establish the source of wealth of a beneficial owner. Further, foreign PEPs were not fully addressed although they posed a significant money laundering risk given their involvement in complex multi-national company structures and cash-intensive businesses.[108]

Perhaps not surprisingly, as a result of the MER Mauritius was required to undergo an enhanced follow-up process. Since then, the FATF/ESAAMLG has noted that Mauritius has made progress on a number of recommended actions. As regards PEPs, the Financial Intelligence and Anti-Money Laundering Regulations 2018[109] introduced enhanced CDD[110] and EDD measures for domestic and foreign PEPs.[111] There are also enhanced requirements introduced for verifying the identity of beneficial ownership of legal persons, trusts and insurance policies, a point of particular significance given the fact of the country being an important off-shore financial centre.[112] However, the country remains on the FATF list of 'Jurisdictions with strategic deficiencies' although in February 2020, the FATF noted that Mauritius had made a 'high-level political commitment to work with the FATF and ESAAMLG to strengthen the effectiveness of its AML/CFT regime'.[113] This is another neat example of the 'persuasive' power of the FATF and African RBs to create the political will in countries to address money laundering effectively.

4.7.4 Mozambique

Mozambique is a member of the ESAAMLG. Its legal system is based on Portuguese civil law. In 2011 Mozambique was evaluated in 2009 and the MER adopted in 2011 by the ESAAMLG Council of Ministers. This highlighted numerous failures to comply with the FATF Recommendations. As a result, several laws were passed including a new AML/CFT law and addi-

---

[108] For the full analysis of FATF Recommendation 12 compliance, see ibid at p. 157.

[109] GN 108 of 2018 and made under sections 17C-E and 35 of the Financial Intelligence and Anti-Money Laundering Act.

[110] See regulations 9 and 10.

[111] See regulations 12 and 14–15.

[112] See in particular, regulations 6 and 7.

[113] http://www.fatf-gafi.org/publications/high-risk-and-other-monitored-jurisdictions/documents/increased-monitoring-february-2020.html#mauritius (accessed 7 June 2020).

tions to the Penal Code providing for a wider scope of predicate offences.[114] However, no National Risk Assessment has been undertaken and further progress on addressing other failures has been extremely slow. This is highlighted in the 9th progress report in 2018[115] where the continued deficiencies identified included weaknesses as regards the operation and powers of the FIU[116] and the lack of a legal framework for dealing with mutual legal assistance[117] and weak asset recovery provisions.[118]

The fact that after nine follow-up reports, Mozambique still has significant money laundering vulnerabilities is disappointing and seemingly demonstrates the lack of political will to take effective action. Inevitably the assessors recommended that Mozambique is required to report bi-annually on progress.[119]

In 2019 a report entitled *Republic of Mozambique: Diagnostic Report on Transparency, Governance and Corruption* (the Diagnostic Report) was published by the International Monetary Fund. The report was prepared by the Government of Mozambique 'in broad consultation with stakeholders' and provides a candid analysis of the efforts made to address AML deficiencies and the on-going AML challenges facing the country. The report identifies high-level corruption as a major money laundering risk and thus, at least impliedly, suggests a lack of political will to take effective action. In addition, low technical capacity, budgetary constraints and lack of institutional autonomy constitute additional on-going constraints.[120]

4.7.5 Mauritania

Mauritania is a member of the MENAFATF. The legal system is a mix of French civil law and of Sharia. In 2018 its MER was adopted by the Plenary of the MENAFATF and highlights starkly the fact that some African countries still

---

[114] Law No.14/2013 and Law No. 35/2014 respectively.

[115] ESAAMLG, *Post Evaluation Progress Report of Mozambique on AML/CFT Measures*, 2018.

[116] In particular the non-implementation of Guidelines relating to the real estate sector due to the failure to pass amendments to the Financial Intelligence Unit Act. In addition, there were still no Guidelines for other DNFBPs as previously recommended by assessors: ibid, at [17]. The country had also failed to address the lack of independence of the FIU: at [20].

[117] This includes the fact there was no recognised Central Authority in place: see ibid, at [24–6].

[118] To address this issue, the assessors noted that there was a proposal to create an Asset Recovery Unit: ibid, at [69].

[119] Ibid, at [82].

[120] Ibid, at [12].

require considerable work in order to comply with FATF standards.[121] Indeed the key finding in the report is that money laundering risks 'are not understood and the general policies are not coordinated among all [AML] entities so as to be appropriately consistent',[122] a point reflected in the fact that the country was not rated 'Compliant' with any of the FATF Recommendations. Deficiencies include ineffective international co-operation measures, a non-functional FIU (Financial Information Analysis Commission (CANIF)), the lack of supervision over DNFBPs and the lack of effective asset recovery provisions.

As regards compliance with FATF Recommendation 12, the report also highlights numerous weaknesses. These included:

- The Central Bank of Mauritania did not issue any circular on determining the conditions for the implementation of due diligence toward PEPs for financial institutions.
- Whilst Article 10 of the AML/CFT law No. 2005/048 required financial institutions to apply EDD to PEPs, it did not take objective measures to detect the origin of their wealth and funds.
- The requirements of EDD did not apply to domestic PEPs.
- There were no instructions requiring financial institutions to obtain the approval of the senior management before establishing or continuing a business relationship as to existing PEPs.

For these reasons Mauritania was deemed partially compliant with Recommendation 12.

As a result of these findings, the report identifies a series of detailed 'priority actions' for Mauritania.[123] The MENAFATF clearly has further significant work to persuade Mauritania to comply with its FATF obligations.

4.8 OVERVIEW

The continent-wide reach of the African RBs means that all African states, no matter what their legal systems, are part of the FATF 'family'. This means they are all required to comply with the AML standards set out in the FATF Recommendations.

Unlike other AML instruments, the FATF has the 'teeth' to impose its will on individual countries that do not achieve technical compliance with their AML obligations or which do not implement them in an effective manner.

---

[121] MENAFATF, *Islamic Republic of Mauritania: Mutual Evaluation Report*, Manama, 2018.

[122] Ibid, at p. 3.

[123] Ibid, at [39–44].

The mutual evaluation process is an extraordinary example of the pressure that can be brought on countries to develop the political will to do so. This is due in no small part to the mutual evaluation country reports which provide detailed information and critical analysis on every aspect of their compliance with the FATF Recommendations. The follow-up process means that there is no escape.

The individual country reports together with money laundering typologies exercises carried out by the African RBs provide invaluable information as to money laundering vulnerabilities throughout Africa. This has led to considerable AML activity, particularly with the introduction of new laws and institutions. Yet it remains work in progress, with many countries still failing to comply fully with their AML obligations and requiring a series of constant reviews from the African RBs. Whilst much depends upon the political will, the need to develop further technical assistance and training is undeniable.

Civil society has a key role to play. Given the information available through country reports, 'Trends' reports and the like, CSOs must commit to raising public awareness of the individual country vulnerabilities and bring pressure on government to address them. This means shining a light on dark corners such as the operation of company and land registries and the extent to which supervisory bodies such as local law societies are carrying out their AML duties.

PART III

Developing and maintaining effective national AML strategies in African states

5. PEPs and the role of FIUs and regulators

5.1 INTRODUCTION

In South Africa, the ABSA Bank made 72 suspicious transaction reports (STRs) to the Financial Intelligence Centre[1] (the national FIU) in relation to accounts held by the Oakbay Group, which had connections to numerous PEPs. In 2015, concern about possible money laundering activity then led to the ABSA Bank and three other banks in South Africa closing their accounts with the Group.[2]

Jayesh Shah made several transfers of large sums of money from a Swiss bank account into an account with the HSBC Bank in London. Suspecting the funds were criminal property, the bank made a series of STRs to the UK FIU. The bank then refused Mr Shah's instructions to remit some of the money back to the Swiss bank, citing that it was 'complying with its UK statutory obligations'. As a result of the STR, the Metropolitan Police launched an investigation, including obtaining an order requiring HSBC to produce information about Mr Shah's account. The freezing of the accounts also came to the attention of the Zimbabwe FIU. As a result, the Zimbabwean authorities froze and then seized his local investments causing him losses of over US$300,000,000.[3]

The nature of money laundering means that criminal funds can move rapidly through financial institutions and DNFBPs both nationally and transnationally and this inevitably makes it extremely challenging to follow the money trail. This calls for agencies at the national level that are empowered to receive and analyse financial information and to share this with other domestic investigative and prosecutorial agencies as well as with AML agencies in other jurisdictions. As a former President of the FATF has noted, the 'effective use of

---

1 Under the provisions of the Financial Intelligence Centre Act 38 of 2001.

2 See *Minister of Finance v Oakbay Investments (Pty) Ltd and Others* [2017] All SA 150 (GP) (North Gauteng High Court, Pretoria). The case is considered in Section 5.4.3 below.

3 *Shah and Another v HSBC Private Bank (UK) Ltd* [2012] EWHC 1283 (QB). The facts are drawn from [1] to [17].

financial intelligence is a critical factor in identifying and tracking criminals, including through the exchange of information at the domestic and international levels'.[4] This is particularly important in cases where PEPs are involved in corruption-related financial transactions. The Oakbay and Shah cases neatly illustrate the critical AML role of national FIUs in this respect.

This chapter critically examines the AML role and potential effectiveness of FIUs in African countries, especially as regards PEPs. Section 5.2 considers the role and organisation of FIUs in general. Section 5.3 then reviews the work of the Egmont Group of FIUs and its three African regional groups. Section 5.4 considers the organisation and role of FIUs in Africa whilst Section 5.5 examines their operation at the transnational level. Section 5.6 then explores the strategies for establishing, strengthening and maintaining effective FIUs in Africa. The role of financial regulators and supervisors is closely linked to that of an FIU and this is considered in Section 5.7. Section 5.8 provides a conclusion to the chapter.

5.2 ABOUT FIUs

5.2.1 Definition

The definition of a FIU is set out in FATF Recommendation 29:

> Countries should [i.e. must] establish a financial intelligence unit (FIU) that serves as a national centre for the receipt and analysis of: (a) suspicious transaction reports; and (b) other information relevant to money laundering, associated predicate offences and terrorist financing, and for the dissemination of the results of that analysis.

The FIU should be able to obtain additional information from reporting entities and should have access on a timely basis to the financial, administrative and law enforcement information that it requires to undertake its functions properly.[5]

---

4 See 'Remarks by FATF President Marshall Billingslea' at the FATF Ministerial Meeting, Washington DC, 12 April 2019.

5 This definition is used by the Egmont Group of Financial Intelligence Units: see *Egmont Group of Financial Intelligence Units Charter*, 2013 and revised 2018, at [1.1] (the Egmont Charter).

Much of this work takes place through receiving and analysing, STRs made by financial institutions and DNFBPs. In doing so, FIUs must undertake two types of analysis:

1. 'Operational analysis': this with the aim of identifying specific targets such as PEPs and their associates; to follow the money trail and to provide links between the laundering and the predicate offence(s).
2. 'Strategic analysis': i.e. using the data to identify money laundering trends and vulnerabilities.[6]

As noted below, numerous African countries have established FIUs.[7]

5.2.2 FIU Models

The Egmont Group of FIUs has identified four FIU 'models': judicial, law enforcement, administrative, and hybrid.

1. The judicial model is established within the judicial branch of government wherein 'disclosures' of suspicious financial activity are received by the investigative agencies of a country from its financial sector such that the judiciary powers can be brought into play, for example seizing funds, freezing accounts, conducting interrogations, detaining people, conducting searches, etc.
2. The law enforcement model implements AML measures alongside already existing law enforcement systems, supporting the efforts of multiple law enforcement or judicial authorities with concurrent or sometimes competing jurisdictional authority to investigate money laundering.
3. The administrative model is a centralised, independent, administrative authority, which receives and processes information from the financial sector and transmits disclosures to judicial or law enforcement authorities for prosecution. It functions as a 'buffer' between the financial and the law enforcement communities.
4. The hybrid model serves as a disclosure intermediary and a link to both judicial and law enforcement authorities. It combines elements of at least two of the FIU models.[8]

---

6 See Interpretive Note to FATF Recommendation 29 B 3 and Section 5.4.4 below.

7 A list of FIUs in Africa is provided at the end of this chapter.

8 Egmont Group, 'Financial Intelligence Units' https://egmontgroup.org/en/content/financial-intelligence-units-fius (accessed 7 June 2020).

The FATF does not 'prejudge a country's choice of a particular model'[9] and the UNCAC Working Group on the Prevention of Corruption has found that the 'structures, responsibilities, functions and independence of such units varied and [that] States have adopted models that best suit their legal, constitutional and administrative arrangements'.[10] Thus in some countries, the FIU performs a purely administrative function by collating, analysing and then distributing intelligence and information derived from STRs to law enforcement or other relevant investigatory bodies. In others, the FIU also has an investigative role with the possible powers to prosecute and seize and freeze assets. As noted below, in African countries FIUs are largely based on the law enforcement model i.e. a buffer between the financial community and the law enforcement agencies.

5.3 THE EGMONT GROUP OF FIUs AND THE AFRICAN REGIONAL GROUPS

5.3.1 The Role of the Egmont Group

The Egmont Group[11] describes itself as a 'united body of 164 Financial Intelligence Units'[12] whose role is to provide a forum for FIUs around the world in order to:

> improve cooperation in the fight against money laundering and financing of terrorism and to foster the implementation of domestic programs in this field, especially in the areas of information exchange, training and the sharing of expertise.[13]

It continues to play 'a vital role in increasing the effectiveness of FIUs worldwide' including providing access to the Egmont Secure website through which financial intelligence is shared.[14] For example, the FIU in Mauritius has reported that membership of the Egmont Group has provided it with wider access to information exchange and international co-operation, whilst such

---

9 Interpretive Note to FATF Recommendation 29.A1.

10 UNCAC Working Group on the Prevention of Corruption report, *Measures to prevent money-laundering (article 14 of the UNCAC)*, 2015, CAC/COSP/WG.4/2015/2.

11 Named after the location of its first meeting at the Egmont Palace in Belgium.

12 See Egmont Group 'About the Egmont Group'. https://egmontgroup.org/en/content/about (accessed 7 June 2020).

13 See the Egmont Charter, p. 6.

14 See generally the Egmont Group, *Statement of Purpose and its Principles for Information Exchange between Financial Intelligence Units for Money Laundering and Terrorism Financing Cases*, 2013 (the Egmont Statement of Purpose).

membership also means that the FIU encounters fewer challenges in obtaining co-operation from its counterparts in other countries.[15]

The FATF requires that as a matter of priority all national FIUs apply for membership of the Egmont Group.[16] However, the Egmont Group will not admit to its membership an FIU that does not have an adequate legal basis for its functions, fails to meet the definition of an FIU, refuses to co-operate with other FIUs, or is unable to demonstrate its operational status.[17]

A significant number of African countries have already done so. Efforts continue to encourage all FIUs to apply for membership,[18] with the process being facilitated with the assistance of other FIUs.[19]

FIUs must comply with the Egmont Group, *Principles for Information Exchange between Financial Intelligence Units* (the Egmont Principles). These are 'binding'[20] and 'cases of significant and relevant non-compliance' can lead to suspension and expulsion from the Group.[21] For example, in 2017 the Nigerian FIU was suspended from membership following concerns about the protection and confidentiality of information held by it[22] as well as its legal basis and operational independence. It was then threatened with expulsion unless appropriate legislation protecting its independence was forthcoming. This led to the passing of the Nigerian Financial Intelligence Unit Act 2018. As

---

15 ESAAMLG report, at [117] and [150].

16 Interpretive Note to FATF Recommendation 29.

17 *Egmont Group of Financial Intelligence Units: Support and Compliance Process*, 2015, p. 3 (the Egmont Support Process).

18 Heads of FIUs reportedly presented a document to the ESAAMLG Council of Ministers setting out the arguments for all FIUs in the region to join the Egmont Group: see *East and Southern Africa Region report to the Egmont Group*, 2019, 1. As at 30 March 2020, action is still awaited.

19 For example the CENTIF (FIU) in Benin was assisted in its successful application to join the Egmont Group by the FIUs of Senegal and France: GIABA report, at [174]. The FIU in Mozambique reportedly secured support from South Africa for its application for Egmont membership: see ESAAMLG, *First Round Mutual Evaluations: Post Evaluation Progress Report of Mozambique on AML/CFT Measures*, 2018, at p. 2 (the ESAAMLG Mozambique report). The Forum of the FIUs of GIABA member states also supports FIUs applying for membership of the Egmont Group.

20 At p. 3. Although as with the FATF Recommendations, the Principles refer throughout to 'should' rather than 'must'.

21 See the Egmont Support Process, p. 18.

22 The Egmont Principles require that international co-operation between FIUs should be based upon a foundation of trust: see General Framework at [7]. In addition, information received, processed, held or disseminated by requesting FIUs must be securely protected, exchanged and used only in accordance with agreed procedures, policies and applicable laws and regulations: at [28].

a result, the Egmont Group lifted the suspension of Nigeria from all Egmont Group events and activities.[23]

5.3.2 The African Regional Groups

The Egmont Group is divided into eight regional groups, three of which are based in Africa. The West and Central Africa Region consists of FIUs in 14 jurisdictions[24] whilst the Middle East and North Africa (MENA) Region includes FIUs in Algeria, Egypt, Morocco, Sudan and Tunisia. The East and Southern Africa Region comprises the members of the ESAAMLG, although only 10 are full members of the Egmont Group.

According to the Egmont Group Charter, the main roles of the regional groups are: supporting and contributing to the activities of the Egmont working groups;[25] facilitating the support and sponsorship of non-Egmont member FIUs in the region to join the Egmont Group and preparing a regional plan. In practice, each regional group has developed an action plan. The MENA regional plan, for example, focuses on assisting non-Egmont FIUs from the region to attain Egmont Group membership, and 'promoting synergy between the Egmont Group and the MENAFATF' to strengthen the implementation of the FATF standards. In addition, training, technical assistance and FIU capacity building matters are addressed.

In practice, the African RBs also play a role in evaluating the capacity of FIUs to carry out the role required by the FATF Recommendations and the Egmont Group. For example, the ESAAMLG MER noted that the Zambian FIU had significant weaknesses in both its organisation and powers, which meant it was not able to meet fully the Egmont Group criteria. The response was the enactment of the Financial Intelligence Centre Act 2010, which sought to address these shortcomings.

---

[23] See the 11th GIABA Follow-up Report on Nigeria.

[24] Benin, Burkina Faso, Cameroon, Cape Verde, Chad, Congo-Brazzaville, Cote D'Ivoire, Gabon, Ghana, Mali, Niger, Nigeria, Senegal, Togo.

[25] These are the Legal Working Group, Operational Working Group, Training Working Group, IT Working Group and the Outreach Working Group. These provide a range of technical assistance services to FIUs: see further, Egmont Support Process, p. 5.

5.4 ROLE OF AFRICAN FIUs AT THE NATIONAL LEVEL

5.4.1 Receiving STRs

FATF Recommendation 20 requires that a financial institution (and a DNFBP) must be required by law to report promptly to the FIU where 'it suspects or has reasonable grounds to suspect that funds are the proceeds of criminal activity'. Such suspicion can arise during the establishment or course of the customer relationship, or when conducting occasional transactions.[26] Whilst such action violates a person's constitutional right to privacy, it is a justifiable infringement as being necessary to facilitate the effective investigation of money laundering and other financial crimes.[27] It must also be mandated to receive reports on cash transactions/wire transfers.[28]

The FATF has emphasised that STRs remain 'critical in the fight against corruption and money laundering'[29] as they can be the first signs of suspicious activity by a PEP. Indeed, in practice they have 'uncovered corruption activity, triggered corruption investigations and been used to support on-going financial investigations of corrupt activity'.[30] As the Shah case highlights, STRs also operate as a restraining order that prevents a PEP from accessing their suspect funds unless and until the FIU has given its approval.

FATF Recommendation 21 prohibits financial institutions, their directors, officers and employees from disclosing to a customer that an STR has been made to the FIU.[31] This undermines the banker-client relationship and may inevitably cause significant economic harm to customers. For example, in the case of Shah, noted earlier, the customer incurred huge losses as a result of the STRs made by the HSBC to the UK FIU and further action by the

---

26 Interpretive Note to FATF Recommendation 10 A1. Compare the Shah and Thiam cases. The Financial Reporting Centre in Kenya may impose civil penalties for a failure to make STRs: see Proceeds of Crime and Anti-Money Laundering (Amendment Act) 2017 section 24B.

27 For a useful analysis of the point see the decision of the High Court of Lesotho in *Metsing v Director General, Directorate on Corruption and Economic Affairs* [2015] LSHC 1 and the discussion in Section 8.4 below.

28 See FATF Recommendation 16 and the accompanying Interpretive Note.

29 See FATF Best Practices paper, at [82]. For example, in Rwanda Article 8 of Presidential Order No. 27/01 provides that the FIU 'can request any reporting entity to transmit, without charge, the information, documents and registries necessary to exercise their functions as set forth in this Order. The entity receiving the request is obliged to respond accordingly.' See also Law 74/2019 of 29 January 2020.

30 FATF, Best Practices Paper, [81].

31 DNFBPs have somewhat similar obligations: see FATF Recommendation 28.

FIU in Zimbabwe. As a result, he brought an action against the HSBC Bank claiming, amongst other things, that their failure to carry out his instructions constituted a breach of contract. The High Court in London ruled that there was an implied term in the contract between the customer and the bank which permitted the bank to refuse to execute his payment instructions in the absence of 'appropriate consent' where it suspected a transaction constituted money laundering. This is a useful precedent for financial institutions and DNFBPs in other countries facing similar arguments from PEPs. In practice, in some countries, statutory provisions grant immunity from civil and criminal liability to reporting persons as a result of making an STR in good faith.

In order to improve the effectiveness of the reporting system, the FATF has emphasised the need for a partnership approach whereby the FIU and other regulatory authorities work together with financial institutions and DNFBPs by providing:

- guidance or detailed instructions on PEPs requirements;
- typologies and indicators of corruption-related money laundering; and
- feedback on STRs relating to corruption, where possible.[32]

In practice, the limited number of STRs being made by reporting entities to FIUs remains a major issue in many African countries and the African RBs as well as individual FIUs have all noted the adverse impact this has on their work.[33] Of particular concern is the lack of reporting by DNFBPs. This is highlighted in the 2017 GIABA Annual Report, which reveals that of the 3,681 STRs submitted by reporting entities in the region to FIUs, over 93 per cent were submitted by banks. Lawyers and real estate agents both made just four reports each.[34] This is a startling statistic given the use made of them in facilitating money laundering and highlights the need for capacity building for regulators and supervisors in the sectors with low reporting rates.[35]

The ESAAMLG has highlighted the same issue. For example, in 2013 the MER on Mozambique criticised the lack of effective supervision of DNFBPs

---

[32] FATF Best Practices paper, p. 23.

[33] For example, in the period 2013–2017 the number of STRs on procurement corruption by 10 countries totalled just 88: see ESAAMLG, *Procurement Corruption in the Public Sector and Associated Money Laundering in the ESAAMLG Region*, 2019, p. 51 (the ESAAMLG Procurement report).

[34] GIABA report p. 107.

[35] For example, the MERs on The Gambia and Liberia noted that both had significant gaps in their supervision of DNFBPs. The FIU in Sao Tome and Principe has also reported challenges in ensuring compliance by the local Bar Association with AML reporting requirements: GIABA report [54], [205] and [158] respectively. See further Section 5.7.

and the lack of enforceable requirements for financial institutions to identify PEPs. As a result, Law 14/2013 was designed to address the shortcomings.[36] Even so, in 2018 the FIU (GIFiM) reported that the real property and insurance sectors remained particularly vulnerable to the laundering of the proceeds of corruption.[37] In a progress report the ESAAMLG later noted that DNFBPs still failed to comply with their legal obligation to file STRs.[38] Similarly, reviewers in their MER on Malawi noted 'with concern' that the majority of STRs analysed by the Financial Intelligence Authority were from financial institutions with limited or no filing by DNFBPs including those carrying high money laundering risks.[39]

These failings highlight the need for relevant regulatory authorities to oversee the activities of their members more effectively and to impose financial sanctions when there is a failure to comply with AML regulations.[40]

Other useful sources of financial intelligence can come from asset declaration information by PEPs and their tax returns.[41] Here co-operation between FIUs and tax authorities as well as effective cross-border cooperation in exchanging tax information for tracking illicit financial flows is seen as an important mechanism for increasing access to beneficial ownership information on PEPs.[42]

5.4.2 Obtaining 'Virtual' and other Information

In practice, the power to compel the production of records or other documents held by financial institutions and DNFBPs plays a key part in many FIU investigations.[43] This pre-supposes that the document(s) in question are within the 'jurisdiction'. Today, financial and many company records are almost entirely electronic and are often held on servers located abroad or at the offices of a parent company in another jurisdiction. Obtaining such information is a challenge common to all AML bodies. An additional challenge comes from the development of virtual assets and virtual asset service providers. These issues are discussed at Section 8.2.2 below.

---

36 IMF, 'Republic of Mozambique: Diagnostic Report on Transparency, Governance and Corruption' Washington DC, 2019, p. 12.

37 Ibid, 12. The purchase and sale of precious stones and metals was also identified as a vulnerable sector.

38 ESAAMLG report, p. 12.

39 ESAAMLG, *Malawi: Mutual Evaluation Report*, 2019, p. 40.

40 See FATF Recommendation 28(b) and the discussion in Section 5.7 below.

41 FATF Best Practices paper, at [81–3] and [87].

42 Noted in the GIABA 2018 report, at [425].

43 See FATF Recommendation 31 and the discussion in Section 8.2 below.

5.4.3 Analysing STRs

An FIU is responsible for analysing STRs and other financial information. The analysis may focus either on each single disclosure or a series of transactions (such as in the Oakbay case) and is designed to identify specific targets such as persons, assets or transactions, to follow the money trail or determine links between corruption (or other predicate) offences and money laundering.[44]

An FIU must have the power to obtain further information to assist with its analysis. A good illustration is that of the Financial Intelligence Authority in Malawi, which has the power to inspect financial records and to 'compel the production of or access to any record, document or information and make notes and take copies' of such records.[45] In addition an FIU must have the right to request information from other agencies, such as an anti-corruption commission and/or law enforcement bodies. This is not universal, with some countries being criticised by the ESAAMLG for, amongst other things, limiting the power of an FIU to request additional information to those financial institutions making the STRs.

Following an analysis, information may be referred to the relevant AML and/or law enforcement authorities for further investigation and possible prosecution. In Mauritius, where there are reasonable grounds to suspect that a person has acquired unexplained wealth, a report may be made to the Integrity Reporting Board, which may then seek an unexplained wealth order from a judge.[46]

Making an STR itself may also involve a political dimension. As noted earlier, 72 STRs were made by the ABSA Bank to the South African Financial Intelligence Centre regarding the accounts of Oakbay Investments (Pty) Ltd (Oakbay). The Group was controlled by the Gupta family, which had close links to several South African PEPs, including the then President, Jacob Zuma. Thus, following the notice given by the ABSA Bank and three other banks terminating their contractual relationship with Oakbay and closing their bank accounts, the company sought assistance from the South African government. The Minister of Finance was asked to intervene due to the 'dire implications' of the actions of the banks to its continued business operation in Africa and with it the prospect of serious job losses. In *Minister of Finance v Oakbay Investments (Pty) Ltd and Others*[47] the High Court of South Africa ruled that the Minister of Finance was not compelled by law to interfere in a private

---

44 See Interpretive Note to FATF Recommendation 29.

45 Section 8 Financial Crimes Act 2017.

46 Sections 9(1) and 14(1) Good Governance and Integrity Reporting Act 2015. On unexplained wealth orders, see Section 10.3 below.

47 [2017] All SA 150 (GP) (North Gauteng High Court, Pretoria).

dispute between a bank and its client. In a further significant ruling, the court held that a member of the National Executive of the ruling party acting alone and/or on behalf of the Cabinet, including the President, was also not empowered to intervene in such matters. This is a welcome decision as it emphasises the duty of financial institutions to fulfil their AML obligations without political interference from PEPs and their associates.

5.4.4 Analysing Money Laundering Trends

Undertaking a strategic analysis designed to identify money laundering related trends and patterns forms an essential role for FIUs.[48] Relatively few African countries have undertaken such an analysis and both the GIABA and ESAAMLG have identified this as a significant weakness. There are some interesting exceptions. For example, on the basis of an analysis of STRs, the FIU in Cote d'Ivoire identified several trends including those relating to corruption and cybercrime.[49] Other countries have identified major money laundering trends as including the use of companies both to conceal beneficial ownership and through which to move illicit funds, trade based money laundering, and investment in real estate.[50] This is clearly an area which requires strengthening.

Some FIUs have the additional responsibility for making freezing orders against suspected proceeds of crime. For example, in one case the FIU in Cote d'Ivoire froze and seized some FCFA25 billion and also obtained freezing orders in Europe of funds worth over 1 million euros.[51] Similarly, the FIU in Togo froze FCFA52 million in a bank account on the basis of an STR.[52]

5.4.5 Coordination and Co-operation between AML Agencies

The need for effective coordination with and between AML agencies[53] is emphasised in FATF Recommendation 2:

> Countries should [must] ensure that policy-makers, the financial intelligence unit (FIU), law enforcement authorities, supervisors and other relevant competent authorities, at the policy-making and operational levels, have effective mechanisms in place which enable them to cooperate, and, where appropriate, coordinate domes-

---

48 Interpretive Note to FATF Recommendation 29 [3].
49 GIABA report, at [166].
50 ESAAMLG Procurement report, p. 50.
51 GIABA report [164].
52 Ibid, [184].
53 See FATF Recommendation 31.

tically with each other concerning the development and implementation of policies and activities to combat money laundering ...

Best Practice Principles require FIUs to have a clear procedure for the dissemination of financial and other relevant information to AML authorities.[54] Having this function enshrined in legislation is good practice. For example, the objectives of the Uganda Financial Intelligence Authority (FIA) specifically include facilitating the exchange of information with competent law enforcement agencies.[55]

Co-operative arrangements are becoming increasingly common and having the arrangement formally recognised is useful.[56] This is often achieved through the signing of a MOU. For example, in 2016 the Ugandan FIA signed a MOU with the Inspectorate of Government to share information on money laundering and other forms of IFFs.[57] Similarly, in Mauritius two tripartite MOUs were signed in 2018, one between the Bank of Mauritius, Financial Services Commission and the FIU and the other between the Bank of Mauritius, the FIU and the Independent Commission Against Corruption.[58] The Forum of the FIUs of GIABA member states also facilitates the signing of MOUs.[59]

In some countries, the FIU is also responsible for coordinating AML policies. For example, the Angolan FIU coordinates a regular meeting of an inter-governmental group with a view to assessing AML strategies including coordinating the National Risk Assessment exercise.[60]

---

[54] FATF Best Practices paper, at [81–3] and [87].

[55] See Section 38A Anti-Money Laundering Act 2013 as inserted by the Anti-Money Laundering (Amendment) Act 2017.

[56] For example, FIUs have reportedly provided law enforcement authorities with information concerning procurement corruption and money laundering activities by PEPs, which has proved useful in AML actions: see ESAAMLG Procurement report, p. 46.

[57] See URN news report, 'IGG, Financial Intelligence Authority to Jointly Fight Money Laundering' 1 June 2016 https://ugandaradionetwork.net/story/igg-financial-intelligence-authority-sign-mou-to-fight-money-laundering (accessed 7 June 2020). The Inspectorate of Government is established under Article 223 of the Constitution of Uganda with the mandate to investigate and prosecute money laundering, corruption and related offences See also section 3 of the Inspectorate of Government Act 2002.

[58] See ESAAMLG report, p. 107. Lesotho has also reported that with the support of the FIU, in two corruption cases the Directorate on Corruption and Economic Offences was able to seize and confiscate proceeds of crime worth almost US$115,000: ibid, p. 88. The FIU in Mozambique (GIFiM) has also signed MOUs with a range of domestic AML agencies.

[59] For example, at the 13th meeting of the Forum in 2018, MOUs were signed between the FIUs of Liberia, Cote d'Ivoire, The Gambia, Nigeria and Sao Tome and Principe: GIABA 2018 report, at [411].

[60] ESAAMLG report, pp. 66–7.

Following appropriate analysis, a FIU may share information with investigative or other related authorities. For example, in 2018 the Zambian FIU sent 80 reports of suspected money laundering and terrorist financing to local law enforcement agencies involving some US$520 million.[61] The GIABA report also notes that FIUs in Benin, Cote d'Ivoire, Guinea, Liberia and Togo reported forwarding STRs on a regular basis to the appropriate prosecutorial agency.

The potential effectiveness of such co-operation is highlighted in the Cashgate case where the sharing of information between the Malawi FIA and law enforcement agencies helped significantly in the pursuit of the misappropriated public funds. As the MER on Malawi explains:

> The country successfully identified, investigated and prosecuted some ML cases on the basis of the financial intelligence and other sources of information. The competent authorities have good coordination and cooperation in the investigation of complex crimes by sharing information and establishing joint teams as demonstrated by some successful ML cases resulting from the Cashgate cases.[62]

5.4.6 Training and Capacity Building

The FATF Best Practice Principles emphasise that FIU staff involved in the analysis of STRs must be sufficiently trained to understand the indicators of corruption. However, the MERs on numerous African countries highlight both the absence of suitably qualified, trained and experienced members within FIUs in operational and strategic analysis as well as a lack of ICT equipment and technology and other resources. This inevitably adversely affects their ability to analyse STRs and other financial information effectively.[63]

In response, the GIABA continues to focus on providing appropriate training and capacity building.[64] Similarly the other African RBs as well as development agencies also provide some training and technical assistance in order to strengthen FIUs. However, considerably more work is required and

---

[61] See Zambia Financial Intelligence Centre, *Money laundering and terrorist financing: Trends 2018*, 2018, p. 7. The FIU in Sao Tome and Principe received six STRs from financial institutions with two being passed on to the Public Ministry for further action: GIABA report [157].

[62] ESAAMLG, *Malawi: Mutual Evaluation Report*, 2019, at [13].

[63] See the ESAAMLG report, p. 57. See also the comments on Ethiopia and Rwanda: ibid, at pp. 81 and 136.

[64] Ibid, 108. GIABA has held a series of capacity building workshops for FIUs and other AML agencies in conjunction with, amongst others, the Egmont Group, the African Development Bank and the European Union: see GIABA 2018 report, pp. 59 et seq.

this is an area in which further donor financial assistance and technical support are needed.

5.4.7 FIUs and Civil Society

FIUs rarely enjoy a high public profile. Given the sensitive nature of their work, this is not surprising. Yet providing regular public briefings on money laundering trends and challenges can raise public awareness and understanding of national AML issues and enhance the effectiveness of its work. Involving CSOs and media organisations is a helpful part of developing this role.

The Financial Intelligence Centre (ZFIC) in Zambia provides an excellent example. Section 5(2)(e) of the Financial Intelligence Centre Act 2010 requires the ZFIC to provide the public with information concerning money laundering trends. In doing so, it is mandated to publish a regular 'Trends' report. The 2018 report provides the public with a wealth of information on money laundering typologies including highlighting the involvement of PEPs. Not surprisingly, it led to considerable public debate on the activities of PEPs, not least because the total value of suspected corruption offences amounted to ZMK4.9 billion.

This is good practice and is one which should be widely followed elsewhere. As noted in Section 2.8.1.4, PEPs are vulnerable when CSOs and the media play an active role in scrutinising their activities. Information obtained from 'Trends' reports provide a helpful basis for doing so.

5.5 CO-OPERATION BETWEEN FIUs AT THE TRANSNATIONAL LEVEL

FIUs are the crucial agency for the exchange of financial information at the transnational level. The *Egmont Group Statement of Purpose* states that FIUs 'should exchange information with foreign FIUs'.[65] They must therefore have an 'adequate legal basis for providing co-operation on money laundering and associated predicate offences ... and exchange information freely, spontaneously and upon request, on the basis of reciprocity'.[66] FIUs should use the most efficient means to co-operate[67] and be able to conduct enquiries on behalf of foreign FIUs.[68]

[65] The Egmont Statement of Purpose makes it clear that this can be 'administrative, law enforcement, judicial or other agencies': at [9]. See further the FBME case below.

[66] Egmont Statement of Purpose at [9–10].

[67] Ibid, at [15].

[68] Ibid, at [16].

In practice numerous FIUs in African countries have developed transnational links to facilitate information sharing and evidence gathering on AML issues particularly through the signing of MOUs. For example, the FIA in Malawi has signed 21 MOUs with other FIUs, 10 of which are in the ESAAMLG region, whilst the FIU in Cote d'Ivoire has entered into a co-operation agreement with the FIU in Namibia.[69] Similarly, the Mozambique FIU has signed MOUs with the FIUs of Angola, Cape Verde, Lesotho, Ethiopia, Swaziland, Namibia, Brazil, South Africa, Malawi, Uganda, Zambia and Zimbabwe.[70]

Of course, if the exercise of coercive powers is required in another country, a mutual legal request must be made by the FIU (or other AML agency). Unusually, the Financial Intelligence Centre of Ethiopia itself serves as the central authority for mutual legal assistance (MLA) and extradition requests.

Given the secrecy surrounding money laundering by PEPs and restrictions on their domestic capacity, FIUs in African countries can greatly benefit from obtaining financial information and evidence from their foreign counterparts. In doing so, it is essential that the appropriate procedure is clearly set out. An excellent model is provided by the Money Laundering (Exchange of Information) Regulations, 2018 in Uganda.[71] These provide that the FIA or any 'competent authority'[72] may receive a request for information from a 'foreign counterpart'.[73] Regulation 3(2) provides that this may be made:

(a) electronically; through a secured reporting system established by the competent authority;
(b) electronically by secured mail;
(c) in writing and submitted by hand or registered post; or
(d) by facsimile.

Regulation 3(3) then sets out the type of information that a competent authority may share with a foreign counterpart. This includes:

(a) information relating to suspected or confirmed money laundering;
(b) information relating to the financing of terrorism; and
(c) information relating to any criminal activity.

---

69 GIABA report at [167].

70 ESAAMLG Mozambique report, at [7].

71 SI 2018 No. 40 and made under sections 38A and 114 of the Anti-Money Laundering Act, 2013.

72 Defined as 'investigative, prosecuting, judicial, regulatory or supervisory authorities of the Government of Uganda': regulation 2.

73 Defined as 'a body in a country outside Uganda which performs functions similar to those of a competent authority': regulation 2.

The importance of providing adequate information to enable a request to be complied with satisfactorily is highlighted in regulation 4. This provides that a competent authority 'shall ensure that every request for information by a foreign counterpart:

(a) states the reason for the information requested;
(b) contains sufficient proof to support the request for information including satisfying the requirements of sub-regulation (2);
(c) is accompanied with proof that the request is linked to an on-going investigation;
(d) states the purpose for the information requested; and
(e) confirms that the request complies with the law of the country establishing the foreign counterpart.'

Interestingly, there is no provision for a refusal by the FIA to disclose information. As the information is made in the form of a 'request', presumably the FIA or other competent body has the right to refuse to provide assistance, albeit that it is normal to provide the requesting state with reasons for doing so.

In providing assistance, regulation 3(5) provides that competent authority shall:

(a) use the most efficient and secure means to share information with a foreign counterpart;
(b) establish controls and safeguards to ensure that any information to be shared with a foreign counterpart—

    (1) is used only by the foreign counterpart requesting for the information; and
    (ii) is used only for the purpose for which the information is requested;

(c) ensure that the foreign counterpart maintains appropriate safeguards to keep the information shared confidential.

This emphasises that confidentiality is a fundamental aspect of the work of an FIU and this applies equally as regards the exchange of information. This is particularly important in highly sensitive, potentially politically charged investigations involving PEPs. The restriction on the use of the information is also important, although in practice it is usual to have a proviso that such information may also be used for another purpose with the written consent of the requested state.

The effectiveness of transnational co-operation is well illustrated in the FBME Bank case. The bank had operated in Tanzania for some years with the FIU having no suspicion of any illegality in its operations. However, in 2016 the US FIU, the Financial Crimes Enforcement Network (FinCEN), issued a 'Final Rule' against FBME under section 311 of the PATRIOT Act 2010 i.e. that the bank was a financial institution involved in transnational money laundering. In 2017 the US District Court, District of Columbia, upheld this ruling.[74] The information concerning these transnational money laundering activities was then passed to the AML authorities in Tanzania with the result that the Bank of Tanzania revoked the licence of the FBME Bank.[75]

The case highlights again the fact that whilst PEPs may be in a position to control or influence domestic AML investigations, they are vulnerable to foreign investigations and the willingness of foreign FIUs to share information with their counterparts.[76]

5.6 TOWARDS STRENGTHENING FIUs IN AFRICAN STATES

5.6.1 The Effectiveness of FIUs in Practice

The effectiveness of FIUs in practice is somewhat mixed. The GIABA and ESAAMLG have both highlighted the lack of functioning FIUs in several countries[77] although the latter has noted that the FIUs in its region are 'generally considered to be credible and have enhanced the level of collaboration between law enforcement and private sector institutions'.[78]

It follows that in order to carry out its mandate effectively, as with other AML agencies, an FIU must be operationally independent and autonomous.[79] As Kreutner rightly asserts '[t]here is now a common and undisputed consensus with academia, practitioners and other experts alike that institutions in

---

74 *FBME Bank v Mnuchin* 249 F. Supp. 3d 215 (D.D.C. 2017).

75 See also the *Shah* case noted in Section 5.4.1 above.

76 See also Section 2.8.2 above.

77 See for example, the GIABA MER on Guinea, 2012, at [20] and the very critical analysis of the Mozambique FIU in the ESAAMLG, *Post Evaluation Report on Mozambique*, 2018, pp. 6–11. As noted earlier, the Egmont Group suspended the Nigeria FIU having raised concerns about its legal basis and operational independence. The Nigerian Financial Intelligence Act 2018 was swiftly enacted to address the deficiencies.

78 ESAAMLG report, [149].

79 Interpretive Note to FATF Recommendation 29 E8. See also Musonda Simwayi and Muhammed Haseed, The role of Financial Intelligence Units in combating money laundering: A comparative analysis of Zambia, Zimbabwe and Malawi, (2012) 15(1) *JMLC* 112–34.

the anti-corruption field shall be independent from those that fall under their remit'.[80]

This means that an FIU (and other AML bodies) must be able to 'carry out its functions freely'[81] and be 'independent, and subject only to the Constitution and the laws ... and must exercise their powers and perform their functions without fear, favour or prejudice'.[82] This requires the development of a series of effective 'building blocks'.

5.6.2 A Firm Legal Foundation

Unlike other AML bodies such as anti-corruption commissions and Offices of the Auditor General, which are enshrined in most national constitutions, FIUs in Africa are essentially creatures of statute. This is unfortunate, for entrenching of an FIU in the national constitution would provide it with a measure of protection against any attempt by PEPs to weaken it through a statutory amendment.

In the absence of constitutional protection, an FIU must be, and be seen to be, an autonomous body. A useful illustration is the FIA in Malawi. Established by the Financial Crimes Act 2017 (FICA), it is the 'principal national agency responsible for preventing and combating financial crimes' and 'shall not, in its functions, be subject to the direction, or control or influence of any person, authority or entity which may compromise its operational independence'.[83] In Nigeria, the FIU is now established as an 'independent agency and operationally autonomous [body which] for the purposes of institutional location is domiciled in the Central Bank of Nigeria'.[84]

However, such autonomy is threatened particularly where the FIU is located within another AML or government structure. For example, in Kenya the Financial Reporting Centre is located within the National Treasury[85] and in Tanzania it is an extra-ministerial department within the Ministry of Finance.[86]

---

80 Martin Kreutner, 10 guiding principles and parameters on the nation of anti-corruption bodies, in Martin Kreutner (ed.), *Practice Meets Science, Contemporary Anti-Corruption Dialogue*, Vienna, IACSS, 2010, p. 51.

81 Interpretive Note to FATF Recommendation 29 E8.

82 The wording taken from section 182(1) Constitution of South Africa.

83 Financial Crimes Act 2017 (FICA) section 3(1) and (3).

84 See the Financial Intelligence Act 2018, section 2(2) and (3). This provision satisfied the Egmont Group, which in October 2018 lifted the suspension of Nigeria from membership of the Group.

85 It was established under section 21 of the Proceeds of Crime and Anti-Money Laundering Act 2009. Curiously the first Director was not appointed until 2017.

86 Section 4 Anti-Money Laundering Act 2006.

It is also essential that the core functions of an FIU are distinct from those of any other authority.[87] Thus in their MER on Uganda, the assessors raised concerns that there was a system of dual reporting whereby financial institutions under the supervision of the Bank of Uganda (BOU) were required to make STRs both to the FIU and the BOU. This made it unclear as to whether there was a single national authority as well as an appropriate process for governing the protection of information.[88]

5.6.3 Appointment and Security of Tenure of Office-holders

It is essential to provide for a demonstrably fair, open and public appointment procedure for heads of FIUs. Not only is this a useful publicity exercise to raise awareness about the role of an FIU, it is also a confidence-building exercise for civil society and donors in the integrity, independence and competence of the body. Similar principles apply to anti-corruption commissions and other AML bodies.

There are a variety of approaches here. The most common is for the President to make the appointment.[89] To avoid undue presidential influence, Malawi provides a helpful example for others to follow. Here the position of the Director General of the FIA must be publicly advertised with the relevant minister then being required to select two to three candidates for the position. The President may then appoint one of those candidates. If all the candidates are rejected, the process is repeated. Whilst the President makes the actual appointment, this is also subject to confirmation by the Public Appointments Committee of the National Assembly.[90] Such provisions are welcome as they have the potential to raise public awareness of the FIA whilst incorporating transparency into the appointment process.[91]

The Director General of the FIA is appointed for five years, renewable once, and can be removed only in circumstances similar to the removal of a senior judge.[92] This is a strong provision and one that other African countries should

[87] Interpretive Note to FATF Recommendation 29 E8.

[88] ESAAMLG, *Uganda Mutual Evaluation Report*, 2016, at [12].

[89] In some countries, this is subject to approval/confirmation by another body. For example the Director of the Nigerian FIU is appointed by the President, subject to confirmation by the Senate: section 5(1) Nigerian Financial Intelligence Unit Act 2018.

[90] Sections 6–8 Financial Crimes Act 2017 (FICA).

[91] See also the discussion on the appointment of the Auditor General, Section 7.4 below.

[92] FICA, section 8. A similar provision applies to the Director of the Nigerian FIU: see section 5(3) Nigerian Financial Intelligence Unit Act 2018.

adopt.[93] In order to avoid a situation where the post of Director General is left open for a lengthy period, any vacancy must be filled within six months or until the vacancy is filled.[94] Unusually, but usefully, in some countries, the qualifications for appointment are set out.[95]

It is this attention to practical details that is so important when seeking to protect the independence of an FIU and the position in Malawi provides a helpful model for other African countries to follow.

5.6.4 Adequate Funding and Resources

Operational independence is fundamental to an effective FIU. This means it must enjoy financial autonomy and be provided with adequate financial, human and technical resources.[96]

The Malawi FIA again provides a useful example, albeit with reservations. The FICA provides that its funding consists of money appropriated annually by the National Assembly with other funding coming from penalties imposed under the Act, fees charged and grants, gifts and donations made to the FIA, subject to the prior approval of the minister.[97] This raises two key issues over financial independence which are of general importance. Firstly, whilst the FIA is responsible for preparing an annual budget, this is submitted to the National Assembly by the minister.[98] Without more, the FIA is seemingly at the mercy of the minister as to what budget is actually submitted to the National Assembly. Further, the FIA may be 'punished' by a budget cut for failing to adhere to presidential or ministerial wishes regarding an investigation. A direct submission to the National Assembly is clearly preferable. Secondly, there is no justification for ministerial approval for the receipt of

---

[93] Compare the position in Nigeria where the President 'may remove the Director of the FIU from office subject to confirmation by the Senate that the Director can no longer carry out his[/her] duties as provided under the Act': ibid, section 5(5). Such a provision seemingly provides little protection for the incumbent.

[94] FICA, section 6(8).

[95] For example, in Tanzania the Director of the FIU must have 'adequate knowledge and experience ... relevant for the execution of their functions': section 5(1) Anti-Money Laundering Act 2006. See further Eugene Mniwasa, The financial intelligence unit and money laundering control in Tanzania, (2019) 22(3) *JMLC* 543–62, at 552. See also section 5(2) Nigerian Financial Intelligence Unit Act 2018.

[96] Interpretive Note to FATF Recommendation 29 E8. In Nigeria, staff of the FIU are 'appointed on terms and conditions as are applicable to law enforcement, security agencies and related services': section 7(2) Nigerian Financial Intelligence Unit Act 2018.

[97] FICA section 12(1).

[98] FICA section 13.

outside funding, especially in that no grounds for such a refusal are specified. To ensure transparency however, a preferable approach is to enable an FIU to receive grants, gifts or donations from donors provided these are disclosed to the legislature or similar body.[99]

Arguably, a suitable model is that of the Inspectorate of Government in Uganda, which is entitled to 'enjoy an independent budget appropriated by Parliament and controlled by the Inspectorate'. Further that:

> It shall be the duty of the State to facilitate the employment by the Inspectorate of such adequate and qualified staff as are needed to enable the Inspectorate to perform its functions effectively and efficiently.[100]

This emphasises the importance of maintaining the independence of an FIU both in theory and in practice.

5.6.5 Operational Issues

There are two key issues here. Firstly, in view of the complexity of financial investigations and analysis, an FIU must be able to attract and retain the necessary expert and experienced staff. In order to do so, they should enjoy enhanced pay and benefits over those applicable to staff in the general public service.

Secondly, maintaining the confidentiality of the financial information is a priority for all FIUs. This requires having in place processes designed to ensure that staff maintain high professional standards, including standards concerning confidentiality, and should be of high integrity and be appropriately skilled.[101] As noted earlier, concern over the lack of security and confidentiality of financial information was another reason that led to the Egmont Group suspending the Nigerian FIU from membership.

5.7 THE ROLE OF FINANCIAL REGULATORS AND SUPERVISORS

The FATF Recommendations[102] require countries to ensure that financial institutions and DNFBPs are subject to adequate regulation and supervision and are implementing their AML responsibilities effectively. In this context, 'supervisors' are those 'designated competent authorities or non-public bodies

---

99 See for example, section 11(1) Nigerian Financial Intelligence Unit Act 2018.

100 Article 229 Constitution of Uganda.

101 Interpretive Note to FATF Recommendation 29 E10. See also Section 7.5 above.

102 FATF Recommendations 26 and 28 respectively.

with responsibilities aimed at ensuring compliance by financial institutions (financial supervisors) and/or DNFBPs with requirements to combat money laundering…'.[103] In African countries, the regulation of financial institutions generally falls under the purview of the Central Bank[104] or other public body[105] although this oversight may be reinforced by other financial sector regulators.[106] Some African countries have established a single agency to supervise the non-banking sector[107] whilst in others there are a plethora of regulatory bodies. Some are public bodies[108] whilst others are non-public bodies with a statutory obligation to supervise specific sectors such as casinos,[109] accountants, lawyers and real estate agents. Unusually in some countries FIUs undertake a supervisory role. Thus in the Seychelles, the FIU is the sole AML supervisor with power to supervise all reporting entities[110] to ensure that they comply with the provisions of the Anti-Money Laundering Act 2006.[111] Unusually, in Lesotho the FIU is the supervisory authority for motor vehicle dealers and real estate agents. Interestingly, here corruption remains the most prevalent predicate offence, with the FIU tracing the laundering of most of these proceeds through the real estate and motor vehicle sectors.[112] This suggests that an FIU might well take a more active supervisory and regulatory role over the non-financial sector.

However, in many cases, key sectors remain unregulated. For example, in Eswatini, real estate agents are not regulated and, as the ESAAMLG has noted,

---

[103] See FATF Recommendations 2012, General Glossary. Supervisors must have adequate powers to oversee and ensure compliance by financial institutions with their AML obligations: FATF Recommendation 27.

[104] For example, Bank of Botswana, Central Bank of Eswatini and Central Bank of Kenya.

[105] For example, the Banking and Financial Supervision Commission in Madagascar.

[106] Such as the Capital Markets Authority and Insurance Regulatory Authority (Kenya).

[107] For example, the Financial Services Commission in Mauritius regulates the non-banking financial services sector and global business: ESAAMLG report, p. 103.

[108] For example, in Botswana the Non-Bank Financial Institutions Regulatory Authority; and in Eswatini the Financial Services Regulatory Authority. In Malawi the Financial Intelligence Authority carries out joint inspections with the self-regulatory bodies.

[109] See the special requirements regarding the supervision of casinos set out in FATF Recommendation 28.

[110] The supervisory power covers accountants and auditors, lawyers, real estate agents, high value dealers, casinos, financial institutions and other non-bank financial institutions: see ESAAMLG report, p. 127.

[111] This is also the position in Nigeria: see Nigerian Financial Intelligence Unit Act 2018, section 19(1).

[112] See further ESAAMLG report, pp. 88 and 90.

this is a growing business that has attracted foreign buyers and that 'large cash transactions are sometimes used to settle real estate payments, with lawyers and accountants as main facilitators'.[113] Given the prevalence of corruption as regards precious metals and stones in many countries,[114] it is also surprising that these AML obligations are not consistently applied to dealers.[115]

There are examples of good practice[116] and enforcement against non-co-operative bodies. For example, financial sector regulators in Kenya have enforced administrative sanctions and penalties arising from AML violations, including in 2018 the imposition by the Central Bank of Kenya of a fine of US$3.92 million on five banks arising from AML 'lapses'.[117] Even so, the paucity of STRs made to FIUs, especially from DNFBPs noted earlier[118] has rightly raised concerns that despite having statutory powers in some cases, the supervisory mechanisms in many countries are ineffective or non-existent. For example, in Eswatini, supervisory authorities have the power to enforce the AML provisions by imposing an administrative penalty/sanction on an accountable institution for failing to comply with its AML obligations.[119] It is not clear as to whether such provisions have ever been utilised. Similarly, the GIABA 7th and 8th follow-up reports on Liberia both highlighted the fact that the country had still not commenced the supervision of DNFBPs nor provided

---

[113] ESAAMLG report, p. 76. Similarly, in Zambia there is no regulator overseeing the activities of property developers, an area that is particularly vulnerable to money laundering: see Zambia Financial Intelligence Centre, *5th Money Laundering and Terrorist Financing Trends Report 2018*, Lusaka, 2018, p. 13 and the discussion in Section 4.6.2 above.

[114] The Luanda Papers allege that in 2012, Sindika Dokolo, the husband of Isabel dos Santos, signed a highly beneficial and lucrative agreement with the Angolan state diamond company, Sodiam: See 'Isabel dos Santos: Africa's richest woman "ripped off Angola"' https://www.bbc.co.uk/news/world-africa-51128950?intlink_from_url=&link_location=live-reporting-story (accessed 5 June 2020).

[115] A point made by the ESAAMLG in respect of many member countries: see, for example, the comments on Angola, Madagascar and Malawi: ESAAMLG report, pp. 93, 96 and 100 respectively.

[116] For example, in Sao Tome and Principe, the FIU and Central Bank reportedly undertook a joint on-site supervision of two private banks to ascertain compliance with AML requirements.

[117] ESAAMLG report, p. 84. In Kenya financial sector regulators including the Central Bank of Kenya, the Capital Markets Authority and the Insurance Regulatory Authority have increased collaboration with the Financial Reporting Centre (the FIU in Kenya): ESAAMLG report, p. 84.

[118] See Section 5.4.1 above.

[119] See section 35 of the Money Laundering and Financing of Terrorism Prevention Act 2011 and section 35 *bis* (1)(a) of the Money Laundering and Financing of Terrorism (Amendment) Act 2016.

any sector specific guidelines.[120] Here specific statutory provisions requiring the appointment of AML supervisors are needed.[121]

5.8 OVERVIEW

FIUs play a key role in combating money laundering by PEPs and it is encouraging that the past few years have seen their establishment in most African states.[122] It is also significant that the MERs carried out by the African RBs have focused considerable attention on the operation of FIUs and this has assisted in analysing their operation and effectiveness. These raise a number of practical issues that potentially affect the operation of FIUs.

The effectiveness of FIUs in fighting money laundering largely depends upon receiving, compiling and analysing financial information. This requires the active assistance of financial institutions and DNFBPs in making the necessary STRs. The MERs indicate that there is a serious failure to do so, particularly on the part of the latter. Yet the real estate sector, dealers in gold and precious stones and lawyers are particularly vulnerable to money laundering by PEPs. It is essential that effective measures are in place to 'persuade' such entities to commit to making appropriate STRs.

---

120 In the 9th Follow-up Report on Liberia, reviewers noted the Money Laundering Terrorist Financing Preventive Measures and Proceeds of Crime Bill 2018 had been drafted, which was designed to address this deficiency. It has yet to be enacted (June 2020).

121 For example the MER on Uganda is critical of the fact that there were no provisions in the Anti-Money Laundering Act explicitly providing for the appointment of AML supervisors: ESAAMLG *Uganda Mutual Evaluation Report 2016*, p. 5.

122 As at 30 March 2020 these are: Algeria: Financial Intelligence Processing Unit (CTRF); Angola: Unidade de Informação Financeira (UIF-Angola); Benin: Cellule Nationale de Traitement des Informations Financières du Bénin (CENTIF); Burkina Faso: National Financial Information Processing Unit (CENTIF-BF); Cameroon (National Agency for Financial Investigation), Cape Verde: Cape Verde UIF (UIF); Chad: Agence Nationale d'Investigation Financière du Tchad (ANIF); Cote d'Ivoire (CENTIF-CI); Egypt (Egyptian Money Laundering Combating Unit); Congo-Brazzaville: Agence Nationale d'Investigation Financiere (ANIF); Ethiopia (Ethiopian Financial Intelligence Centre), Gabon (National Agency for Financial Investigation), Ghana: Financial Intelligence Centre Ghana (FIC); Malawi (FIU); Mali (CENTIF-MALI); Mauritius (FIU); Morocco (Financial Information Processing Unit); Namibia (FIC); Niger: National Financial Intelligence and Processing Unit of Niger (CENTIF); Nigeria (FIU); Senegal (CENTIFSENEGAL); Seychelles (FIU); South Africa (Financial Intelligence Centre); Sudan: Financial Information Unit (FIUSU); Tanzania (FIU); Togo: Togo Financial Intelligence Unit (CENTIF Togo); Tunisia (Tunisian Financial Analysis Centre); Uganda (Financial Intelligence Authority); and Zambia (FIC).

This requires the establishment and maintenance of effective regulators and supervisors with powers to impose effective sanctions for failures by financial institutions and DNFBPs to comply with their AML obligations and the willingness to do so. However, the MERs indicate that not every country has put in place the necessary regulatory and supervisory framework and that, where this exists, weaknesses remain. There is also little evidence to indicate that the imposition of administrative or criminal sanctions for failures to comply with AML obligations is widespread.

As regards FIUs themselves, there is much to admire. The majority are now members of the Egmont Group, which has produced demonstrable benefits. In addition, co-operation and coordination with AML agencies both domestically and transnationally are increasing with some positive results. This is encouraging. However, the MERs on a significant number of countries reveal that more is needed to enhance the effectiveness of FIUs.

Firstly, as FIUs are not enshrined in national constitutions, they are especially vulnerable to undue influence by PEPs. It is therefore vital that their independence, including their budget and security of tenure for senior officers, is clearly provided for in the enabling legislation.

Secondly, the MERs on several countries highlight gaps in the AML legislation relating to FIUs. Addressing these gaps is an on-going process and requires a constant review of domestic AML legislation.

Thirdly, a recurrent point from the MERs is the need to provide further training and technical assistance to FIUs. African RBs and development agencies already offer some such assistance but this is an area that needs considerable further attention and donor support.

Fourthly, given the limitations on the making of STRs, FIUs must also actively look for alternative sources of information. Encouraging whistleblowers to make reports is essential. Promoting a reward system might be considered.[123] The Panama Papers and the Luanda Papers highlight the usefulness of 'super-whistleblowers' but having in place effective provisions at the domestic level is also necessary. Reviewing the asset declarations and tax returns by PEPs may also provide useful financial information as well as accessing social media platforms involving PEPs.[124]

Fifthly, the development of virtual currencies and mobile money has brought new challenges for FIUs. This requires on-going assistance from the Egmont Group and the FATF to assist in addressing these issues.

---

[123] See for example, section 10(d) Good Governance and Integrity Reporting Act 2015 (Mauritius).

[124] See further Section 8.4.1.

Finally, it is important to highlight the supportive role of CSOs and the media. As the example from Zambia demonstrates, these can assist in raising awareness both of the work of FIUs and to follow up on cases involving PEPs referred to in the FIU 'Trends' report.

The work of the Egmont African regional groups and the African RBs themselves in reviewing the operation of FIUs and in critically evaluating their capacity to fulfil the requirements of the FATF and the Egmont Group is also commendable. This emphasises the need for on-going scrutiny of compliance with their standards. The progress made in this respect over the past few years emphasises the effectiveness of 'gentle persuasion' mechanisms.

Overall, assessing the impact of FIUs in African states on combating money laundering is not clear. Whilst some have been able to assist in asset recovery, the number of convictions resulting from STRs is alarmingly low. For example, in 2018 STRs received by FIUs in 15 GIABA member states totalled 12,675.[125] From these 393 reports were filed for judicial action and yet no convictions were reported. As the GIABA 2018 report bluntly puts it, the 'data shows an ever increasing number of STRs but investigation remains at very low levels'. This may not reflect the entire picture as the GIABA 2018 report goes on to note that 'there are real challenges with obtaining information from the law courts relevant to assessing and understanding the outcomes of the AML/CFT efforts'.[126] How many of these STRs relate to PEPs is nowhere recorded but almost inevitably many will so refer. This disconnect between STRs and investigations and convictions is alarming and the GIABA is rightly conducting an independent investigation of the issue with a view to addressing the challenges.

---

[125] GIABA 2018 report, Table 8.2. 10,346 of the STRs were filed with the Nigerian FIU. No STRs were seemingly reported by the FIU in Liberia. In 2018 the Comoros reported 30 STRs received by the FIU, which resulted in 13 investigations and three reports made to the Prosecutor. There is no indication as to whether any prosecutions resulted: GIABA 2018 report, at [169].

[126] Ibid, at [518].

6. PEPs and constitutions as AML instruments

6.1 CONSTITUTIONS AS AML INSTRUMENTS

It is curious that the relationship between constitutions and combating money laundering by PEPs has received little attention. As the supreme law of a country,[1] the national constitution bestows powers and protections designed to enable PEPs to carry out their duties effectively. However, as a former Chief Justice of South Africa, Justice Ismail Mohammed, has observed, a constitution is not simply a document which mechanically defines the structures of government and the relations between the government and the governed, but it is:

> [a] mirror reflecting the national soul, the identification of the ideals and aspirations of a nation; the articulation of the values binding its people and disciplining its government.[2]

Thus the fundamental values of a nation are enshrined in its national constitution and given that 'corruption and maladministration are inconsistent with' those values,[3] it has a key role to play in 'disciplining' PEPs and thereby upholding good governance and accountability. Its role in preventing money laundering by PEPs comes through providing for institutional safeguards such as a supreme audit authority[4] and an anti-corruption/AML body or bodies as

---

1 See for example, Article 10 of the African Charter on Democracy, Elections and Governance, which provides that 'State Parties shall entrench the principle of the supremacy of the constitution in the political organization of the State'.

2 *S v Acheson* 1991 (2) SA 805 (Nm) at 813 A-B. See also the comments of the Supreme Court of Ghana in *Taffour v Attorney General* (1980) GLR 637 at 647–8 and the views of Aguda JA in *Unity Dow v Attorney General* [1992] LRC Const 623 at 668.

3 Chaskalson, P. in *South African Association of Personal Injury Lawyers v Heath* [2000] ZACC 22; 2001 (1) BCLR 77 at [4] (Constitutional Court of South Africa).

4 See Chapter 7 on the role of the Auditor General.

well as provisions requiring financial transparency[5] including a requirement for PEPs to declare their assets.[6]

Yet a national constitution can also impact adversely on national AML efforts. Thus implementing several of the FATF Recommendations causes difficulties in that they potentially infringe constitutional rights and make it harder to investigate and successfully prosecute PEPs.[7] In addition, as PEPs 'control the controls' they are often in a position to undermine the effectiveness of the constitutional AML agencies.[8]

6.2 CONSTITUTIONS IN AFRICAN STATES

The structure of constitutions in African states varies significantly. Some adopt a federal model whilst others adopt a unitary model. In the case of Nigeria, for example, a presidential system is adopted. Elsewhere, in Anglophone Africa a parliamentary system is more the norm. The colonial influence remains strong. Thus the constitutions in Francophone African states largely follow the format of the former colonial power, being concise and providing only minimal detail.[9] A few, such as the Namibian and South African Constitutions, were drafted internally as part of the constitutional transition process.

For the reasons noted in Section 6.2.1, the constitutions in Anglophone African countries form the main focus of attention in Part III of the book.

6.2.1 Structure of the Anglophone African Constitutions

1. *Common constitutional principles*

The constitutions of most Anglophone African countries (the African Constitutions)[10] remain largely based on the Westminster export model. Although replaced or much amended, they still retain a similar and recognisable structure. Thus the documents are long, elaborate, technical and detailed and are designed to be as exhaustive as possible. They detail the powers of

---

5 See Section 5.6.

6 See Section 5.4.1.

7 See the discussion in Chapters 8 and 9 below.

8 See Section 8.6 below.

9 The independence constitutions of Mozambique and Angola had more the character of a programme for action than including any regulatory law: see M Hall and T Young, Recent constitutional developments in Mozambique, (1991) 35(1) *Journal of African Law* 102.

10 Ghana, Kenya, The Gambia, Lesotho, Malawi, Namibia, Nigeria, South Africa, Uganda, Zambia and Zimbabwe. Reference is also made to the Namibian Constitution where appropriate.

PEPs and the limitations on their exercise, including the mechanisms and institutions designed to 'discipline its government'.

They include a justiciable and detailed Bill of Rights. These frequently include a range of new generation rights which potentially enhance their role as AML instruments, for example, the inclusion of freedom of information provisions.[11]

2. *Common legal language*

The decisions of the superior courts in Anglophone African states are almost invariably written in English. This greatly facilitates the sharing and development of constitutional principles. This is further enhanced by effective law reporting systems in many states which provide a wealth of comparative material. Judges have made commendable use of such material in their rulings on constitutional issues, with several being of particular importance as regards AML issues.[12]

3. *Common interpretation of constitutional principles*

Adopting a liberal approach to *locus standi* is imperative, especially when allegations of abuse of power by PEPs are in issue, for those whose rights 'are allegedly trampled upon must not be turned away from the court by procedural hiccups'.[13] As Lugakingira J neatly put it:

> In matters of public interest litigation this court will not deny standing to a genuine and bona fide litigant even when [s/he] has no personal interest in the matter ... where the court can provide an effective remedy.[14]

An excellent example is the successful challenge by a civil society organisation in Kenya to limits placed on access by the Auditor General to sensitive government financial information.[15]

Adopting a liberal approach to constitutional interpretation depends upon the ability and willingness of judges to interpret the document in a manner that will fulfil its role as the 'mirror' of the nation. In doing so, courts in several African states have adopted the approach to constitutional interpretation set

---

[11] See Section 8.4.3 below.

[12] See for example, section 7.2.1 below.

[13] See Egonda-Ntende J in *Rwanyarara v S* (1998) Court of Appeal of Uganda, unreported, at p. 3.

[14] *Mtikila v Attorney General* (1994) High Court of Tanzania, unreported at p. 11.

[15] See *Transparency International (TI Kenya) v Attorney General*, [2018] eKLR discussed in Section 7.3.3 below.

out in the case of *R v Big M Drug Mart Ltd.*[16] In considering the interpretation of the Canadian Charter of Rights and Freedoms, Dickson J in the Supreme Court of Canada stated:

> This Court has already, in some measure, set out the basic approach to be taken in interpreting the Charter. In *Hunter v Southam Inc* [1984] 2 SCR 145, this Court expressed the view that the proper approach to the definition of the rights and freedoms guaranteed by the Charter was a purposive one. The meaning of a right or freedom guaranteed by the Charter was to be ascertained by an analysis of the purpose of such a guarantee; it was to be understood, in other words, in the light of the interests it was meant to protect.[17]

Dickson J then went on to state:

> In my view this analysis is to be undertaken, and the purpose of the right or freedom in question is to be sought by reference to the character and larger objects of the Charter itself, to the language chosen to articulate the specific right or freedom, to the historical origins of the concept enshrined, and where applicable, to the meaning and purpose of the other specific rights and freedoms with which it is associated within the text of the Charter. The interpretation should be ... a generous rather than legalistic one, aimed at fulfilling the purpose of a guarantee and securing for individuals the full benefit of the Charter's protection.[18]

Adopting such a liberal approach to interpretation enables the Constitution to play an effective AML role.

6.2.2 The African Constitutions and Combating Money Laundering

The African Constitutions provide for a range of institutions and strategies that can combat money laundering by PEPs. They also provide judges, researchers and CSOs with a wide range of comparative material that can be used to enhance AML action. Yet as the following section demonstrates, other provisions present opportunities for PEPs to undermine the very values that the Constitution articulates simply by using their power to ‘control the constitutional controls’.

---

[16] [1985] 1 SCR 295; 18 DLR (4th) 321.

[17] Ibid, at [116].

[18] Ibid, at [117]. See also similar views expressed by the Zimbabwe Supreme Court in *In re Munhemeso* 1994(1) ZLR 49 and the Constitutional Court of South Africa in *S v Zuma* 1995 (4) BCLR 401.

6.3 PEPs AND THE POWER TO UNDERMINE A CONSTITUTION BY CONSTITUTIONAL MEANS

Whilst the national constitution is the supreme law, PEPs are in a unique position to 'control the constitutional controls' and thus undermine the very safeguards designed to combat money laundering. In essence the constitution itself becomes a potential vehicle for facilitating and supporting money laundering. This results largely from insufficient institutional autonomy, ineffective or inadequate oversight and accountability mechanisms and impunity for PEPs.[19]

In essence there are two key questions: firstly, whether constitutions can control PEPs or whether they are controlled by PEPs; and secondly, to what extent the implementation of the FATF Recommendations is limited by the enjoyment of constitutional rights by PEPs. These raise several issues that are discussed in the following chapters.

6.3.1 PEPs and the Power to Appoint and Remove Office-holders of Constitutional AML 'Safeguarding' Institutions

Constitutions provide for a range of institutions that play important AML roles including Offices of the Auditor General and anti-corruption/AML commissions. Yet providing for a range of constitutional AML bodies is not an end in itself for these must be, and be seen by citizens as, independent and effective institutions.

A fundamental aspect of this is the requirement for a demonstrably fair and independent appointment procedure for office-holders in such institutions. Yet in many constitutions, PEPs enjoy the power of appointment and removal of key office-holders and the power of the purse i.e. control over the financing of AML institutions.

6.3.2 PEPs and the Use and Abuse of Presidential Pardons

The presidential power of pardon is enshrined in most constitutions. Whilst an important tool to remedy any injustice, it also facilitates the pardoning of a PEP following a conviction for a corruption-related and/or money laundering

---

[19] See for example, the IMF, *Republic of Mozambique: Diagnostic Report on Transparency, Governance and Corruption*, 2019, IMF Country Report No. 19/276, at [11] and [12].

offence. In essence the abuse of this power undermines the criminal justice system.[20]

The criminal justice system is also undermined when there is a 'pre-emptive' pardon i.e. where the President agrees to a 'deal' whereby a PEP is not prosecuted perhaps in exchange for the return of at least part of the laundered proceeds of crime.[21]

6.3.3 PEPs and Control over National Security Spending

Constitutions provide PEPs with control over national security spending.[22] However, the secrecy surrounding national security can facilitate the laundering of the proceeds of crime and potentially undermine freedom of information laws and effective scrutiny by the Auditor General.[23]

6.3.4 PEPs, Constitutional Rights and the FATF Recommendations

The FATF Recommendations contain a series of obligations that potentially conflict with the enjoyment of constitutional rights and provide challenges to effective investigations and prosecutions.

For example, the right to privacy is enshrined in several African Constitutions. In addition, strict data protection laws often limit access by law enforcement agencies to the personal information of PEPs and their associates. However, several of the FATF Recommendations involve requiring AML investigators and prosecutors to have power to access such personal information.

Similar issues arise as regards PEPs and the right to a fair trial. Yet these can inevitably impact on the effectiveness of AML investigations. For example, the constitutional right to consult a lawyer and legal professional privilege impact on the power to investigate the affairs of PEPs and the admissibility of evidence.

6.4 THE CHALLENGES

Given this reality, there are twin challenges. Firstly, to ensure that constitutions and constitutional safeguards are robust enough to be capable of 'persuading' even the most powerful of PEPs to 'commit' to good governance or at least to limit the opportunities for PEPs to undermine the constitution by constitutional

---

20 For a full discussion see Chapter 11 below.

21 See Section 11.9 below.

22 See Section 2.5 above.

23 For a full discussion see Chapter 7 below.

means. Secondly to ensure that constitutional rights do not unduly interfere with effective AML investigations and prosecutions. These points are explored in the following chapters.

7. Preventing money laundering by PEPs: the constitutional role of the Auditor General

7.1 ADDRESSING CORRUPTION LEAKAGES IN THE PUBLIC SERVICE[1]

In 2013 forensic investigations carried out by the Auditor General in Malawi revealed that enormous sums of government money had been unlawfully appropriated from up to 10 ministries through the manipulation of the government computer system. This revelation brought to light the 'Cashgate' scandal with subsequent investigations by the Malawi Anti-Corruption Bureau leading to the prosecution and conviction for money laundering and other offences of a series of PEPs and their accomplices.[2]

The Cashgate and Thiam cases highlight the fact that corruption by PEPs causes 'leakages' at multiple points in the public sector, for example through corruption in government procurement and the looting of state assets.[3] Of particular contemporary concern are the allegations of the misuse of funds received from international donors and development agencies for the procurement of equipment and medication required to address during the 2020 Covid-19 pandemic as well as the associated government contracts being awarded without due diligence checks.[4] This is then followed by the 'outflow leakages' through the laundering of the proceeds of corruption. The challenge is to have in place effective independent oversight bodies enshrined in the

---

[1] Part of this chapter is drawn from John Hatchard, The role, independence and accountability of the Auditor General: A comparative analysis, (2018) 30(2) *Denning Law Journal* 51. Reproduced with the kind permission of the publisher.

[2] See further Section 1.1.

[3] See Section 2.1 above for a discussion on the Thiam case. For a useful diagram on corruption leakages in the public sector see International Monetary Fund, *Fiscal Monitoring: Curbing Corruption* 2019, Figure 2.3. For further discussion on PEPs, procurement corruption and money laundering see Section 2.5 above.

[4] 'Fighting corruption during the coronavirus pandemic', Global Initiative report, 3 June 2020. Available at www.globalinitiative.net (accessed 30 June 2020).

national constitution designed to safeguard the integrity of public finances and public procurement, to detect and deter money laundering and to hold PEPs to account for any wrongdoing. For example, offices of the ombudsman investigate complaints from members of the public into alleged maladministration by public officials, anti-corruption commissions investigate and prosecute corruption and money laundering, whilst human rights commissions offer a vehicle through which individuals and groups can seek to enforce their constitutional rights against the government.

As the supreme audit authority, including the Auditor General in this framework of 'state institutions supporting constitutional democracy'[5] emphasises that this is not an isolated and somewhat remote office but part of a scheme that is designed to ensure that the good governance values and AML safeguards enshrined in the Constitution apply to the daily administration of the country. In essence, such institutions form an additional branch of government.

The constitutional mandate of the Auditor General is to audit and to report annually to the legislature on the use of public funds with a view to ensuring that 'good governance' values of integrity, transparency and accountability in public finances are fully respected.[6] Indeed, respondents to the study by the ESAAMLG on public sector procurement and money laundering identified reports by Auditors General as providing significant assistance to law enforcement agencies in investigating such criminality and recovering the proceeds of crime.[7] The office-holder is thus potentially a key player in both preventing and identifying money laundering by PEPs.

This chapter assesses critically the extent to which, in practice, Auditors General can and do play an effective AML role, especially in the face of efforts by PEPs to undermine their work. In doing so, the chapter focuses on the constitutional role, powers and independence of the Auditor General enshrined in the African Constitutions.[8]

The chapter is divided into the following parts. Section 7.2 explores AML safeguards and the constitutional role of the Auditor General whilst Section 7.3 considers the basic provisions for developing an effective auditing role.

---

[5] A phrase used to describe such institutions in chapter 9 of the Constitution of South Africa 1996.

[6] See for example, Article 10 Constitution of Kenya and the Preamble to the Constitution of Zimbabwe.

[7] ESAAMLG, *Procurement Corruption in the Public Sector and Associated Money Laundering in the ESAAMLG Region*, 2019 (the ESAAMLG Procurement report), p. 46.

[8] As noted in Section 6.2.1 these comprise the Constitutions of Ghana, Kenya, The Gambia, Lesotho, Malawi, Namibia, Nigeria, South Africa, Uganda, Zambia and Zimbabwe. This chapter does not seek to consider the constitutional position of the Auditor General in each country.

Sections 7.4 and 7.5 then analyse the constitutional provisions in support of individual and institutional autonomy of the office and office-holder. Section 7.6 examines the mechanisms to support and oversee the work of the Auditor General whilst Section 7.7 critically assesses the constitutional safeguards on the removal of the Auditor General. Section 7.8 then provides a conclusion.

7.2 AML SAFEGUARDS AND THE CONSTITUTIONAL ROLE OF THE AUDITOR GENERAL

7.2.1 The 'Ally of the People'

Article 10 of the UNCAC emphasises the need for each State Party to take the necessary measures 'in accordance with the fundamental principles of its domestic law', to 'enhance transparency in its public administration, including with regard to its organisation, functioning and decision-making processes, where appropriate'. This includes taking steps to ensure fiscal integrity, transparency and accountability in government and the public service. Further the UNCAC CoSP has acknowledged that 'efficient, accountable and transparent service delivery is one of the key components in building an anti-corruption environment in the public sector'.[9] The key role played by Auditors General in enhancing this goal is echoed in Article IX of the Commonwealth Principles,[10] which were endorsed by Commonwealth Heads of Government in 2003.

As Yilmaz and Beris have pointed out, accountability addresses a number of elements including providing for transparency in the use of public funds and public accessibility to such information.[11] However, the key to accountability is 'control'. This requires an independent audit body or bodies to ensure fiscal integrity i.e. that the powers of PEPs are not abused or misused and that there is accountability for retaining 'sound and transparent public expenditure and financial management systems'.[12] This has the dual purpose of both encourag-

---

9 CoSP Resolution 6/6 of 2015, *Follow-up to the Marrakech declaration on the prevention of corruption*, 2015, Preamble.

10 Commonwealth (Latimer House) Principles on the Accountability of and Relationship between the Three Branches of Government. Article IX states 'Independent bodies such as ... Auditors General ... and similar oversight institutions can play a key role in enhancing public awareness of good governance and rule of law issues'.

11 Serder Yilmaz and Yakup Beris, Good governance and the emergence of a new accountability agenda, in Gabor Peteri (ed.), *Finding the Money: Public Accountability and Service Efficiency through Fiscal Transparency*, Open Society Initiative, 2008, p. 30.

12 Ibid.

ing 'ethical behaviour by making unethical behaviour hard to accomplish and easy to detect' and helping to bring to light any abuse of power.[13]

The position of the Auditor General is enshrined in all the African Constitutions[14] and as the supreme audit authority, the office-holder has responsibility for auditing on an annual basis the accounts of all government and other state institutions,[15] publishing an annual report, and submitting this to the legislature for scrutiny and debate. Thus the office-holder is the key constitutional figure in overseeing the proper use of public resources and, if necessary, of publicly exposing any abuse of public funds and potential money laundering activity. This role is neatly explained in the Kenyan case of *Transparency International (TI Kenya) v Attorney General*:[16]

> the Auditor General is an ally of the people. While Parliament is the peoples' representative, the Auditor General provides Parliament with accurate and independently derived audit information on state organs and public bodies expenditure [and] thus ensures that there is public sector accountability.[17]

The effective performance of this responsibility is neatly highlighted by the Cashgate scandal where as a result of forensic investigations by Malawi's Auditor General:

> In September 2013, gates to what was meant to be a clandestine and non-detectable criminal syndicate of fraudsters and money launderers were flung open. Information revealing an unprecedented fiscal scandal gradually unfolded in a manner an unsuspecting observer would have been forgiven to think was a masterfully scripted piece of fiction. It was a shocking reality. Billions of Kwacha had been embezzled from the national fiscus by some unscrupulous people.[18]

---

13 Ibid.

14 Thus a statutory provision referring to the Auditor General as the 'statutory' head of the office violates the Constitution: see *Transparency International (TI Kenya) v Attorney General*, [2018] eKLR at [83].

15 See for example, Article 226(3) Constitution of Kenya.

16 [2018] eKLR at [5]. The case is considered in detail below.

17 In the case of *Re the Matter of the Independent Electoral and Boundaries Commission of Kenya* [2011] eKLR, the Supreme Court of Kenya also helpfully described independent commissions and bodies such as the Office of the Auditor General as 'people's watchdogs' [59].

18 Per Kapindu J in *R v Lutepo* [2015] MWHC 491 at [1] (High Court of Malawi).

7.3 TOWARDS AN EFFECTIVE AUDITING ROLE

Requiring Auditors General to 'exercise their powers and perform their functions without fear, favour or prejudice' is a constitutional imperative.[19] Yet, as the Constitutional Court of South Africa has rightly pointed out, the work of the Auditor General 'inherently entails the investigation of sensitive and potentially embarrassing affairs of government',[20] and those of PEPs in particular. In order to enable Auditors General to carry out their constitutional role of effective public sector auditing and the prevention of money laundering, eight Core Principles (the Core Principles) were recognised in the Mexico Declaration on Supreme Audit Authority Independence (the Mexico Declaration).[21] These cover issues relating to independence, security of tenure, investigative powers and unrestricted access to information. These Core Principles are noted throughout this chapter.

7.3.1 Establishing and Maintaining an Independent Office

Core Principle 2 states that the independence of the Auditor General is an essential requirement for proper public sector auditing. This emphasises the fundamental requirement of enshrining the independence of the office and office-holder in the Constitution and this is discussed below.

7.3.2 Providing 'A Sufficiently Broad Mandate'[22]

In carrying out their constitutional role effectively, Auditors General must be empowered to audit all state bodies or public entities. In some constitutions, the specific bodies and entities are listed.[23] For example, Article 187(2) of the Constitution of Ghana provides:

> The public accounts of Ghana and of all public offices, including the courts, the central and local government administrations, of the Universities and public

---

[19] Constitution of South Africa 1996, Section 181(2).

[20] *Ex parte Chairperson of the Constitutional Assembly: In re Certification of the Constitution of the Republic of South Africa, 1996* [1996] ZACC 26; 1996 (4) SA 744 (CC); 1996 (10) BCLR 1253 (Constitutional Court of South Africa) (First Certification), at [163].

[21] Agreed at the XIX Congress of the International Organization of Supreme Audit Authorities (INTOSAI). The African Organization of Supreme Audit Institutions collaborates with the INTOSAI.

[22] Core Principle 3.

[23] For a useful discussion on the scope of the Auditor General's powers see *Khumalo v Auditor General* [2013] SZHC 56 (High Court of Swaziland).

> institutions of like nature, of any public corporation or other body or organisation established by an Act of Parliament shall be audited and reported on by the Auditor General.

Similarly, Section 188(1) of the Constitution of South Africa provides:

> The Auditor General must audit and report on the accounts, financial statements and financial management of (a) all national and provincial state departments and administrations; (b) all municipalities; and (c) any other institution or accounting entity required by national or provincial legislation to be audited by the Auditor General.

A key to a successful audit is unrestricted access to all relevant documentation or premises.[24] This is emphasised in Article 187(3) of the Constitution of Ghana:

> the Auditor-General or any person authorised or appointed for the purpose by the Auditor-General shall have access to all books, records, returns and other documents relating or relevant to those accounts.

Access to sensitive 'national security' information provides a particular challenge for there are several examples where PEPs have laundered stolen state assets under the cover of spurious 'national security' needs. This focuses attention on the extent to which Auditors General enjoy in practice the 'unrestricted access to information' required for carrying out their functions,[25] including that relating to expenditure on 'national security'. This was the focus in the High Court of Kenya case of *Transparency International (TI Kenya) v Attorney General* (the TI case).[26]

7.3.3 The TI Case

In this important case, the petitioners submitted that a number of sections of the Public Audit Act 2015 were unconstitutional both in purpose and effect as they tended to 'interfere with the independence and mandate of the Auditor General, an independent constitutional office'.[27] The Constitution of Kenya provides, amongst other things, that the Auditor General is 'subject only to the Constitution and the law and independent and not subject to direction or

---

24 Core Principle 4 refers to 'unrestricted access to information'.
25 Core Principle 4.
26 [2018] eKLR.
27 Ibid, at [77].

control by any person or authority'.[28] Further, that in carrying their constitutional mandate the 'Auditor General may audit and report on the accounts of *any entity* that is funded from public funds' (emphasis added) and '[a]n audit report shall confirm whether or not public money has been applied lawfully and in an effective way'.[29]

One provision of the Public Audit Act that was challenged was section 40. Mwita J noted the section required the Auditor General 'to hold a pre-audit meeting at the highest level to agree on areas to audit and the appropriate audit approach when auditing national security organs and even allows the vetting of officers to conduct the audit'.[30] In addition, he noted that section 42 of the Public Audit Act barred the Auditor General from questioning government policy objectives during audits.

In an impressive and thoughtful judgment, Mwita J declared these sections unconstitutional. Having discussed the constitutional provisions relating to the independence of the Auditor General he continued:

> Flowing from the exposition above, it leaves no doubt on the unconstitutionality of sections 40 and 42 of the Act ... The Auditor General has a constitutional obligation under Article 229(4)(h) to audit and report on the accounts of state organs public bodies and any entity funded by public money. This cannot be done if the Auditor General has to seek permission by holding meetings with higher authorities as proposed by section 40 before carrying out the audit. Subjecting officers to vetting before audit would leave room for state organs and public bodies to decide who to audit them.

As regards the limitations imposed in section 42, as Mwita J explained:

> The Auditor General cannot also confirm the viability of the policy objectives funded by the people of Kenya when section 42 suggests that he should not question policy objectives funded by the people. This has the effect of stifling his independence. A statute cannot seek to impose conditions on the Auditor General's audit approaches *when the Constitution gives him mandate to do his work without direction or control from any person or authority*. This violates national values and principles of governance including integrity, transparency and accountability in Article 10 and financial openness in Article 201 of the Constitution (emphasis added).[31]

---

[28] Article 249(2) Constitution of Kenya.

[29] Article 229(5) and (6).

[30] [2018] eKLR at [118].

[31] Ibid, at [118] and [119]. Article 10 of the Constitution of Kenya states: 'The national values and principles of governance in this Article bind all State organs, State officers, public officers and all persons' when carrying out their public functions. These values include 'good governance, integrity, transparency and accountability'.

It followed that the wide constitutional mandate of the Auditor General included the right to scrutinise spending by *all* entities that were publicly funded and this included the National Intelligence Service, the Kenya Defence Force and the National Police Service.

Given the vast sums of money lost by states when national security becomes a veil for corruption and money laundering by PEPs, requiring transparency in spending on 'national security' is a milestone in seeking to prevent such criminality.[32] Understandably public confidence and trust in national security financing requires an appropriate balance between secrecy and transparency. This emphasises the importance of having a demonstrably independent appointee holding the office of Auditor General.

The case also emphasises the supremacy of the constitution. Thus any attempt to undermine or restrict the constitutional role and powers of the Auditor General by legislation must be declared unconstitutional. This recognises the role of the Auditor General as the 'ally of the people' and the critical importance of providing for an independent watchdog body.

The right of the Auditor General in Zambia to scrutinise defence procurement contracts was also noted by Peter Smith J in *Attorney General for Zambia v Meer Care and Desai.*[33] Here the failure to do so had enabled former President Chiluba and his accomplices to launder large sums of looted government assets. The position in the other African jurisdictions is not clear. Perhaps it is time for the CSOs in those jurisdictions to follow the lead of TI Kenya and test the matter in the courts.

7.4 PROTECTING THE INDEPENDENCE OF THE OFFICE-HOLDER 1: THE APPOINTMENT PROCESS

As with other oversight bodies, it is essential that the appointment of the Auditor General is made through a demonstrably fair and transparent procedure.[34] This is essentially a confidence-building exercise for government, public officials, citizens, civil society and donors alike in the integrity, independence and competence of the appointee. Whilst considerable attention has been paid in modern constitutions to the appointment process of members of other oversight bodies, the position of the Auditor General often remains unsatisfactory.

---

[32] For a helpful discussion on this area see Transparency International (UK), *Out of the Shadows: Promoting Openness and Accountability in the Global Defence Industry*, London, 2016.

[33] [2007] EWHC 952.

[34] See further Section 8.6.

There are three key issues here: (1) the qualifications for appointment; (2) the nomination process; and (3) the appointment process itself.

7.4.1 Qualifications for Appointment

In South Africa the Auditor General must be 'a fit and proper person to hold that office. Specialised knowledge of, or experience in, auditing, state finances and public administration must be given due regard in appointing the Auditor-General.'[35] More specifically, in Kenya the Auditor General must 'have extensive knowledge of public finance or at least ten years' experience in auditing or public finance management'.[36]

Few of the other African Constitutions lay down any specific qualifications for appointment. This is surprising as a suitable background is surely a prerequisite for any such appointment and should be expressly provided for in the constitution.

7.4.2 Nominating the Candidate for Appointment

In most of the African Constitutions it is the President who has the sole power to nominate the candidate.[37] There is no justification for this position for it does not bring with it any confidence in the independence of the President's choice. A preferable approach is for the nomination to emanate from a separate body. This is the position in Nigeria[38] and Namibia,[39] where the recommendation for appointment is made by the Federal Civil Service Commission and Public Service Commission respectively. Of course, it raises the question as to the independence of the Commissions themselves. Thus in Nigeria the Commission comprises a chairman and not more than 15 other members, who 'shall, in the opinion of the President, be persons of unquestionable integrity and sound political judgment'.[40] In Namibia there is a stronger formulation. The Public Service Commission consists of a 'chairperson and not less than three nor more than six other persons nominated by the President and

---

[35] Section 193(3).

[36] Constitution of Kenya, Article 229(2).

[37] It is recognised that separate legislation may make provision for the selection process but it is argued that the appointment process is so fundamental that it must be enshrined in the Constitution to avoid any weakening of the procedure by subsequent legislation.

[38] Constitution of Nigeria, section 86(1); Constitution of Namibia, Article 127(1).

[39] Constitution of Namibia, Article 32(3)(i).

[40] Constitution of Nigeria, 3rd Schedule, at [10].

appointed by the National Assembly by resolution'. It 'shall be independent and act impartially'.[41]

7.4.3 The Appointment Process

The African Constitutions contain a variety of procedures concerning the appointment process albeit with the legislature being involved in most jurisdictions.[42] The most common procedure is for the President to appoint the Auditor General 'with the approval of the legislature'[43] or 'subject to ratification' by the legislature.[44] This is a weak approach, for the President is able to hand-pick their chosen candidate and then have the (normally) co-operative legislature rubber-stamp the appointment by a simple majority. A stronger formulation is found in the Constitution of Malawi, which provides that the appointment must be confirmed by the National Assembly by a majority of the members present and voting.[45]

In South Africa the support of at least 60 per cent of the members of the National Assembly is required.[46] The rationale for such a requirement was noted by Mogoeng CJ in the Constitutional Court of South Africa in *Helen Suzman Foundation v President of the Republic of South Africa and Others*:[47]

> in the case of the Public Protector and Auditor-General the Constitution goes further, requiring that the recommendation be approved by a supermajority. These are the two institutions of accountability whose gaze ... is fixed firmly on the political branches; their task 'inherently entails investigation of sensitive and potentially embarrassing affairs of government'.[48]

---

[41] Constitution of Namibia, Article 112(3). There is also a concern that the bodies making the recommendation are themselves subject to scrutiny by the Auditor General.

[42] Article 70(1) of the Constitution of Ghana provides: 'The President shall, acting in consultation with the Council of State, appoint ... the Auditor-General'. Given the presidential influence over the Council, this does not hold out strong hopes of an independent assessment of the matter.

[43] For example, in Namibia, Uganda, Zimbabwe and Kenya.

[44] For example, in Zambia.

[45] Section 184(1).

[46] Section 193(5).

[47] [2014] ZACC 32; 2015 (1) BCLR 1 (CC); 2015 (2) SA 1 (CC) [159].

[48] Quoting from the case of *Ex parte Chairperson of the Constitutional Assembly: In re Certification of the Constitution of the Republic of South Africa, 1996*, above at [163].

In Nigeria the appointment is subject to confirmation by the Senate,[49] which has the power to reject a presidential nomination.[50]

7.4.4 The Involvement of Civil Society

The role of the Auditor General as the 'ally of the people' raises the issue of public involvement in the appointment process. Regrettably, the only constitution to address this point is the Constitution of South Africa where section 194(6) provides that the 'involvement of civil society in the recommendation process [for the appointment of the Auditor General] may be provided for as envisaged in section 59(1)'. Section 59(1) states that the National Assembly must facilitate public involvement in the legislative and other processes of the Assembly and its committees.

All of the Constitutions provide that the President formally appoints the Auditor General. This is unexceptional. However, the current procedure for appointment in most constitutions arguably provides the President with far too much influence, especially given the perceived weakness of the legislature in many jurisdictions. If the Auditor General is to be, and be seen by the public as being, an 'ally of the people' whose mission as an independent constitutional office-holder is to protect public finances and guard against money laundering by PEPs, then there must be confidence in the transparency and reliability of the appointment process.

Here the objective is the same as with judicial appointments: i.e. to appoint 'a professionally competent person of proven integrity' with candidates being drawn from as wide a pool as possible. It follows that restricting the nomination process to the President is unacceptable and, at the very least, there should be an opportunity for the public involvement in the entire process.

---

[49] Constitution of Nigeria, section 86(1).

[50] In December 2016 the Senate rejected the nomination by President Buhari of Ibrahim Magu as the Chairman of the Economic and Financial Crimes Commission based on an adverse 'security report' from the State Security Service. The power of the Senate to do so was upheld by the Abuja Federal High Court in *Ojamo v Attorney General of the Federation of Nigeria*, 2018, unreported.

7.5 PROTECTING THE INDEPENDENCE OF THE OFFICE-HOLDER II: ADMINISTRATIVE AND FINANCIAL AUTONOMY

Article 187(7) of the Constitution of Ghana neatly encapsulates the independence of the Auditor General:

> In the performance of his functions under this Constitution or any other law the Auditor-General … shall not be subject to the direction or control of any other person or authority…[51]

The office and office-holder must therefore be entirely independent of government[52] including the Public Service Commission (PSC),[53] a key point as the PSC itself is subject to the audit process.

7.5.1 Financial Autonomy

Core Principle 8 states that an Auditor General requires: 'Financial and managerial/administrative autonomy and the availability of appropriate human, material and monetary resources.' This means that the administrative expenses of the office of the Auditor General must be charged on the Consolidated Fund.[54] It also follows that the recruitment of staff and other staffing matters are solely a matter for the office-holder and thus the PSC plays no part in the process. In essence 'the workings of the Auditor General including recruitment and discipline cannot be subject to the Public Service Commission or any other authority' and any provision to the contrary violates such independence.[55]

The importance of the point is illustrated by the fact that in several countries 'advisory boards' have been established which threaten this independence. For example, in Kenya, the Audit Advisory Board (AAB) was established by the Public Audit Act 2015, its principle function being to 'advise the Auditor

---

[51] In the TI case, Mwita J also noted that 'as the [holder] of an independent office, he is subject only to the Constitution and the law and is not subject to direction or control of any person or authority': at [117].

[52] The point was also emphasised by Lord Diplock in *Thomas v Attorney General of Trinidad and Tobago* [1982] AC 113, where he observed that the purpose of such provisions was to insulate members from political interference exercised directly upon them by the government of the day (at p. 124).

[53] A point specifically made in Article 127(3) of the Constitution of Namibia.

[54] This includes all salaries, allowances, gratuities and pensions payable to or in respect of persons serving in the Audit Service: see, for example, Article 187(14) Constitution of Ghana.

[55] Per Mwita J in the TI case [88]. See also his views at [101].

General on how to discharge his/her mandate under the Constitution'. In the TI case, Mwita J highlighted the independence of the Auditor General, which was enshrined in Article 249(2) and which provided that the office-holder is not under 'the direction or control of any person or authority'.[56] The role of the AAB was therefore an 'interference with his institutional and individual independence' which altered the 'constitutional architecture of the independent office of the Auditor General and violated Article 249(2)'.[57] He therefore had no hesitation in declaring the provision inconsistent with the Constitution of Kenya. This is a most welcome ruling and should encourage CSOs in other jurisdictions to seek judicial review of the constitutionality of any domestic legislation adversely affecting the office of the Auditor General.

For Ghana the matter is more complex in that the Audit Service Board (ASB) is established by Article 189 of the Constitution of Ghana. Its membership comprises (1) a chairman and four other members appointed by the President, acting in consultation with the Council of State; (2) the Auditor General; and (3) the Head of the Civil Service or his representative.[58] Its functions directly impact on the independence of the Auditor General. Article 189(2) and (3) provide that 'the appointment of officers and other employees in the Audit Service, other than the Auditor General, shall be made by the ASB, acting in consultation with the Public Services Commission'. Articles 189(2) and (3) also provide that the ASB 'shall, acting in consultation with the Public Services Commission ... determine the terms and conditions of service of officers and other employees in the Audit Service'. These provisions constitute a direct interference with the institutional and individual independence of the Auditor General and are inconsistent with Article 187(7) of Constitution of Ghana, which was noted earlier. This is another fruitful issue for a domestic CSO to take up in the courts.

7.5.2 Security of Tenure

Core Principle 2 states that Auditors General must enjoy security of tenure. Inevitably, this is linked to the term of office for the incumbent. Here the African Constitutions vary considerably. The majority provide for a fixed, non-renewable term with the length varying between five years and 12 years. In Namibia the Auditor General holds office for five years but is eligible for re-appointment.[59]

---

56 TI case at [114].
57 Ibid, at [116].
58 Article 189(1).
59 Constitution of Namibia, Article 127(1).

The danger of a fixed-term appointment is that the experience, expertise and public confidence in the office-holder is likely to be lost. Further, given that there is no constitutional provision relating to the time-frame for appointment of a new office-holder, there may be a lengthy hiatus (deliberate or otherwise) before the new appointment is made by the President. This can significantly affect the operation and effectiveness of the office, especially where on-going investigations into possible criminality by PEPs are concerned.

The different approaches perhaps reflect the uncertainty as to the position of the Auditor General. In practice the African Constitutions almost invariably provide for a fixed-term appointment to other 'national institutions' such as human rights commissions. Yet these are largely multi-member bodies where a periodic change of membership is inevitable. As the work of the Auditor General 'inherently entails investigation of sensitive and potentially embarrassing affairs of government' including any potential wrongdoing by PEPs, the office-holder is in a very different position from those in other national institutions.[60] Given this reality, arguably the office-holder must enjoy the same terms and conditions as that of a senior judge. Suitable illustrations come from Nigeria, where the position of the Auditor General is similar to that of a judge, i.e. s/he holds office until retiring age[61] and from Ghana where the Auditor General is appointed until retirement age.[62]

7.6 SUPPORTING AND OVERSEEING THE WORK OF THE AUDITOR GENERAL

The Chiluba case illustrates the failure of an Auditor General to perform his constitutional responsibilities. The then President of Zambia, Frederick Chiluba, and several of his close associates (all PEPs) looted large sums of state money under the guise of national security needs through what was known as the Zamtrop account. During the entire time the criminality was taking place, the Auditor General remained inactive and also failed in his constitutional duty to make annual reports to Parliament.[63] As Peter Smith J explained in *Attorney General for Zambia v Meer Care & Desai*:

> Mr Siame, the Auditor General failed properly to exercise his duties or alternatively chose not to exercise the duties required of him probably because of the intimidatory

---

[60] The same point applies to the appointment of the Director of an Anti-Corruption Commission.

[61] Constitution of Nigeria, Section 87(2).

[62] Constitution of Ghana, Article 187(12).

[63] See now Constitution of Zambia, Article 121(4).

> nature of Chungu [Chiluba's national security chief and co-conspirator] and the unwillingness of the Auditor General to challenge him and thus the President.[64]

Payments through the Zamtrop account were still subject to scrutiny by the Auditor General yet, as Peter Smith, J noted:

> There are provisions for the issue of certificates to the Auditor General on a quarterly basis. I observe that there were indications of audit approvals in the early 1990s but none has been discovered for the period the subject matter of this action ...

This highlights the pressure PEPs can exert on Auditors General and emphasises once again the significance of maintaining the independence of the office-holder and their staff. It also emphasises the need to ensure that effective 'guarding of the guards' safeguards are in place.

7.6.1 The Role of Parliament

Reflecting Core Principle 5 i.e. the right and obligation to report on their work, a typical constitutional requirement is for the Auditor General to submit his/her report to the legislature within a specified time period after the end of the preceding financial year. A specialist multi-party public accounts committee (or equivalent) is then to review the report and may call any ministers, public officials or others to explain any discrepancies. The annual report may be supplemented by ad hoc reports. The legislature is then required to debate the report of the Auditor General and to make recommendations or give instructions for follow-up action.[65] For example, Article 229(8) of the Constitution of Kenya provides that 'within three months after receiving an audit report, Parliament ... shall debate and consider the report and take appropriate action'.[66] Such a provision should be enshrined in every constitution.

The Chiluba case illustrates the challenge of making such scrutiny effective in practice. The Auditor General was under a constitutional mandate to lay an annual report before Parliament but never did so. Parliamentarians failed to

---

[64] [2007] EWHC 952, at [103–4]. The payments were facilitated through the bribery of a senior PEP in the Ministry of Finance.

[65] Core Principles 5–7 recognise (i) the right and obligation of supreme audit authorities to report on their work; (ii) the freedom both to decide the content and timing of audit reports and to publish and disseminate them; and (iii) the need for effective follow-up mechanisms on their recommendations.

[66] See for example, Articles 187(5) and (6) Constitution of Ghana and section 85(5) Constitution of Nigeria. Article 229(8) of the Constitution of Kenya provides that 'within three months after receiving an audit report, Parliament ... shall debate and consider the report and take appropriate action'.

pursue this. Thus whilst constitutional safeguards did exist their failure meant that Chiluba and his associates were able to carry out their money laundering scheme. In essence, through the intimidation or bribery of key public officials their criminality was hidden from view by the failure of the constitutional safeguards.

The extent to which parliamentary scrutiny is effective in practice is questionable. For example, a report published on behalf of the African Parliamentarians Network Against Corruption found that 'too few African parliaments have effective committee systems, and it is rarely possible to properly scrutinise the behaviour of ministers or the senior civil servants who work with them'.[67] This highlights two potential issues. First, the extent to which the appropriate expertise and experience is available in order for parliamentarians to assess the reports and, if necessary, to take action. Second, given the reality of executive control over parliamentary business, whether there is the commitment or opportunity on the part of parliamentarians to do so.[68]

It means that additional support mechanisms are required.

7.6.2 Whistleblowing and the Obligations of Public Officials

The use of whistleblowers is a potentially vital means by which to break through the secrecy surrounding corruption cases and money laundering involving PEPs. The need for states to develop effective whistleblowing schemes is reflected in Article 8(4) of the UNCAC, which provides that each State Party must consider:

> establishing measures and system to facilitate the reporting by public officials of acts of corruption to appropriate authorities, when such acts come to their attention in the performance of their functions.

The Auditor General clearly falls into the category of an 'appropriate authority'. A CoSP resolution also calls on UNCAC States Parties to establish 'measures and systems to facilitate the reporting of incidents' which may be considered to constitute Convention offences.[69]

---

[67] Joanne Davis, *Parliamentarians and Corruption in Africa: The Challenge of Leadership and the Practice of Politics*, Ottawa, The Parliamentary Centre, 2009.

[68] Akech also suggests that key parliamentary committees are themselves implicated in corruption and therefore take no effective steps to address the reports of the Auditor General: see Migai Akech, Abuse of power and corruption in Kenya, (2011) 18(1) *Indiana Journal of Global Legal Issues* 342, at 342.

[69] UNCAC Conference of States Parties resolution 6/6 of 2015: *Follow-up to the Marrakech declaration on the prevention of corruption*, 2015, at [4].

Given that corruption and money laundering by PEPs requires the assistance or acquiescence of others, both within and outside the public service, information provided by whistleblowers is one of the most common ways in which instances of such criminality are identified.[70] This emphasises the importance of having in place effective whistleblowing laws and mechanisms which facilitate reporting to an appropriate authority, and in particular, the Auditor General.

Arguably, this includes placing a *duty* on public officials to report suspicions of corruption or money laundering within the public service. This is clearly contentious, not least because of the dangers this may well pose to the whistleblower and their family. The argument for doing so is set out neatly in the Explanatory Memorandum to the Council of Europe Code of Conduct for public officials, which notes that whilst this could create tensions among public officials, 'the passive or tolerant attitude of public officials regarding breaches would be more harmful for public administration and society as a whole'.[71]

In fact legislation in South Africa already places a duty on any person who holds a 'position of authority' and who 'knows or ought reasonably to have known or suspected that any other person' has committed a serious corruption offence, including a money laundering offence, to report the fact to any police official.[72] This position is potentially complicated by state security legislation which criminalises the unauthorised disclosure of government documents/information.[73] Given that the Auditor General is specifically authorised to have access to all government documentation, including national security information, there is no reason why such a reporting mechanism is not put in place.

7.6.3 The Role of Civil Society/the Media

In their role of 'Constitution-watchers', CSOs can play a significant supportive role in overseeing the office of the Auditor General.

---

[70] UNODC, *The United Nations Convention Against Corruption: Resource Guide on Good Practices in the Protection of Reporting Persons*, 2015, p. 3.

[71] At [70].

[72] Section 34 Prevention and Combating of Corrupt Activities Act (No. 12 of 2004). See also section 39(1) Prevention and Combating of Corruption Act 2007 in Tanzania. As suggested above, a requirement to report to the Auditor General would be more appropriate.

[73] For example, during his investigation into the corruption by PEPs in Kenya in the Goldenberg affair, Justice Bosire specifically referred to the effect of the law and oath of secrecy on silencing public officials: see Republic of Kenya, *Report of the Judicial Commission of Enquiry into the Goldenberg Affair*, Nairobi, 2005, at p. 842.

The oversight role involves the monitoring of the work of the Auditor General. For example, in the Chiluba case the failure of the Auditor General to submit annual reports to the Zambian Parliament and the failure of parliamentarians to address the matter represented a fundamental breakdown of the constitutional safeguards. By directing media attention to this situation CSOs could have raised public awareness of this failure and called for an explanation. This provides a safe and constructive role for CSOs in that allegations are not being made against PEPs of corruption or money laundering, but rather the highlighting of the Auditor General's failure to fulfil their constitutional mandate.

Where concern arises regarding a failure by the Auditor General to carry out their constitutional mandate, CSOs may also consider lodging a complaint with another constitutional 'watchdog' body. For example, in the Ouko case (see below), the complainant lodged a series of complaints concerning a breach of the constitutional obligations of the Auditor General with the Kenya Ethics and Anti-Corruption Commission. Arguably this also falls within the jurisdiction of the office of the ombudsman (or similar national institution), which has a mandate to investigate complaints of 'maladministration'.

Key supportive work includes undertaking public education initiatives to highlight the constitutional role of the Auditor General. Raising public awareness of the constitutional safeguards and focusing attention on their effective operation (or otherwise) can arguably make a real contribution towards developing transparency and accountability in the management of public affairs. In addition, CSOs can play a useful role in assisting parliamentarians to understand and ensure the implementation of the constitutional safeguards with regard to public sector finance.[74]

In order to assess the work of the office, public access to annual reports of the Auditor General is essential. In the TI case, for example, the petitioner challenged the constitutionality of section 72 of the Public Audit Act, which recognised the right of public access to such reports 'except where such access may unduly jeopardize state security'. It was argued by the petitioner that any limitation on access to the reports must satisfy the test for the limitation on rights and fundamental freedoms enshrined in the Constitution. Whilst not deciding the point, Mwita J noted that any 'limitation on grounds of national security would have to be justified' particularly in view of the right to freedom

---

[74] See for example, *The Abuja Guidelines on the relationship between Parliaments, Parliamentarians and Commonwealth National Human Rights Institutions*, 2004. Available at https://www.agora-parl.org/sites/default/files/guidelines_abujaworkshop.pdf (accessed 7 June 2020).

of information enshrined in Article 35 of the Constitution of Kenya.[75] Thus once published, reports by Auditors General become public documents and it was therefore the constitutional right of every citizen to have access to the document subject to any *constitutional* rather than statutory limitation.

The role of the courts in supporting CSOs should not be overlooked. This is epitomised by the TI case, in which Transparency International (Kenya) had *locus standi* (a point seemingly unchallenged) to lodge a petition in support of the independence of the Auditor General. This generous approach to standing should encourage other CSOs to make use of their own courts to challenge any threats to the independence and work of Auditors General.

7.7 PROCEDURE FOR REMOVING THE AUDITOR GENERAL

7.7.1 Grounds for Removal

Ideally the grounds for removal should be similar to those of a judge. For example the Constitution of Namibia provides: 'The Auditor General may be removed from office by reason of an inability to discharge the functions of his office (whether arising from infirmity of mind or body) or for misconduct.'[76] Similarly, in South Africa the Auditor General may be removed from office only on the ground of misconduct, incapacity or incompetence.[77] In Kenya Article 251(1) the grounds for removal are a serious violation of the Constitution or any other law; gross misconduct, whether in the performance of the member's or office-holder's functions or otherwise; physical or mental incapacity to perform the functions of office; incompetence; or bankruptcy. Less satisfactory is the position in Nigeria where the Auditor General may be removed from office by the President on grounds of an 'inability to discharge the functions of his office (whether arising from infirmity of mind or body *or any other cause*) or for misconduct' (emphasis added).[78]

---

[75] Article 35 provides: that 'Every citizen has the right of access to information held by the State' and that 'The State shall publish and publicise any important information affecting the nation'.

[76] Article 127(4).

[77] Constitution of South Africa, section 194(1).

[78] Constitution of Nigeria, section 87(1).

7.7.2 Procedure for Removal

7.7.2.1 Commencing the removal process

How the removal procedure is commenced requires careful scrutiny as it offers a mechanism for PEPs to intimidate the Auditor General. In most of the African Constitutions, parliamentarians or a parliamentary committee may commence an investigation. For example, section 184(3) of the Constitution of Malawi provides that the 'Public Appointments Committee may at any time inquire as to the competence of the person so appointed to perform the duties of that office and as to the financial probity of a person so appointed, so far as it is relevant to the duties of that office'.

Who else may request that the possible removal of the Auditor General is rarely elaborated in the African Constitutions. The right of an individual to do so was brought into issue in the 2017 decision of the Kenyan High Court in *Republic v Speaker of the National Assembly & 4 others Ex Parte Edward R.O. Ouko* (the Ouko case).[79] Here Article 251(2) of the Constitution of Kenya specifically provides that 'a person desiring the removal of [the Auditor General] on any [relevant] ground may present a petition to the National Assembly setting out the alleged facts constituting that ground'. The National Assembly must then consider the petition and, if it is satisfied that it discloses a ground for removal must send the petition to the President. The President may then suspend the Auditor General pending the outcome of the complaint.

The case raises several issues of general concern. First, the complaint was submitted to the National Assembly by a petitioner, who was the legal representative of an undisclosed complainant who sought the removal of Mr Ouko. The prospect of a series of such petitions being presented to the National Assembly by any number of anonymous individuals is clearly of practical concern, particularly when dealing with them is liable to distract the Auditor General from their work and can be used by political enemies or disgruntled individuals to undermine the work of the office-holder. In the case itself, the anonymous complainant had made a series of complaints concerning Mr Ouko, some of which fell within the scope of Article 251 of the Kenyan Constitution. However, these had already been referred to the Ethics and Anti-Corruption Commission and the Director of Public Prosecutions whose investigations had vindicated Mr Ouko. In essence the petitioner was 'forum shopping'.

Second, the procedure adopted by Parliament was questionable. Here the petitioner was permitted to give unsworn testimony before a parliamentary committee and this was heard without the applicant, Mr Ouko, being given any prior notice of the hearing nor afforded a chance to cross-examine the

---

[79] [2017] eKLR.

petitioner. Further the applicant had not been informed of the precise nature of the allegations against him nor given sufficient time to address them. Whilst not disputing the right of Parliament to deal with the matter and to regulate its own procedures, the applicant argued that there was procedural unfairness in the manner in which the parliamentary committee approached the matter. Odunga J upheld this argument, pointing out that any such action must be constitutional and lawful. Article 47(1) of the Constitution of Kenya specifically provided: 'Every person has the right to administrative action that is expeditious, efficient, lawful, reasonable and procedurally fair.' He therefore held, correctly it is argued, that the Article required a court to look both at the merits and legality of an administrative decision and at the process and procedure adopted.[80] He added that even at common law, fairness in administrative action was paramount.[81]

This point raises a broader question concerning the separation of powers and the right of the courts to question parliamentary proceedings. The Commonwealth (Latimer House) Principles emphasise: 'Parliamentarians must be able to carry out their legislative and constitutional functions in accordance with the Constitution, free from unlawful interference'.[82] However, as Odunga J pointed out, the Constitution is supreme and thus Parliament 'cannot enjoy privileges, immunities and powers which are inconsistent with the fundamental rights guaranteed in the Constitution … Parliamentary privilege does not extend to violation of the Constitution [and where Parliament does so] the Court's jurisdiction would not be defeated….'[83] In doing so he 'associated himself' with a series of decisions from other Commonwealth jurisdictions[84] and affirmed the words of Lord Denning in *Gouriet v Union of Post Office Workers* 'Be you ever so high, the law is above you'.[85]

Odunga J also addressed an argument by the respondents that the parliamentary committee was exercising an administrative function and not a quasi-judicial function. In his view, the issue for the court was not whether the action was described as 'quasi-judicial' or 'administrative' but rather whether Parliament was 'undertaking an act that affects the legal rights and

---

80 At [118]. In doing so, he referred with approval to the decision of the Constitutional Court of South Africa in *Republic of South Africa v South African Rugby Football Union* 2000(1) SA 1, at [135–6], which applied section 33 of the Constitution of South Africa and which is in similar terms to the Kenyan provision.

81 [2017] eKLR, at [79].

82 Ibid, at [III(a)].

83 Ibid, at [81].

84 For example, *Biti v Minister of Justice, Legal and Parliamentary Affairs* [2002] ZWSC 10 (Supreme Court of Zimbabwe) and *Doctors for Life v Speaker of the National Assembly* 2006 (6) SA 416 (Constitutional Court of South Africa).

85 [1977] 1 QB 729, 762, quoting the words of Thomas Fuller.

interests of the applicant to whom the action related'.[86] This was clearly the case here.

As a result, Odunga J issued a declaration that the proceedings conducted by the appropriate parliamentary committee failed to meet the threshold of fair administrative action and ordered that the committee conduct its proceedings in strict compliance with and adherence to Article 47 of the Constitution of Kenya.

7.7.2.2 The removal process

Given the status of Auditor General and the need to avoid the politicisation of the decision, there is a strong case for the decision regarding removal being a matter for the judiciary. This is the position in Kenya where the President must appoint a judicial tribunal of enquiry, which is to investigate the matter 'expeditiously' and must make a binding recommendation upon which the President must act within 30 days.[87] In Ghana, the matter is entirely removed from the legislature with the procedure for removal of the Auditor General being the same as that of a senior judge.[88]

Where the removal process involves the legislature, the approach in South Africa provides an important model. This is commenced by a finding by a committee of the National Assembly of misconduct, incapacity or incompetence on the part of the Auditor General. If the National Assembly then adopts a resolution supported by at least two-thirds of its membership calling for the removal from office of the Auditor General, the President must remove the Auditor General from office. Interestingly, the drafters of the 1996 Constitution provided that the removal process required a simple majority of National Assembly members only. However, the Constitutional Court did not consider that this adequately safeguarded that office-holder's independence and impartiality and the constitutional provision was accordingly amended

---

86 [2017] eKLR, at [112]. In doing so, the judge adopted the words of Lord Denning in *Breen v Amalgamated Engineering Union* [1971] 2 QB 175, who emphasised that whether functions are described as judicial or quasi-judicial or as administrative the body still must act fairly: at p. 190.

87 The tribunal must consist of a person who holds or has held office as a judge of a superior court, at least two persons who are qualified to be appointed as High Court judges, and one other member who is qualified to assess the facts in respect of the particular ground for removal: see Constitution of Kenya, Article 251(5). It is required to investigate the matter expeditiously, report on the facts and make a binding recommendation to the President, who must act in accordance with the recommendation within 30 days.

88 Constitution of Ghana, Article 187(13).

to require a two-thirds majority.[89] Similarly, in Nigeria, the removal of the Auditor General by the President requires approval by a two-thirds majority of the Senate.

The requirement for a super-majority provides a welcome additional safeguard. However, the concern remains that the weakness of legislatures and the dominance of the ruling party in many jurisdictions may inevitably result in the politicisation of the removal decision.

7.8 CONCLUSION

The power of PEPs to control the appointment and operation of the Auditor General can facilitate corruption and money laundering. The challenge is to prevent the abuse of this power and to protect the good governance values of integrity, transparency and accountability enshrined in constitutions. This chapter has argued that as the 'ally of the people', the Auditor General can, and must, play a leading role through overseeing and ensuring fiscal integrity. This has the dual purpose of both encouraging 'ethical behaviour [by PEPs] by making unethical behaviour hard to accomplish and easy to detect' and helping to bring to light any abuse of power. As Klug neatly puts it, such an independent constitutional institution has 'a distinct role in ensuring that the promises of human rights and good governance [enshrined in the constitution] reach down into the daily administration of the country…'.[90]

All the African Constitutions make provision for the office of the Auditor General and, as the Cashgate example from Malawi illustrates, an effective Auditor General poses a threat to corrupt PEPs by '[flinging open] the gates to what was meant to be a clandestine and non-detectable criminal syndicate of fraudsters and money launderers'.[91] Yet the case of Chiluba highlights the pressure that PEPs can exert on office-holders. Thus the real test is the extent to which, in practice, Auditors General enjoy the necessary individual and institutional independence and security of tenure to enable them to carry out their constitutional mandate effectively. This includes enjoying access to all public expenditure, including that relating to national security. However, the chapter has demonstrated that several of the African Constitutions do not adequately protect the office and the office-holder and that there is a need to strengthen key provisions.

---

89 See *Ex parte Chairperson of the Constitutional Assembly: In re Certification of the Constitution of the Republic of South Africa*, above.

90 Heinz Klug, Accountability and the role of independent constitutional institutions in South Africa's post-apartheid constitutions, (2015–2016) 60 *New York Law School Law Review* 153, at 156.

91 The words of Kapindu J in *Republic v Lutepo* [2015] MWHC 492.

A review of the relationship between the Auditor General and the legislature is also required. Retaining the close working relationship between the two as regards fiscal matters remains essential. This includes the supportive role of the legislature through the appropriate scrutiny and follow-up on annual audit reports. There is also an accountability role for the legislature which must follow up any failure by the Auditor General to submit such reports.

Given the weakness of many legislatures, their role in the appointment and removal process of the Auditor General raises serious concerns. In most of the countries under discussion, the present constitutional arrangements arguably do not adequately protect the independence of the office and office-holder in practice. Instead it is argued that the position of the Auditor General should be equated to that of a senior judge including enjoying the same terms and conditions as regards security of tenure and removal.

As an 'ally of the people' the Auditor General requires and deserves active support from CSOs. There are a range of opportunities for doing so, such as publicising the work of the office and monitoring its effectiveness. This requires enjoying public access to the reports of the Auditor General. Challenging attempts to undermine its operation is another key strategy including, where necessary, resort to the courts. The TI case neatly demonstrates how effective such action can be and should encourage CSOs in other countries to challenge any attempt to restrict or undermine the constitutional role of the Auditor General.

To adapt Lord Denning's words noted earlier, 'Be you ever so high, the Constitution is above you'. The Auditor General as a constitutional office-holder has the power to oversee all public spending and the activities of PEPs and thus uphold the good governance values and protect the AML provisions enshrined in the constitution. This will truly make the Auditor General the 'ally of the people'.

8. PEPs, constitutions and investigating money laundering

8.1 CONSTITUTIONAL RIGHTS VERSUS THE FATF RECOMMENDATIONS: THE INVESTIGATORY POWERS OF AML AUTHORITIES

In the Cashgate case of *R v Katengeza*,[1] a private building contractor was suspected of facilitating money laundering by PEPs. Investigators obtained a warrant to access her bank account at the FDH Bank in Lilongwe. With the active co-operation of the bank, significant documentary evidence including bank statements and cheque images was obtained. These played a key part in the successful prosecution of Mrs Katengeza for money laundering.[2]

In this case the FDH Bank was co-operative. This is not always the case. Thus in following the money laundering trail, FATF Recommendation 31 states that 'competent authorities' i.e. 'all public authorities with designated responsibilities for combating money laundering'[3] must be empowered to obtain access to all necessary documents and information for use in investigations, prosecutions and related actions. This includes powers:

- to use compulsory measures for the production of records held by financial institutions, DNFBPs and other natural or legal persons;
- for the search of persons and premises;
- for the taking witness statements; and
- for the seizure and obtaining of evidence.

---

[1] [2016] MWHC 490.

[2] She was charged with 'Having in her possession property knowing or having reason to believe represented the proceeds of crime contrary to section 35(1)(c) Money Laundering, Proceeds of Serious Crime and Terrorist Financing Act'.

[3] In particular, the term includes the FIU, investigating and prosecuting authorities, authorities mandated to seize/freeze and confiscate criminal assets and financial supervisors established as independent non-governmental authorities with statutory powers: see General Glossary to the FATF Recommendations.

In doing so, countries must:

> ensure that competent authorities conducting investigations are able to use a wide range of investigative techniques suitable for the investigation of money laundering [and] associated predicate offences. These investigative techniques include: undercover operations, intercepting communications, accessing computer systems and controlled delivery.

However, seeking to exercise such powers may give rise to constitutional and legal challenges. Thus PEPs may refuse to co-operate in an investigation citing their constitutional right to remain silent (and privilege against self-incrimination) whilst their legal advisers may invoke legal professional privilege.[4] Without access to such information or witnesses, a successful prosecution is potentially seriously jeopardised.

This chapter focuses on the challenge of balancing the constitutional rights of PEPs against providing adequate investigative and evidence-gathering powers to AML agencies in line with the FATF Recommendations. The following two chapters consider similar issues in relation to the prosecution of PEPs and asset recovery.

8.2 COMPULSORY QUESTIONING, ACCESS TO RECORDS AND THE RIGHT TO REMAIN SILENT

8.2.1 Compulsory Questioning of PEPs

The Anti-Corruption Act 2009 in Uganda provides that in investigating corruption cases, the Director of Public Prosecutions or Inspector General of Government have the power to require a public official to answer questions, supply information and disclose documents. Such powers are enjoyed by many anti-corruption/AML investigation agencies in African states. However, the exercise of such powers raises constitutional issues concerning the right against self-incrimination and right to a fair trial. The pre-trial and trial stages require separate consideration.[5]

At the pre-trial stage, accused persons enjoy the constitutional right to remain silent and not to be compelled to make any confession or admission that could be used in evidence against them.[6] On the face of it, such provisions do not apply where the exercise of the compulsory questioning powers by AML

4 See Section 8.3 below.

5 The issues raised at the trial stage are discussed in Chapter 9.

6 See for example, the Constitution of Kenya, Article 49(1)b) and (d).

investigators forms part of an information-gathering or investigation process as the person who is required to answer questions or provide information is not necessarily the subject of a criminal investigation and the questioning occurs prior to any criminal charge(s) being brought against a PEP. Given the constitutional right against self-incrimination, any such information obtained from an accused is not admissible against them at any subsequent criminal trial.[7] However, in principle, if other information such as bank statements or company documents were unlawfully obtained, thus breaching the accused's constitutional right to privacy, they should still be admissible in any criminal proceedings brought against the accused. This rejection of the 'fruit of the poisoned tree' argument was clearly stated by Canadian Supreme Court in *R v Collins*:

> Real evidence that was obtained in a manner that violated the Charter will rarely operate unfairly for that reason alone. The real evidence existed irrespective of the violation of the Charter and its use does not render the trial unfair. ... [T]he evidence obtained as a result of the search was real evidence, and while prejudicial to the accused as evidence tendered by the Crown usually is, there is nothing to suggest that its use at the trial would render the trial unfair ...[8]

These words were approved by the Court of Appeal of Lesotho in *Kopano v R* where the court emphasised that real evidence procured by illegal or improper means does not involve self-incrimination.[9]

Whilst accused persons have the constitutional right to consult their legal representative, the position is less clear when compulsory questioning for investigative purposes is in issue. For example, investigators questioning a PEP using their compulsory powers may be concerned that the presence of a lawyer will prejudice the investigation and thus seek to refuse such access. Arguably, as the PEP is not an 'accused person', the constitutional right of access does not apply. This important point has seemingly not arisen in the African context. The matter was considered in *R (on the application of Lords Reynolds and Taylor) v Director of the Serious Fraud Office*[10] where the High Court of England and Wales was concerned with the exercise of the compulsory questioning powers of the Serious Fraud Office (SFO) under section 2

---

[7] For a helpful example of the point see the decision of the High Court of Lesotho in *Metsing v Director General, Directorate on Corruption and Economic Affairs* [2015] LSHC 1 and the decision of the European Court of Human Rights in *Allan v United Kingdom* (2002) 13 BHRC 652.

[8] [1987] 1 SCR 265 at [37].

[9] [2011] LSCA 19 at [24] and *Metsing v Director General, Directorate on Corruption and Economic Affairs* [2015] LSHC 1 at [92].

[10] [2015] EWHC 865 (Admin).

of the Criminal Justice Act 1987. On the particular facts of the case, the court held that the presence of lawyers for the applicants could prejudice the SFO investigations. However, to clarify the matter, in 2016 new SFO Guidance was issued, which states that a lawyer may only accompany an interviewee if the SFO believes it will assist the purpose of the interview and/or investigation, or that it will provide essential assistance to the interviewee by way of legal advice or pastoral support. The lawyer must apply to the SFO in advance of the interview to explain why any of these reasons is satisfied. Investigators in African states may well wish to follow this approach.

8.2.2 Gaining Access to Financial and Company Records

The power to compel the production of relevant documentation is enjoyed by AML investigators throughout Africa. A good example comes from Malawi, where the FIA has the statutory power to 'inspect any [relevant] record, document or information ... and, obtain or compel the production of or access to any record, document or information and make notes and take copies of whole or any part of the record, document or information'.[11]

Obtaining such information may conflict with the constitutional right to privacy of PEPs.[12] However, it also raises a practical issue concerning gaining access to such documentation. The records of financial institutions and companies are today almost entirely electronic and are often held on a server outside the jurisdiction or, in the case of a local subsidiary, by a parent company in another jurisdiction. In the latter case, obtaining such documentation may require the making of a MLA request. This is often time-consuming and depends upon the willingness and ability of the requested state to provide such assistance.[13]

The decision of the England and Wales High Court in *R (KBR Inc) v Director of the Serious Fraud Office*[14] illustrates a potentially effective alternative approach. KBR Inc was incorporated in the United States but had a UK subsidiary, KBR Ltd, that was being investigated for suspected corruption offences involving payments to foreign PEPs in the Unaoil case.[15] The SFO sought to exercise its section 2 powers in relation to two sets of documents. As

---

[11] Section 5(d) Financial Crimes Act 2017.

[12] See Section 8.4 below.

[13] See Section 8.5.1 below.

[14] [2018] EWHC 2368 (Admin).

[15] It was alleged that Unaoil, a company based in Monaco, was 'engaged at various times by KBR's UK subsidiaries (including KBR Ltd) from 1996 onwards "...ostensibly to provide consultancy services in the oil and gas sectors in the Caspian region, primarily Kazakhstan and Azerbaijan"': at [5].

regards those held on a server outside the jurisdiction, the High Court held that the SFO power to obtain documents 'must have an element of extraterritorial application' and that it was 'scarcely credible that a UK company could resist an otherwise lawful [section 2] notice on the ground that the documents in question were held on a server out of the jurisdiction'.[16]

This then raised the issue as to documents held by foreign companies. Here the Gross LJ was of the view that:

> the extraterritorial ambit of [section 2] is capable of extending to some foreign companies in respect of documents held abroad. For my part, however, I would not go further and say that the reach of [section 2] extended to *all* foreign companies in respect of documents held abroad, subject only to the safeguards or limitations in ss. 1 and 2 of the CJA 1987. As it seems to me, the right answer (to adopt the expression used by Lord Mance, in *Masri*[17] at [10]) is a 'nuanced answer': [Section 2] extends extraterritorially to foreign companies in respect of documents held outside the jurisdiction when there is a sufficient connection between the company and the jurisdiction. It may be noted that the potential relevance of the documents to the investigation is not the basis of the challenge (at [71] emphasis in the original).

On the facts, the court found that there was a sufficient connection between KBR Inc and the UK so as to bring KBR Inc within the jurisdictional reach of section 2.[18]

This is a potentially significant ruling for anti-corruption and AML investigators. Not only does it circumvent the need for MLA, the extraterritorial application of compulsory investigative powers provides real 'teeth' to investigators by enabling them to *demand* documentation from both foreign bribe-paying companies and financial institutions and companies holding documentation on a server outside the jurisdiction as well as obtaining information about the involvement of PEPs in foreign companies. It is an approach that should be widely adopted.

8.2.3 Accessing Land and Company Records

Ready access to up-to-date and accurate records held in land registries can assist investigators identify the ownership of real estate. This is particularly important given the fact that PEPs and their PMLs make considerable use

---

16 Ibid, at [64].

17 *Masri v Consolidated Contractors Int (UK) Ltd (No. 4)* [2009] UKHL 43; [2010] 1 AC 90.

18 As Gross LJ noted, the 'payments central to the SFO's investigation of KBR Ltd (i.e., the KBR investigation) and KBR Ltd's contracts or arrangements with Unaoil required the approval of KBR Inc and were paid by KBR Inc through its US-based treasury function': at [82].

of this sector as part of their money laundering activities. Such information also provides a potentially useful cross-check on the accuracy of asset and income disclosures by PEPs[19] as well as helping to identify any possible tax or accounting offences. Regrettably, in practice, the value of such registries is often limited, with land registries in many African countries failing to maintain up-to-date records. Further, as rural land is often unregistered, the actual ownership of property becomes even more opaque.

Likewise, company registries also often fail to maintain up-to-date and accurate records. In any event, most only contain information as to the legal ownership of a company thus enabling PEPs to conceal their ultimate beneficial ownership. For example, in Mauritius a freely accessible on-line registry contains details of the legal ownership of companies and businesses registered in the country.[20] However, as the ICIJ has noted, the Mauritius Papers leak revealed that 'the registry often shows basic information such as name, type of company, date of incorporation, registered address and status. Information such as the true, or beneficial, owner of the company and its activity is not listed.'[21]

The position regarding trusts is even more problematic with few states holding any formal register and this makes them extremely vulnerable to facilitating money laundering.[22]

In 2009, an ESAAMLG report concluded that in many countries 'company and land transfer registries have been in a dysfunctional state for some time'.[23] An ESAAMLG 2019 report shows little has changed:

> the majority of respondents highlighted significant challenges faced in seeking and collecting information such as the lack of information on beneficial ownership, inadequate information held by Company Registries, Land Registries and other administrative sources.[24]

---

[19] See also Section 8.5 below.

[20] Available at https://companies.govmu.org:4343/MNSOnlineSearch/ (accessed 7 June 2020).

[21] See www.icij.org/investigations/mauritius-leaks/ (accessed 7 June 2020). On addressing beneficial ownership transparency, see Chapter 11.

[22] See further Section 12.3 below. In Uganda, under the Trustees Incorporation Act, trusts which want to acquire land or certain interest in land must register with the relevant Ministry.

[23] Charles Goredema and Jackson Madzima, *An assessment of the links between corruption and the implementation of anti-money laundering strategies and measures in the ESAAMLG region*, Report for the ESAAMLG, 2009, [49].

[24] ESAAMLG report, 51–2.

This calls for urgent action both to ensure that land and company registries contain details of both the legal and beneficial ownership and that they contain readily accessible accurate and up-to-date information. A project to digitalise the registries would be helpful and might be a suitable project for donors. In addition, consideration should be given to providing an AML body, such as a FIU or anti-corruption commission, with the mandate to oversee the operation of the registries.

Making such registries fully accessible to the public is also essential. This will enable CSOs to help identify PEPs through scrutinising both legal and beneficial ownership records. The effectiveness of such activity is highlighted by the work of international CSOs such as Global Witness and Transparency International.[25]

8.3 RIGHT TO CONSULT A LAWYER IN PRIVATE AND LEGAL PROFESSIONAL PRIVILEGE

8.3.1 AML Responsibilities of Lawyers

Lawyers[26] enjoy (or should enjoy) a high degree of credibility and trust. With this comes vulnerability, for their range of services provides PEPs and PMLs with attractive money laundering opportunities. These include buying and selling real estate, managing finances and securities and 'creating, organising or managing legal persons or arrangements'.[27] A client trust account is particularly attractive, through which PEPs can launder their proceeds of crime.[28] In some cases this is the result of innocent or unwitting involvement of lawyers.[29] Other cases may involve wilful blindness or complicity.[30] A further vulnerability for lawyers arises from the fact that many real estate transactions are

---

25 See Section 2.7.2 above.

26 The word includes notaries and other independent legal professionals: see FATF Recommendation 22(d): in essence it covers anyone offering professional legal services.

27 FATF Recommendations 22(d) and 23. Legal arrangements 'refer to express trusts or other similar legal arrangements'. These include *fiducie, treuhand* and *fideocomiso*: see FATF General Glossary. An excellent practical analysis of such conduct is found in Zambia Financial Intelligence Centre *Money Laundering and Terrorist Financing Trends Report 2018*, 2018, Lusaka.

28 For an interesting discussion in the South African context, see A Hamman and R Koen, *Cave Pecuniam*: lawyers as launderers, [2012] *PER* 49.

29 See for example, the decision of the Court of Appeal in *Attorney General for Zambia v Meer, Care and Desai* [2008] EWCA Civ 1007.

30 The activity of James Ibori and Bhadresh Gohill being an excellent example: see Section 2.6.1 above.

cash-based, a point reported by several states including Ghana, Nigeria and Senegal.[31]

Lawyers may also establish off-shore companies and trusts in facilitating states. This is perfectly legitimate activity in itself, but, wittingly or unwittingly, the intention may be to conceal the fact that the ultimate beneficial owner is a PEP and to use the company as a vehicle to enable PEPs to launder their proceeds of crime into a safe haven state.[32]

Lawyers are subject to the full KYC and EDD requirements as well as being required to report suspicious transactions promptly to a FIU[33] and prohibited by law from 'tipping' off a client that they have made an STR.[34] They are also subject to the standards, rules and regulations laid down by their own national Bar Association or similar professional body. Such bodies are responsible for both admitting individuals to the profession as well as sanctioning those whose conduct violates such standards. For example, a failure to adhere to the normal CDD, KYC and/or EDD requirements may breach the professional standards expected of lawyers and render them liable to disciplinary proceedings by their own professional body.[35] Even so, the MERs on many African countries reveal that lawyers make very few STRs and this remains a considerable concern.[36]

8.3.2 AML Obligations and Legal Professional Privilege

The AML obligations of lawyers are limited by legal professional privilege (LPP). The constitutional right of access to justice/to a fair trial encompasses the right of every accused person to consult a lawyer in private. The right to

---

31 See GIABA, *The vulnerabilities of designated non-financial businesses and professions to money laundering and terrorist financing and the adequacy of control measures in West Africa*, Dakar, 2015, [29] and [38]. Although high-value transactions would normally be done through banks: see ESAAMLG report, 41.

32 For an interesting example of the issue, see John Hatchard, Legal practitioners as potential money launderers: Beneficial ownership transparency and PEPs: *Solicitors Regulation Authority v Sharif*, (2019) 31(1) *Denning Law Journal* 189–97.

33 Although countries may permit lawyers to send their STRs to their appropriate professional body, 'provided that there is appropriate forms of cooperation between these organisations and the FIU': Interpretive Note to FATF Recommendation 23 [3].

34 See FATF Recommendation 23.

35 See Hatchard, Legal practitioners as potential money launderers, above.

36 See further Section 7.5 above.

LPP in connection with communications with one's lawyer is broader.[37] LPP refers to the principle that:

> a [person] must be able to consult [their] lawyer in confidence ... The client must be sure that what [s/he] tells [their] lawyer in confidence will never be revealed without [their] consent. Legal professional privilege is thus more than an ordinary rule of evidence, limited in its application to the facts of a particular case. It is a fundamental condition on which the administration of justice as a whole rests.[38]

Thus Interpretive Note to FATF Recommendation 23 specifically states that 'Lawyers, notaries, other legal professionals and accountants acting as independent legal professionals' are not required to report suspicious transactions 'if the relevant information was obtained in circumstances where they are subject to professional secrecy or legal professional privilege'. This would normally cover information lawyers 'receive from or obtain through one of their clients: (a) in the course of ascertaining the legal position of their client, or (b) in performing their task of defending or representing that client in, or concerning judicial, administrative, arbitration or mediation proceedings'. This means that lawyers must consider whether carrying out AML obligations, including making a STR to the FIU, will breach client confidentiality or their client's right to LPP. In addition, the power of an FIU to demand information is also potentially compromised by LPP whilst information subject to LPP is not available for MLA purposes.[39]

LPP itself is often enshrined in legislation. For example, in Kenya section 18(1) of the Proceeds of Crime and Anti-Money Laundering Act 2009 provides that the money laundering reporting requirements do not apply to a 'communication of privileged information between the advocate and the client'.[40] However, it is for each country to determine the matters that fall under LPP or

---

37 For example, section 42(1)(c) of the Constitution of Malawi provides an accused person with the right 'to consult confidentially with a legal practitioner of his or her choice'. See also Article 50 Constitution of Kenya.

38 Per Lord Taylor CJ in *R v Derby Magistrates' Court, ex p. B.* [1996] 1 AC 487, 507D.

39 A point highlighted in the ESAAMLG, *Seychelles Mutual Evaluation Report*, 2018, p. 189.

40 Section 18(2) then provides that this covers the 'giving of advice to [a] client in the course and for purposes of the professional employment of the advocate or in connection and for the purpose of any legal proceedings on behalf of the client'. See Constance Gikonyo, The legal profession in Kenya and its anti-money laundering obligations or lack thereof, (2019) 22(2) *JMLC* 247, at 252.

professional secrecy.[41] As a result, the FATF has noted that there is significant diversity between countries as to the scope of LPP and that:

> this diversity and differing interpretations by legal professionals and law enforcement has at times provided a disincentive for law enforcement to take action against legal professionals suspected of being complicit in or wilfully blind to money laundering activity.[42]

For example, in the MER on Rwanda, the assessors raised concerns about the wide scope of LPP and recommended that it was limited to information: '(a) obtained in the course of ascertaining the legal position of a client, or (b) in performing their tasks of defending or representing that client in, or concerning judicial, administrative, arbitration, or mediation proceedings'. A follow-up report raised concerns that this matter had still not been adequately addressed.[43]

According to a FATF report, in most countries, evidence obtained in breach of LPP or professional secrecy is inadmissible in court. Further, any other evidence obtained as a result of the inappropriately obtained evidence is also inadmissible.[44] Yet given the seriousness of money laundering by PEPs and the manner in which LPP can hamper or even undermine effective AML investigations, it follows that it is only a qualified right.[45] Arguably the constitutional fair trial provisions do not apply if the communications are intended to further a criminal purpose (the 'iniquity exception').[46] As Lord Neuberger set out in *McE v Prison Service of Northern Ireland*:[47]

> However, while these two rights (viz. the right of a person to consult a lawyer in private and the right to legal professional privilege in connection with communications with one's lawyer) are very important, neither can possibly be regarded as unqualified. Both rights can self-evidently be abused for improper, even criminal, purposes; indeed, as a result of such abuse, the rights themselves could fall into disrepute.[48]

---

41 Interpretive Note to FATF Recommendation 23.

42 FATF, *Money Laundering and Terrorist Financing Vulnerabilities of Legal Professionals*, Paris, 2013, p. 8 (FATF legal professionals report).

43 ESAAMLG, *First Round Mutual Evaluations – Post Evaluation Progress Report of Rwanda*, 2017, p. 38.

44 FATF legal professionals report, p. 21.

45 See Lord Neuberger in *McE v Prison Service of Northern Ireland* [2009] UKHL 15; [2009] 1 AC 908 [109].

46 *Brown* [2015] EWCA Crim 1328. See also the FATF legal professionals report, p. 20.

47 [2009] UKHL 15; [2009] 1 AC 908 [109].

48 See also the views of Lord Dyson in *Warren and others v Attorney General for Jersey* [2011] UKPC 10; [2012] 1 AC 22 especially at [36].

In such circumstances, a balance is required between the enjoyment of constitutional rights and facilitating effective AML investigations. It follows that where the 'iniquity exception' applies, a breach of LPP does not in itself render inadmissible any evidence obtained at any subsequent trial nor affect the admissibility of any other evidence obtained as a result of the breach.

8.4 RIGHT TO PRIVACY AND EVIDENCE GATHERING

8.4.1 Constitutional Right to Privacy

This right is enshrined in many of the African Constitutions. For example, Article 31 of the Constitution of Kenya provides that 'Every person has the right to privacy', which includes the 'right not to have ... information relating to their family or private affairs unnecessarily required or revealed; or the privacy of their communications infringed'. Further, the right cannot be limited 'except by law, and then only to the extent that the limitation is reasonable and justifiable in an open and democratic society based on human dignity, equality and freedom, taking into account all relevant factors'.[49]

Article 13(1) of the Namibian Constitution sets out the scope of the right neatly:

> No persons shall be subject to interference with the privacy of their homes, correspondence or communications save as in accordance with law and as is necessary in a democratic society in the interests of national security, public safety or the economic well-being of the country, ... for the prevention of disorder or crime or for the protection of the rights or freedoms of others'.

It follows that the right to privacy is subject to importance limitations and this raises the issue as to how far the enjoyment of the right may be restricted by AML investigations.[50]

---

[49] Article 24(1).

[50] See also section 11 of the Constitution of Lesotho and the decision of the High Court of Lesotho in *Metsing v Director General, Directorate on Corruption and Economic Affairs* [2015] LSHC 1 (see Section 5.4.1 above). The AU Convention on Cyber Security and Personal Data Protection also requires AU member states to put in place a legal and institutional framework designed to protect personal data.

8.4.2 Right to Privacy, AML Investigations and Accessing Electronic Information

This is the era of electronic information and technological innovation which provide not only new opportunities for money laundering by PEPs but also a fresh means of combating the problem. Evidence of money laundering is now to be found in e-mails and on social media platforms such as Whatsapp, LinkedIn, Facebook and Twitter. Access to such information is likely to enhance investigations particularly through life-style audits[51] and the mapping of links between PEPs *inter se* as well as to those linked with them. Evidence gathering through the use of social media also provides a potentially effective supplement to more labour intensive, time-consuming and expensive covert operations. Law enforcement agencies also have the power to confiscate 'instrumentalities' of crime and can therefore confiscate mobile devices and retrieve information from them.

It follows that despite constitutional protection for the privacy of communications, the derogation provisions will enable law enforcement agencies to carry out AML investigations through accessing social media platforms. In addition, many African states have enacted legislation empowering law enforcement agencies to intercept communications albeit with the consent of a judge and, in some cases with consent of the Attorney General.[52] Subject to any general judicial discretion to exclude, such evidence is likely to be admissible at any subsequent trial.[53]

Accordingly African countries must develop the capacity to deal with the digital world through investing in appropriate hardware and software and staff training as well as ensuring that such evidence is admissible at any subsequent trial.

Law enforcement agencies are now using social media platforms to encourage whistleblowing as well as providing information to the public as to their anti-corruption/AML activities.[54] Social media may also be used by

---

[51] For example, using postings by PEPs and members of their families about their property, lifestyle and other assets, especially those located abroad.

[52] For example, the Electronic Communications and Transactions Act 2009, section 8 (Zambia).

[53] Of course, prosecutors must comply strictly with the statutory provisions for admissibility. See for example, *Uganda v Byandala*, 2015, unreported, High Court of Uganda, Criminal Session Case No. 12 of 2015. Here a senior PEP was acquitted on corruption charges when key e-mail evidence was ruled inadmissible due to the failure of prosecutors to comply with the Computer Misuse Act 2011 and Electronic Transactions Act 2011. I am grateful to Grace Atwongyeire for this information.

[54] For example, the Anti-Corruption Commission in Namibia, the Anti-Corruption Bureau in Malawi and the Zimbabwe Anti-Corruption Commission. See also the role of the Zambia Financial Intelligence Centre, discussed at Section 5.4.7.

anonymous whistleblowers to disclose information about money laundering or other criminality by PEPs. This is a strategy that is both cost-effective and potentially a significant AML tool.

Obtaining the disclosure of information by social media companies which generate and/or store electronic data and which are located abroad poses a different problem. In such cases, MLA requests to their 'home' countries are required in order to obtain such information. However, the introduction of Overseas Production Orders (OPOs) provides a possible alternative approach. For example, in the UK, the Crime (Overseas Production Orders) Act 2019 grants law enforcement agencies and prosecuting authorities the power to apply for and obtain electronic data directly from service providers (those who create, process, communicate or store electronic data) for the purposes of criminal investigations and prosecutions. Such orders may only be used when permitted under an international co-operation arrangement between the UK and the country where the subject of the order is located.[55] In practice, the task of developing such arrangements may take many years to complete. Even so, OPOs illustrate the need for the development of new and imaginative techniques and initiatives to facilitate money laundering investigations.[56]

8.4.3 Freedom of Information versus the Right to Privacy

Article 9 of the AU Convention requires each State Party to 'adopt such legislative and other measures to give effect to the right of access to any information that is required to assist in the fight against corruption and related offences'. Article IV of the Declaration on Principles of Freedom of Expression in Africa (the Windhoek Declaration)[57] also states that 'the right to information shall be guaranteed by law' and that:

> Public bodies hold information not for themselves but as custodians of the public good and everyone has a right to access this information, subject only to clearly defined rules established by law.

---

[55] See UK Government 'Crime (Overseas Production Orders) Act 2019: Explanatory Notes to the Act', http://www.legislation.gov.uk/ukpga/2019/5/notes/division/1/index.htm (accessed 7 June 2020).

[56] Even then, investigators are still faced with the problem of the encryption of end-to-end messaging.

[57] Adopted by the African Commission on Human and Peoples' Rights at its 32nd Ordinary Session.

In 2011 these principles were re-affirmed by the African Platform on Access to Information.[58] Article IV is particularly significant in that it emphasises the responsibility placed on governments to respect the right of 'everyone' to access government-held information as well as to take positive steps to ensure that there is an independent mechanism in place to enforce this right.

Despite these initiatives, at the national level, a UNESCO survey has reported that the constitutions of only 17 African states specifically include the freedom of information whilst only a few African states have passed freedom of information laws. This is disappointing especially given the importance of access to such information in an AML context.

In practice, much will depend upon the particular type of information that is sought and from which individual or body. This was made clear by Ackermann J in the Constitutional Court of South Africa in *Bernstein and Others v Bester NO and Others*[59] where he stated:

> The truism that no right is to be considered absolute, implies that from the outset of interpretation each right is always already limited by every right accruing to another citizen. In the context of privacy this would mean that it is only the inner sanctum of a person, such as his or her family life, sexual preference and home environment, which is shielded from erosion by conflicting rights of the community ... Privacy is acknowledged in the truly personal realm, but as a person moves into communal relations and activities such as business and social interaction, the scope of personal space shrinks accordingly.[60]

This approach is demonstrated by the decision of the High Court of South Africa in *Centre for Social Accountability v Secretary of Parliament and Others*.[61] The case centred on the so-called 'Travelgate' affair in which several South African parliamentarians were accused of malpractice over claims for travel expenses. A local CSO sought access to certain relevant documents relating to the affair under the Promotion of Access to Information Act, 2 of 2000. The parliamentary authorities refused to release certain information. Alkema J, having referred to the case of *Bernstein*, amongst others, made a key distinction. Thus information about the personal lives of members of Parliament, including 'his or her personal preferences and beliefs, how he or she choose

[58] See Preamble, at [8]. The African Platform on Access to Information working group was formed in 2009 in order to initiate a campaign to promote Access to Information in Africa around the twentieth anniversary of the Windhoek Declaration. It consists of media related CSOs from around Africa: see further www.africanplatform.org (accessed 7 June 2020). Article 9 of the African Charter on Human and Peoples' Rights also provides that 'Every individual shall have the right to receive information.'

[59] [1996] ZACC 2; 1996 (4) BCLR 449 (CC).

[60] At [67].

[61] [2011] ZAECGHC 33; 2011 (5) SA 279 (ECG); [2011] 4 All SA 181.

to live his or her personal life, what they do on vacation in the privacy of their holiday home' were their own business and of no concern to the state and protected by privacy laws. The same applied as to 'how they spend their money and how much money they have to spend'.[62] However, information as to how they executed their parliamentary duties including 'whether or not they obey the rules of Parliament and act in accordance with the code of conduct which society expects from its members of Parliament' was the business of the state. The state had the right to know, and through the state, so did members of society who had elected the members of Parliament in an open and democratic society.[63] Accordingly, an order was made to release the information relating to claims in respect of travel vouchers issued to members of Parliament in their official capacities.

This is surely the correct approach, although the exclusion of access to the personal finances of parliamentarians seemingly overlooks the vital point that asset and income declarations by public officials (and their families) are key good governance/AML mechanisms and such information is not only the 'business of the state' but also arguably of members of the public. This point is emphasised in Article 7(1) of the AU Convention, whereby State Parties commit themselves to 'require all or designated public officials to declare their assets at the time of assumption of office [and] during their term in office in the public service'.[64]

An accurate asset and income register can protect honest PEPs against false allegations of misuse of public office and instil public confidence in their integrity. It can also provide an early warning system of improper conduct on the part of a PEP. Indeed the register can also provide cogent evidence of money laundering or other misuse of public office.

It also means that a failure on the part of a PEP to comply with their obligation to register their interests *in itself* constitutes a disciplinary and potentially a criminal offence. Indeed providing for possible criminal liability for non-compliance provides a useful alternative to illicit enrichment charges, especially in those states which may have constitutional difficulties in criminalising such conduct. For example, Diepreye Alamieyeseigha, whilst governor of Bayelsa State in Nigeria, allegedly accumulated a wide range of assets principally from the theft of public funds and the receipt of bribes for the award of public contracts. For a variety of reasons, prosecutions for bribery and money laundering proved impossible but Alamieyeseigha was finally convicted on six charges of making false declarations of assets. Significantly,

62 At [80].

63 Ibid.

64 See also UNCAC Article 8(5).

he also caused two of his off-shore companies to plead guilty to 23 counts of money laundering. This opened up the way for proceedings both nationally and internationally to recover the proceeds of crime from both Alamieyeseigha himself as well as the companies. A potentially neat and effective way of dealing with corrupt conduct and money laundering. As noted in Section 2.8.8.1 above, in 2019 the Chief Justice of Nigeria, Walter Onnoghen, was stripped of office for failing to declare foreign bank accounts.

8.5 OBTAINING EVIDENCE FROM ABROAD: AFRICAN STATES AND INTERNATIONAL CO-OPERATION

Given the transnational nature of money laundering, obtaining evidence from abroad as well as assistance in finding and freezing the proceeds of crime is an essential part of any AML regime. Part G of the FATF Recommendations contains a range of provisions relating to international co-operation, with Recommendation 36 requiring countries to implement fully the Palermo Convention and the UNCAC, both of which contain detailed provisions relating to such co-operation.

8.5.1 Mutual Legal Assistance (MLA)

FATF Recommendation 37 states that 'Countries should [must] rapidly, constructively and effectively provide the widest possible range of mutual legal assistance in relation to money laundering, associated predicate offences and terrorist financing investigations'. In addition, countries must ensure they have the power to identify, freeze, seize and confiscate laundered property or instrumentalities in response to a MLA request(s).[65]

MLA is 'any assistance given by the requested state [to the requesting state] in respect of investigations, prosecutions or proceedings in a criminal matter'.[66] Strictly speaking, a formal MLA request is only required where the requested state is being asked to exercise a coercive power or to obtain a court order, for example to undertake a search of premises, obtain bank or business records or trace or freeze the proceeds of crime.[67] When making requests for such co-operation, the requesting state must make their best efforts to provide 'complete, factual and, as appropriate, legal information, including any need

[65] FATF Recommendation 38.

[66] Article 2(1) SADC Protocol on Mutual Legal Assistance.

[67] Article 46 of the UNCAC provides a comprehensive set of provisions for effective MLA requests and FATF Recommendation 36 requires countries to take immediate steps to become party to and fully implement the UNCAC.

for urgency, to enable a timely and efficient execution of the request'.[68] Requested states must not prohibit or place unreasonable or unduly restrictive conditions on the provision of exchange of information or assistance.[69] However, constitutional constraints may mean a request cannot be accepted, for example, due to constitutional restrictions on the provision of privileged information or to limitations on the exercise of domestic powers.

The experience of African states as regards the effectiveness of MLA varies considerably. On the positive side, Malawi has reportedly made numerous requests to foreign counterparts especially with regard to investigations of the Cashgate scandal and generally the responses were very beneficial. On the negative side, many African countries have reported difficulties and these are often highlighted in their MER reports. There are two commonly identified practical difficulties. Firstly, the failure of requested states to provide any assistance at all. For example, between 2011 and 2014, law enforcement agencies in Zimbabwe made 424 MLA requests but only 90 resulted in any response. Secondly, delays in responding to MLA requests. Given the ease with which the proceeds of crime can be moved, investigating money laundering often requires a rapid response to a MLA request. However, for example, Botswana has reported that the average turnaround time for MLA requests was two years and that in most cases the responses were inadequate.[70] There is no doubt that MLA processes are complex and time-consuming and many African countries still lack the capacity to deal with them efficiently. There is also the possibility that political interference by PEPs can also undermine the operation of the MLA process.[71]

In practice, problems with the MLA process mean that, where possible, other forms of co-operation must be utilised.

8.5.2 Other Forms of International Co-operation

FATF Recommendation 40 requires countries to 'ensure that their competent authorities can rapidly, constructively and effectively provide the widest range of international co-operation in relation to money laundering, associated predicate offences and terrorist financing'.

---

[68] Interpretive Note to FATF Recommendation 40. For a detailed analysis of the MLA process, see John Hatchard, *Combating Corruption: Legal Approaches to Supporting Good Governance and Integrity in Africa*, Edward Elgar, 2014, pp. 300–17.

[69] Ibid.

[70] See generally, ESAAMLG, *Botswana: Mutual Evaluation Report*, 2017, at [8.1].

[71] A point made in Section 2.5 above.

8.5.2.1 International Criminal Police Organisation (Interpol) and other AML-related networks

All African countries are members of INTERPOL and make use of its services as a channel to request assistance from law enforcement agencies in other jurisdictions. For example, in 2013 and 2017 the Zimbabwe Police Service made 42 requests for information through INTERPOL and of these 31 responses were received and the information provided used in the investigation and prosecution of money laundering cases.

Other networks such as the Asset Recovery Inter-Agency Network for Southern Africa and the Southern African Regional Police Chiefs Co-operation Organisation have also proved of assistance.

8.5.2.2 Financial intelligence units (FIUs)

As noted in Chapter 5, co-operation between national FIUs through the signing of MOU is now commonplace. The development of the Forum of Financial Intelligence Units of GIABA member states is also proving effective.[72]

8.5.2.3 Financial supervisors

There is increasing assistance and exchange of cross-border intelligence sharing between financial supervisors. For example, the Bank of Mauritius, which is the regulator for all financial institutions under the Banking Act, has entered into a series of MOUs with its foreign counterparts, which provide for mutual assistance and the exchange of financial and other related information. Similar arrangements exist in respect of the Financial Services Commission, which regulates the non-banking financial services sector.[73]

8.5.2.4 Using domestic investigatory powers in a extraterritorial setting

As noted in Section 8.2 above, a liberal interpretation by the courts of the domestic powers of anti-corruption/AML agencies can provide them with extraterritorial jurisdiction in relation to the obtaining of documentation including financial and company records.

8.6 TOWARDS ESTABLISHING EFFECTIVE AML INVESTIGATIVE BODIES

FATF Recommendation 30 requires countries to have designated law enforcement authorities with 'responsibility for ensuring that money laundering [and predicate offences] are properly investigated through the conduct of a finan-

---

72 See Section 5.5 above.

73 ESAAMLG, *Mutual Evaluation Report of Mauritius 2016*, pp. 185–6.

cial investigation'. This includes 'developing evidence which can be used in criminal proceedings'.[74] Enforcement authorities 'should also have sufficient powers to identify, trace and initiate freezing and seizing of assets'.[75]

It is not uncommon for money laundering investigations to involve several agencies. In addition to the police service, many African states have introduced an anti-corruption commission (ACC), AML investigations unit[76] or similar body[77] with a mandate that includes investigating corruption and money laundering.

Some ACCs also enjoy prosecutorial power as well as acting both as an asset recovery agency and as a code of conduct bureau for public officials. However, other African states have chosen a different approach and incorporated an anti-corruption/AML mandate into other institutions. Thus such responsibilities are given to the office of the ombudsman in, for example, Rwanda (Office of the Ombudsman); South Africa (Public Protector) and Uganda (Inspector General of Government). Here linking anti-corruption/AML work with the wider mandate of addressing 'maladministration' within the public service is potentially useful. Thus in reality the real issue is to identify which body is (or bodies or persons are) best able to carry out AML investigations effectively and to ensure effective co-operation between agencies.[78]

8.7 CONSTITUTIONAL PROTECTION FOR INVESTIGATORS AND PROSECUTORS

Entrenching an AML agency in the national constitution provides the most effective protection against attempts by PEPs to undermine it. The key 'building blocks' towards establishing an effective and independent body comprise security of tenure for office-holders, adequate funding and resources and the ability to attract and retain the necessary expert and experienced staff.[79]

---

[74] Interpretive Note to FATF Recommendation 30 [2].

[75] Interpretive Note to FATF Recommendation 30 [6].

[76] See for example, the Prohibition and Prevention of Money Laundering Act No. 14 of 2001 (Zambia).

[77] These include Algeria, Angola, Benin, Botswana, Burkina Faso, Burundi, Cameroon, Congo, Cote d'Ivoire, Egypt, Ethiopia, Gabon, The Gambia, Ghana, Guinea, Kenya, Lesotho, Libya, Madagascar, Malawi, Mauritius, Mozambique, Namibia, Nigeria, Senegal, Seychelles, South Africa, Swaziland, Tanzania, Togo, Tunisia, Uganda, Zambia and Zimbabwe.

[78] For a full discussion see John Hatchard, *Combating Corruption*, above, chapter 7.

[79] See the discussion regarding financial intelligence units at Section 5.6 above and the Auditor General at Section 7.5 above.

In addition, the courts must rigorously protect the independence of anti-corruption and AML agencies. For example, in *Kamau v Ethics and Anti-Corruption Commission*,[80] the President of Kenya had directed the Commission to expedite the handling of corruption cases involving certain PEPs. The Constitutional Court held that in making the direction the President exceeded his mandate as it could reasonably be perceived as undue interference with the Commission in the discharge of its mandate. It therefore infringed the independence of the Commission enshrined in Article 249(2) of the Constitution of Kenya. In so holding, the Court of Appeal noted the words from *In Re The Matter of the Interim Independent Electoral Commission*:[81]

> It is a matter of which we take judicial notice, that the real purpose of the 'independence clause', with regard to Commissions and independent offices established under the Constitution, was to provide a safeguard against undue interference with such Commissions or offices, by other persons, or other institutions of government. Such a provision was incorporated in the Constitution as an antidote, in the light of regrettable memories of an all-powerful presidency that, since Independence in 1963, had emasculated other arms of government ... The several independent Commissions and offices are intended to serve as 'People's watchdogs' and, to perform this role effectively they must operate without improper influences, fear or favour: this, indeed, is the purpose of the 'independence clause'. While bearing in mind that the various Commissions and independent offices are required to function free of subjection to 'direction or control by any person or authority', we hold that this expression is to be accorded its ordinary and natural meaning; and it means that the Commissions and independent offices, in carrying out their functions, are not to take orders or instructions from organs or persons outside their ambit.

These principles are applicable to all anti-corruption/AML bodies.

8.8 CONCLUSIONS

The FATF Recommendations place a wealth of obligations and responsibilities on AML investigative authorities that are essential in the fight against money laundering by PEPs. Yet in order to fulfil them, regard must be had to constitutional issues.

The power of PEPs to undermine key AML agencies must be addressed by providing effective constitutional protections for them with the courts jealously upholding their independence and operation. Here CSOs can play a use constitutional 'watchdog' role, for example, by overseeing the operation and performance of AMLs bodies and bringing judicial challenges when there are threatened breaches of their constitutional mandate or operation.

---

80 [2017] eKLR.

81 Const. App. No. 2 of 2011.

PEPs are entitled to enjoy constitutional rights, including the right to a fair trial, to LPP and the right to privacy. However, these are not absolute and the courts must ensure that appropriate limitations are applied in order to prevent abuse and to facilitate AML investigations.

International co-operation remains a key to AML investigations. The reality is that greater efforts are needed to facilitate effective co-operation between AML agencies.

Finally, it is essential to recognise that investigating money laundering by PEPs can be a dangerous activity and tribute must be paid to those who face personal danger in doing so.[82]

---

[82] For example, the Cashgate scandal in Malawi broke in September 2013 when the former Budget Director, Paul Mphwiyo, was shot in a failed assassination attempt. Issa Njauju the Director of Corporate Services of the Malawi Anti-Corruption Bureau was murdered in July 2015, allegedly in connection with the Cashgate investigations: see Alan Bacarese, 'Malawi's Cashgate Crisis: An African Corruption Metaphor or a Sign of Hope?' Basel Institute on Governance, 2015.

9. Prosecuting PEPs

9.1 INTRODUCTION

The successful prosecution of PEPs (and their subsequent inability to return to public office) followed by the forfeiture of their proceeds of crime is the ideal. In practice, there are numerous difficulties in doing so. As a result, different approaches to asset recovery are also essential. These issues are all discussed in this chapter and the next. This chapter explores prosecutorial challenges whilst Chapter 10 is devoted to asset recovery.

9.2 PEPs AND ADDRESSING PROSECUTORIAL CHALLENGES

The MERs on numerous African countries reveal the paucity of successful prosecutions of PEPs for money laundering offences. This is confirmed in a 2019 ESAAMLG report on the laundering of the proceeds of procurement corruption. In the 10 countries studied, between 2013 and 2017 there were 682 cases of money laundering investigated resulting in just 66 convictions (a rate of 9.6 per cent) with the vast majority occurring in Ethiopia (28), South Africa (17) and Malawi (15).[1]

There are two practical reasons for this situation. Firstly, as noted in the previous chapter, investigators and prosecutors continue to experience considerable challenges in evidence gathering. Secondly, in corruption cases involving PEPs, prosecutors rarely conduct parallel financial investigations to identify potential money laundering charges.[2]

According to an ESAAMLG study, limited institutional capacity and expertise amongst investigative agencies were the primary factors explaining this situation.[3] This is disappointing as the failure to bring parallel proceedings reduces the chances of a successful criminal conviction and thereby limits the

---

1 ESAAMLG report, pp. 38–9. See also the GIABA 2018 report, Table 8.2.

2 A useful example of parallel proceedings is the Cashgate case of *R v Karonga* [2018] MWHC 1 discussed in Section 9.6.

3 See also the comments of reviewers in the MERs on Senegal: see GIABA 2018 report, [154].

chances of recovering the proceeds of crime through the making of a criminal confiscation order.[4] Further, it fails to make use of the financial information provided by FIUs and other AML agencies.[5]

The lesson is clear: as a matter of policy, prosecutors must be equipped, trained and encouraged to undertake parallel money laundering prosecutions.

9.3 PEPs AND PLEA BARGAINS

Article 37(2) of the UNCAC requires State Parties to 'consider the possibility, in appropriate cases, of mitigating punishment of an accused person who provides substantial co-operation in the investigation or prosecution' of a corruption offence.[6] In practice, plea bargains are a potentially effective way for prosecutors to obtain evidence about money laundering by PEPs as well as facilitating the recovery of proceeds of crime.

9.3.1 The Cashgate Experience

Two Cashgate cases from Malawi illustrate the operation of plea bargains in money laundering cases involving PEPs. The case of *R v Senzani* provides a simple example. Here a former Principal Secretary in the Ministry of Tourism in Malawi entered into a plea bargain in which she pleaded guilty to money laundering charges and agreed to return over MK62 million representing the proceeds of crime in return for a lighter sentence.[7] The case of Leonard Karonga[8] is more significant as it demonstrates that such bargains are a potentially vital means of obtaining information about PEPs, syndicate and grand corruption and resultant money laundering activities. It also sets out the basic principles upon which a trial court should base a decision as to whether to permit a plea bargain.

Karonga, a former senior official in the Malawi Ministry of Tourism (and therefore a PEP) pleaded guilty to conspiracy to defraud and to several counts of money laundering and facilitating money laundering.[9] The case involved a sum of MWK520 million, which he had used to purchase six Marco Torino

---

4 ESAAMLG report, at p. 47. See further Section 10.2 below.

5 See Section 5.4.

6 FATF Recommendation 31 also requires countries to ensure investigators enjoy a wide range of investigative techniques. Whilst not mentioned as an example, the use of plea bargains is one such technique.

7 2013, unreported, Malawi High Court.

8 *R v Karonga* [2018] MWHC 1.

9 Contrary to section 35 of the Money Laundering, Proceeds of Serious Crime and Terrorist Financing Act 2006. On the issue of sentencing, see Section 9.6 below.

buses, and the further laundering of some MWK3.25 billion. His plea of guilty was accompanied by a Witness Assistance Agreement in which he provided extensive information to law enforcement officials concerning the whole Cashgate affair. This was seemingly part of his bargain with the state in the hope of some reduction in sentence in return.

In principle, and particularly where a case involves a PEP, any such agreement must be transparent and requires an assessment by a judge in open court. As Mwila J noted in *Karonga*, bargains between the prosecution and defence were common in Malawi but were entirely informal and always occurring outside the formal court process. He rightly viewed this as unsatisfactory and therefore embarked on a comparative analysis of plea bargains mechanisms.[10] From this and supplemented by guidelines issued by the Director of Public Prosecution,[11] he drew some important basic principles which are of general application in relation to plea bargains involving PEPs in money laundering and related cases.

1. The parties may negotiate the charge(s) on which the prosecution will proceed.[12]
2. The bargain may involve a decision by the prosecution not to proceed with the case.[13]
3. Possible concessions regarding sentence must be carefully considered by the prosecution to take into account the impact on victims and the public and on the prospects of successfully prosecuting others involved in the criminality.
4. The set of facts the prosecution will proceed on for the purpose of sentencing must be agreed and the implications fully understood by the accused.
5. The prosecution (and the defence) may suggest an appropriate sentence.
6. The bargain cannot override judicial discretion which the court exercises in order to protect the rights of the accused to a fair trial: in particular to protect a vulnerable defendant from possible manipulation or exploitation.

---

[10] Mwila J referred to the position in the United States, Canada, Australia and the United Kingdom. It is noteworthy that no African jurisdiction was considered: an indication of either a lack of information or the lack of a formal process elsewhere.

[11] DPP of Malawi, *Guidelines issued by the Director of Public Prosecutions: Plea Discussions in Cases of Serious or Complex Fraud and the Prosecutor's Role in Sentencing*, 2015.

[12] This emphasises the importance of prosecutors reviewing cases involving PEPs with a view to determining the most appropriate charge(s) to bring. As noted earlier, a parallel charge of money laundering may be highly desirable.

[13] A transparent decision-making process overseen by a court is essential in these circumstances.

7. It is fundamental that the court is satisfied that the bargain is both fair and ethical.

The use of plea bargains is seemingly not well established in African states. Arguably these should follow the principles established in Malawi for, as the *Karonga* case highlights, they can be of fundamental importance in successfully investigating and prosecuting syndicate and grand corruption as well as money laundering cases.

9.4 PEPs AND CONSTITUTIONAL IMMUNITIES

Constitutional immunities exist in order to protect the dignity of the President or other PEPs and allow them to exercise their duties appropriately.[14] It is when those powers are abused, that issues arise as to the scope of such immunity.

9.4.1 Presidential Immunity

A typical constitutional provision states that: 'The President shall not, whilst in office as President, be personally liable to any civil or criminal proceedings in court.'[15] This immunity is entirely appropriate so long as the powers are exercised in accordance with the presidential oath of office in which the President-elect undertakes to well and truly perform the functions of the office and to preserve, protect and defend the Constitution. However, a sitting President may face accusations of involvement in money laundering, corruption and/or abuse of office. Here there is normally a constitutional option to seek their removal from office. For example, the Constitution of Uganda[16] provides for the removal of the President if 'he or she has dishonestly done any act ... which is prejudicial or inimical to the economy ... of Uganda'. This requires a constitutionally mandated investigation process that is transparent and objective. The African Constitutions all provide for a formal investigation process that normally involves the legislature and judiciary although there is no agreement as to the final decision-maker on the matter.[17]

---

[14] See for example, the decision of the Botswana Court of Appeal in *Motswaledi v Botswana Democratic Party* [2009] BWCA 111.

[15] Constitution of Ghana, Article 57(5).

[16] Article 107(1)(b)(2).

[17] A discussion of the procedure is beyond the scope of this chapter. For a full discussion see John Hatchard, Presidential removal: Unzipping the constitutional provisions, (2000) 44 *Journal of African Law* 1.

In most African countries personal liability becomes enforceable at the end of the presidential term of office. As the Constitutional Court of Uganda has explained:

> Even the Chief Executive of the country in the person of the President, is accountable for actions/omissions in his/her personal capacity once he/she leaves office.[18]

There are exceptions. For example, in Cameroon a 2008 constitutional amendment provides immunity for the President even after leaving office.[19] The Constitution of Zambia also provides an outgoing President with continued immunity from prosecution although the National Assembly may lift this,[20] as indeed occurred in the case of former President Rupiah Banda.[21] This approach has some merit in that it 'encourages' incumbents to leave office with some protection against possibly facing politically motivated accusations of corruption and/or money laundering but allows them to be called to account where appropriate.

9.4.2 Immunities Enjoyed by other PEPs

The granting of immunities to other PEPs is a matter of some controversy. The potential abuse of immunity provisions is highlighted by the appointment of Teodorin Nguema Obiang as Vice-President of Equatorial Guinea, an office that is not provided for in the Constitution and which was seemingly done with the intention of preventing criminal investigations against him taking place in other countries.[22]

An attempt to extend presidential immunity to a Vice-President was firmly rejected by the Constitutional Court of Uganda in *Bukenya v Attorney General.*[23] Here a former Vice-President of Uganda was charged with abuse of

---

[18] *Bukenya v Attorney General*, 2011, Constitutional Court of Uganda Constitutional Petition 30 of 2011 (no page numbering). Available at http://www.ulii.org/ug/judgment/constitutional-court/2011/9 (accessed 7 June 2020).

[19] Article 53(3) Constitution of Cameroon.

[20] Article 43(3) provides: 'No person who has held, but no longer holds, the office of President shall be charged with a criminal offence or be amenable to the criminal jurisdiction of any court in respect of any act done or omitted to be done by him in his personal capacity while he held office of President, unless the National Assembly has, by resolution, determined that such proceedings would not be contrary to the interests of the State.'

[21] See 'Communication' from Katai Mwinga, 'The process of removing the immunity of a former President: The Zambian experience', Inter-Parliamentary Union, 2014.

[22] Aspects of the Obiang case are considered in Sections 10.3.4 below and 14.7.1.

[23] *Bukenya v Attorney General*, above.

office contrary to section 11 of the Anti-Corruption Act 2009 and fraudulent practice contrary to section 95(1)(d) of the Public Procurement and Disposal of Public Assets Act 2003. He argued that the acts in question were done whilst he was carrying out his official Vice-Presidential duties and that the charges therefore contravened the immunities of the Presidency. The Constitutional Court accepted that the Vice-Presidential role included deputising for the President but noted that the office-holder was a Presidential appointee who derived his/her mandate from the office of the President. The Constitution of Uganda specifically provided that '[w]hile holding office, the President shall not be liable to proceedings in any court'[24] and thus such immunity was strictly limited to the President.

In Nigeria, constitutional immunity for PEPs is taken to an extreme by virtue of Section 308(1)(a) of the Constitution of Nigeria 1999. This provides that 'no civil or criminal proceedings shall be instituted or continued against a person to whom this section applies during his term in office'.[25] The section applies not only to the President but also the Vice-President, state governors and deputy state governors. Given that there are 36 states in Nigeria, this effectively provides immunity from prosecution for over 70 senior public officials during their terms in office. Section 308 remains the subject of much debate. Kehinde has suggested that it is needed to protect incumbents against politically motivated and/or frivolous prosecutions which can deflect them from the exercise of their functions. This argument has merit in respect of the Head of State but extending such immunity further is completely unacceptable as it can inevitably encourage abuses of power and provide unwarranted protection for corrupt PEPs.[26] Indeed there has been widespread concern over allegations of corruption and money laundering made against numerous Nigerian state governors and according to Nuhu Ribadu, the former Chairman of Nigeria's Economic and Financial Crimes Commission, approximately 31 of Nigeria's 36 state governors were involved in such criminality, including Ibori of Delta State, Alamieyeseigha of Bayelsa State, and Dariye of Plateau State.[27] Section 188 of the Constitution of Nigeria provides for the removal of a state governor

---

[24] Article 98(4).

[25] This immunity applies to proceedings brought even before the official took office: see *IMB Securities PLC v Tinubu* (2001) 45 WRN 1.

[26] See further the thoughtful discussion by S Kehinde, The immunity clause under the Nigerian 1999 Constitution, (2016) *The Lawyers Chronicle.* Available at http://thelawyerschronicle.com/index.php?option=com_content&view=article&id=54:the-immunity-clause-under-the-nigerian-1999-constitution-&catid=39:constitutional-law&Itemid=43 (accessed 5 June 2020).

[27] See http://www.guardian.co.uk/global/2010/mar/19/nigeria-goodluck-jonathan-umaru-yaradua (accessed 7 June 2020).

or deputy governor by the House of Assembly of the particular state on much the same grounds as that of the President and this was used to remove from office James Ibori, the then governor of Delta State.

Constitutional provisions granting limited immunity to judicial officers are commonplace. A typical provision is found in Article 128(4) of the Constitution of Uganda:

> A person exercising judicial power shall not be liable to any action or suit for any act or omission by that person in the exercise of judicial power.

Such protection for official acts is essential as it enables judges to act fearlessly and impartially in the discharge of their judicial duties as it will be difficult for the judges to function if their actions in court are made subject to legal proceedings either civil or criminal.[28] It has no application to extra-judicial activities they may undertake.

Parliamentarians enjoy parliamentary privilege but this does not extend to acts of corruption or money laundering.[29]

9.4.3 PEPs and Immunities in an International Setting

Given that an offence of money laundering is committed in every jurisdiction through which the proceeds of crime pass or are located, it follows that domestic immunity for PEPs has limited application in an international setting. The Vienna Convention on Diplomatic Relations 1961 requires states to grant diplomatic immunity to officials of foreign states whilst they are in office in respect of their official acts. Heads of State also enjoy such immunity, as emphasised in *Tachiona v Mugabe:*

> The potential for harm to diplomatic relations between affected sovereign states is especially strong in cases ... essentially as it entails branding a foreign ruler with the ignominy of answering personal accusations of heinous crimes.[30]

Presidential immunity ceases as soon as the incumbent leaves office.

The issue of whether constitutional immunity provisions apply to other PEPs came before the English courts in 2006 in *R (Alamieyeseigha) v Crown Prosecution Service.*[31] Here Diepreye Alamieyeseigha, the then serving gover-

---

[28] Statement of Objects and Reasons in the Judges (Protection) Act 1985 (India).

[29] See for example, *R v Chaytor* [2010] UKSC 52.

[30] 169 F. Supp. 2d 259, 291 (S.D. N.Y. 2001). See also the views of Lord Browne-Wilkinson in *R v Bow Street Magistrates ex parte Pinochet (No. 3)* [2000] 1 AC 142 at page 201G.

[31] [2005] All ER (D) 348; [2006] Crim LR 669.

nor of Bayelsa State in Nigeria, was arrested and charged by the Metropolitan Police in London with three counts of money laundering. He sought to challenge his arrest and prosecution on the basis that as a Nigerian state governor he enjoyed immunity from prosecution under section 308 of the Constitution of Nigeria (see above) and consequently was entitled to sovereign immunity under English law. This argument was firmly rejected by the High Court on the ground that as Bayelsa State was a constituent part of the Federal Republic of Nigeria and therefore was not entitled to state immunity, the Governor and Chief Executive of Bayelsa State was also not entitled to state immunity in criminal proceedings.[32]

A PEP convicted of a money laundering offence in another jurisdiction may also have their proceeds of crime subject to forfeiture. For example, James Ibori, a former Governor of Delta State in Nigeria, was convicted in a London court of money laundering. He was sentenced to a lengthy period of imprisonment as well as having a criminal confiscation order imposed on him.[33]

Countries may seek to use honorary consulships or membership of international governmental organisations to protect PEPs or their associates from corruption or money laundering charges in other jurisdictions. A blatant attempt to do so was made in the case of Pierre Falcone. He was detained in France pending an investigation into allegations of his involvement with tax fraud, influence peddling, and corruption of public officials associated with arms sales in Angola. Following his release on bail he fled to Angola where the then President, Eduardo dos Santos, appointed him the representative of Angola to UNESCO. Falcone then claimed diplomatic immunity from criminal prosecution in France. Unsurprisingly, the French authorities denied his claim on the ground that his arms trafficking activities were not a function of his diplomatic status.[34]

9.5 PEPs AND THE CONSTITUTIONAL RIGHT TO CONFRONT ONE'S ACCUSERS

Like any individual, PEPs are entitled to enjoy the constitutional right to a fair trial, which includes the presumption of innocence and privilege against self-incrimination. Also included is the right to know and confront one's

---

32 *Nigeria v Santolina Investment Corp and Ors* [2007] EWHC 3053.

33 'Nigeria ex-Delta State Governor James Ibori Guilty Plea' *BBC News Report* 27 February 2012 https://www.bbc.co.uk/news/world-africa-17181056 (accessed 7 June 2020).

34 See the report of the United States Senate Permanent Subcommittee on Investigations Committee on Homeland Security and Governmental Affairs, *Keeping Foreign Corruption out of the United States: Four Case Histories*, 2010, at page 251.

accuser. The enjoyment of this right may inevitably impact on prosecutions, particularly as regards the protection of whistleblowers and witness anonymity.

9.5.1 The Importance of Whistleblowers

The vulnerability of PEPs and their money laundering exploits to information provided by whistleblowers was noted in Section 2.8.1.6. In practice it is essential to provide adequate protection to whistleblowers and to facilitate their giving evidence at the trial. Article 5(6) of the AU Convention requires State Parties to 'adopt legislative and other measures to protect informants and *witnesses* in corruption and related offences, *including protecting their identities*' (emphasis added).

In particular the following constitute the minimum requirements as regards individuals:

- Effective whistleblower protection legislation. This should be along the lines of the Protected Disclosures Act (No 26 of 2000)(South Africa) and the Whistleblower Protection Act 2017 (Namibia). Such legislation must provide a safe alternative to silence particularly when the reporting of corruption or money laundering by PEPs impacts on national security issues;
- The protection must apply to both those in the public and private sectors;
- The protection must extend to the close family members of the whistleblower;
- Given the potential deleterious effect on individual career prospects, holistic and adequate financial compensation must be readily available;
- Legal practitioners should be available to offer pro bono assistance to bona fide whistleblowers;
- There must be adequate provision made for anonymous reporting (see below).

9.5.2 The Pre-trial Stage, Constitutional Rights and 'Trial by Ambush'

Protecting whistleblowers from reprisals is a key part of any anti-corruption/AML strategy. This must include protecting their identity and encouraging the making of anonymous reports.[35] Even so, the desire to preserve such anonymity conflicts with a constitutional provision or statutory requirement that prior to trial the prosecution disclose all witness statements to the defence including

[35] See for example, the Witness Protection Act 2006 and Witness Protection (Amendment) Act 2010 (Kenya) which, amongst other things, establish a Witness Protection Agency.

details identifying the maker of the relevant statement(s). The issue here is that the right to a fair trial normally incorporates the right of the accused to be given 'adequate facilities for the preparation of his or her defence'. In *Juma and Others v Attorney General of Kenya*[36] the High Court of Kenya explained this right as follows:

> The accused must be given and afforded those opportunities and means so that the prosecution does not gain an undeserved or unfair advantage over the accused; and so that the accused is not impeded in any manner and does not suffer unfair advantage and prejudice in preparing his defence, confronting his accusers and arming himself in his defence and so that no miscarriage of justice is occasioned.[37]

Significantly, the court recognised that this is not an absolute right and that a trial judge has the power to refuse disclosure 'where there are grounds for fearing that disclosing a statement might lead to an attempt being improperly made to persuade a witness to make a statement retracting [their] original one, to change [their] story, not to appear in court or otherwise to intimidate [them]'.[38]

Similarly, in *Attorney General v Soon Yeon Kong Kim and Kwanga Mao*[39] the Constitutional Court of Uganda agreed that 'the right to a fair hearing contains in it the right to a pre-trial disclosure of material statements and exhibits ... [and] in an open and democratic society, courts cannot approve of trial by ambush. The right to a fair hearing envisages equality between the contestants in litigation.'[40] However, it was again recognised that the rule was subject to limitations and that the trial judge had the discretion to refuse disclosure where, for example, the state established by evidence the need to protect witnesses from intimidation or protect disclosure of the identity of informers.[41] Neither case seemingly involved money laundering charges[42] but the approach of both courts is helpful because of the recognition that, particularly in cases involving PEPs, there is clearly a strong argument for the judge to uphold pre-trial witness anonymity in the circumstances envisaged in *Soon*.

---

36 (2003) AHRLR 179 (KeHC 2003).

37 At [12].

38 Ibid, at [30].

39 [2008] UGCC 2.

40 At p. 12.

41 In *Juma*, above, the court recognised that protection of the identity of informers was 'well covered by separate rules related to informer privilege and exceptions thereto (see *Marks v Beyfus* [1890] 25 QBD 494) and any rules with respect to disclosure would be subject to this and any rules of immunity': at [26].

42 In both *Juma* and *Soon* neither law report identifies the charges against the accused.

9.5.3 The Trial Stage

Despite the availability of forensic evidence in the form of financial statements, business documents and the like, witness testimony is still often crucial in money laundering cases. Depending upon the jurisdiction, in order to provide protection for a witness when giving evidence, the trial judge may have a variety of measures available. These can include allowing the witness to give evidence behind a screen so as to avoid a face-to-face confrontation with the accused,[43] permitting the witness to give evidence by way of a video link or ordering a closed hearing, and/or prohibiting any disclosure of the identity of the witness by the media.[44] Appropriate legislation is required to enable evidence to be given in such circumstances. These measures still enable the accused to know the identity of the prosecution witness, to have an opportunity to cross-examine them and to test the reliability of their testimony. In addition, the trial judge (and assessors or other triers of fact) can judge the demeanour of the witness at all times. As a result, such measures raise no fair trial or equality issues.

The tension arises when measures are taken which either exclude or at least significantly limit the right of accused persons to confront their accusers in circumstances where this evidence potentially brings into play the 'sole or decisive rule' i.e. 'if the conviction of an accused is solely or mainly based on evidence provided by witnesses whom the accused is unable to question at any stage of the proceedings, [their] defence rights are unduly restricted'.[45] There are three such measures to consider.

The first is concealing the *identity* of a witness. Here the witness testifies at the trial but steps are taken to ensure that no details which might identify them are revealed at any time to the accused or their legal representatives,[46] for example using voice changer technology for the witness whilst giving evidence at the trial.[47] Without such knowledge, the accused inevitably has,

---

43 Although the witness remains visible to the rest of the court.

44 See also Article 32(2)(b) of UNCAC.

45 *Unterpertinger v Austria* 24 November 1986, 33, Series, No. 10 and *Lucà v Italy* Case 33354/96, ECHR 2001.

46 Of course, this pre-supposes that the witness also enjoys pre-trial anonymity. In addition, legislation is required to prohibit the asking of questions to any other witness which might reveal the identity of the person seeking anonymity: see, for example, section 44(1) Anti-Corruption Act 2009 (Uganda).

47 A MENAFATF report notes that this is used in several countries in the region: see MENAFATF *Typologies Report on Money Laundering and Corruption*, 2017, p. 33.

at best, a very limited opportunity to confront their accuser(s) in a meaningful manner.[48]

The second measure permits the admission of an out-of-court statement made by the witness rather than requiring their attendance at the trial. For example, suppose that a key witness makes a statement to the ACC alleging money laundering on the part of an accused PEP but then refuses to give evidence at the trial on the grounds that they are too frightened to do so, perhaps because there is no way of concealing their identity. Depending on the jurisdiction, in such circumstances the trial judge may permit the prosecution to adduce the previous statement at the trial as evidence of the truth of its contents. Here the identity of the witness is disclosed but the accused has no opportunity to confront their accuser at the trial. In African common law and Roman-Dutch law jurisdictions this brings into play the hearsay rule. i.e. that 'any statement of fact other than one made, of [their] own knowledge, by a witness in the course of oral testimony' is inadmissible at a criminal trial.[49] This reflects the policy behind the sole or decisive rule.

A third measure is what might be termed the 'double protection' scenario. Here not only is the pre-trial statement admitted at the trial via the 'fearful witness' exception but also the identity of its maker is withheld from the accused. This has the advantage of offering witnesses anonymity as well as sparing them the ordeal of giving evidence at the trial. From the defence perspective, such a scenario completely undermines the right to confrontation.

The challenge is to establish a system that (1) protects the constitutional rights of the accused and addresses the danger that the incriminatory evidence of the witness may be untrue either by design[50] or simply erroneous;[51] but (2) provides adequate protection to bona fide witnesses. Neither the applicability of the sole or decisive rule nor the constitutionality of the hearsay rule in criminal cases has seemingly yet been considered by a court in Africa. Given its importance, it is surely just a matter of time before this occurs. This makes the 2011 decision of the Grand Chamber of the European Court of Human Rights in the case of *Al Khawaja and Tahery v United Kingdom*[52] all the more inter-

---

48 Of course, where there are a limited number of persons who could have supplied this information, the accused may be able to make an educated guess as to their identity.

49 Lord Phillips in *Horncastle* [2009] UKSC 14 at [20]. Section 3(4) of the Law of Evidence Amendment Act 45 of 1988 in South Africa defines hearsay evidence as 'evidence, whether oral or in writing, the probative value of which depends upon the credibility of a person other than the person giving such evidence'.

50 For example, the case is brought for political reasons against a former PEP who has now fallen out of political favour.

51 See *Kostovski v The Netherlands*, 1989, Series A, No. 166, at [142].

52 [2011] ECHR (GC).

esting and pertinent, especially as the decision is applicable to both common law and civil law jurisdictions and is based on the provisions of Article 6(3)(d) of the European Convention on Human Rights, which are widely replicated or incorporated in constitutions throughout Africa.[53]

In this case, the two applicants were separately convicted of criminal offences largely on the evidence of out-of-court statements of witnesses, one now deceased and the other who refused to give evidence due to fear. The Grand Chamber accepted that the 'sole or decisive rule may have been developed in the context of [civil law] systems which permitted a defendant to be convicted on evidence of witnesses whom he did not have an opportunity to challenge', but that it also reflected the strict common law rule against hearsay. Thus also it recognised that although there were substantial differences in legal systems and procedures, including different approaches to the admissibility of evidence in criminal trials, ultimately the Court 'must apply the same standard of review under Article 6(1) and 3(d), irrespective of the legal system from which a case emanates'.[54]

The Grand Chamber was clearly very aware of the considerable practical implications of a rigid application of the sole or decisive rule. In particular, the untimely death, intimidation or disappearance of the key prosecution witness (perhaps facilitated by the accused or their associates) could lead to the collapse of the prosecution. As a result, the Court concluded that, 'where a hearsay statement [or evidence from an anonymous witness] is the sole or decisive evidence against a defendant, its admission as evidence *will not* automatically result in a breach of Article 6(1)'.[55] However, in such circumstances, the Grand Chamber ruled that the trial court 'must subject the proceedings to the most searching scrutiny'. They noted that in each case the prime concern of the court is to evaluate the *overall fairness* of the criminal proceedings.[56] In making this assessment the court must take into account a triangulation of interests and 'look at the proceedings as a whole having regard to the rights of the defence but also to the interests of the public and the victims that crime is properly prosecuted and, *where necessary, to the rights of witnesses*' (emphasis added).[57] This is a decision of major interest as regards cases involving

---

[53] Article 6(3)(d) states that everyone charged with a criminal offence 'has the right to examine or have examined witnesses against him and to obtain the attendance and examination of witnesses on his behalf under the same conditions as witnesses against him'.

[54] *Al Khawaja and Tahery* at [130].

[55] At [147].

[56] Applying *Taxquet v Belgium* ECHR [GC], 2010, No. 926/05, at [84].

[57] See, amongst many authorities, *Doorson v The Netherlands*, ECHR (GC) 1996, Reports of Judgments and Decisions 1996-II, at [70].

PEPs in that it recognises that the rights of the accused are not the paramount consideration.

In order to carry out this balancing act, the Grand Chamber identified two requirements. Firstly, the court must be satisfied that there is a good reason for the non-attendance (or anonymity) of a witness. This was self-evident where the witness had died but each case needed careful evaluation where it was based on fear. Here the court must consider whether there are sufficient existing safeguards that protect the right to a fair trial and this is the central question which applies irrespective of the legal system from which the case emanated.[58]

Secondly, at the same time where a conviction is based solely or decisively on the evidence of absent witnesses, the Court must subject the proceedings to the most searching scrutiny. Thus,

> when a conviction is based solely or to a decisive degree on depositions that have been made by a person whom the accused has had no opportunity to examine or to have examined, whether during the investigation or at the trial, the rights of the defence may be restricted to an extent that is incompatible with the guarantees provided by Article 6 (the so-called 'sole or decisive rule').[59]

9.5.4 Overview

Maintaining an appropriate balance between the constitutional right to a fair trial and facilitating prosecutions in money laundering cases remains difficult. Given the potential seriousness of such cases, it is in the public interest to encourage reporting by offering adequate and effective protection for witnesses. In essence, it is up to the courts to resolve the tension by taking steps to ensure the overall fairness of the proceedings. This requires taking into account the rights of the accused, but balancing these with the interest of victims of corruption and money laundering and the public interest in combating such crimes.

As the Panama Papers and Luanda Papers highlight, perhaps the future lies with 'super-whistleblowers', both anonymous or otherwise, whose revelations shatter the secrecy that PEPs seek to maintain and thus provide the cogent evidence that is needed to convict the criminals and recover the proceeds of crime.

---

[58] The Court has consistently assessed the impact that the defendant's inability to examine a witness has had on the overall fairness of his trial.

[59] *Al Khawaja and Tahery* at [119].

9.5.5 PEPs: the Presumption of Innocence and the Burden of Proof

Article 7(1)(b) of the African Charter on Human and Peoples' Rights and numerous national constitutions provide that every accused person has the right to be presumed innocent until proved guilty by a competent court or tribunal. Even so, the challenge of proving money laundering or corruption offences, particularly when dealing with PEPs, means that it is not uncommon for a statute to place the legal burden of proof, either expressly or impliedly, on the accused on a specific exculpatory issue.

The approach to interpreting whether a statute impliedly places the legal burden of proof on an accused was helpfully clarified by the Privy Council in *Beezadhur v Independent Commission against Corruption.*[60] The appellant was convicted of money laundering offences contrary to the Financial and Anti-Money Laundering Act 2002 in Mauritius. Section 5 of the Act imposed criminal liability for certain cash deposits unless these constituted 'exempt transactions'. The question arose as to where the legal burden of proof lay on this issue. On an appeal from the Supreme Court of Mauritius, the Privy Council set out the general principle to be applied in such cases. Lord Carnwath, delivering the judgment of the Board, stated:

> Section 10 of the Constitution [of Mauritius] provides:
> '(2) Every person who is charged with a criminal offence –
> (a) shall be presumed to be innocent until he is proved or has pleaded guilty; …
> (11) Nothing contained in or done under the authority of any law shall be held to be inconsistent with or in contravention of –
> (a) subsection (2)(a), to the extent that the law in question imposes upon any person charged with a criminal offence the burden of proving particular facts; …'
>
> Section 10 gives expression to a fundamental rule of the common law, that the general burden of proof in criminal cases lies on the prosecution. That rule is subject to a well-established exception, the best known statement of which is probably in the judgment of Lawton LJ in *R v Edwards* [1975] QB 27, 39-40. He described the line of authority which 'over the centuries' had evolved an exception to the fundamental rule:
>
>> 'This exception … is limited to offences arising under enactments which prohibit the doing of an act save in specified circumstances or by persons of specified classes or with specified qualifications or with the licence or permission of specified authorities. Whenever the prosecution seeks to rely on this exception, the court must construe the enactment under which the charge is laid. If the true construction is that the enactment prohibits the doing of acts, subject to provisos, exemptions and the like, then the prosecution can rely upon the exception.'
>
> The exception has been held equally relevant where the general rule is enshrined in a constitutional provision (see *A-G for Hong Kong v Le Kwong-kut* [1993] AC 951,

60 [2014] UKPC 27.

968–70, relating to article 11(1) of the Hong Kong Bill of Rights, which provided: 'Everyone charged with a criminal offence shall have the right to be presumed innocent until proved guilty according to law.') at [25–26].

The Board concluded that section 10(11)(a) 'was intended to give constitutional effect to the common law principle enunciated in cases such as *R v Edwards* and applies whenever the relevant law … interpreted in the light of that principle, has the effect of placing the burden of proof on the defendant'. Accordingly, if that effect was clear from the form of the provision in issue, it did not need to be spelt out in express terms. In the present case, the Supreme Court of Mauritius was right to hold that, in accordance with section 10(11)(a), it was for the defendant to show that the transaction was within one of the exempt categories.

Such an approach is commendable as it is in the public interest and overcomes the practical reality that it is sometimes impossible or unduly burdensome for the prosecution to be required to prove all elements of an offence to the criminal standard.[61]

9.6 SENTENCING PRINCIPLES IN MONEY LAUNDERING CASES INVOLVING PEPs AND THEIR ASSOCIATES

The Interpretive Note to FATF Recommendation 3 states that countries must ensure that '[e]ffective, proportionate and dissuasive criminal sanctions ... apply to natural persons convicted of money laundering'. These should also apply to legal persons unless this is not possible due to 'fundamental principles of domestic law'.[62]

The Cashgate cases of *Republic v Lutepo*[63] (*Lutepo*) and *Republic v Karonga* (*Karonga*) provide an excellent analysis of the sentencing principles in money laundering cases involving PEPs. In *Lutepo*, the accused was convicted of facilitating money laundering involving some MWK4.2 billion and conspiracy to defraud.[64] As regards mitigating circumstances, Kapindu J in the High Court of Malawi took into account that Lutepo was a first offender, had on his own

---

[61] See also *S v Chogugudza* [1996] LRC 683 (Supreme Court of Zimbabwe) and *S v Meaker* 1998 (2) SACR 73 (Constitutional Court of South Africa). Hopefully courts in other African countries will adopt this approach when determining the constitutionality of reverse onus provisions in money laundering and corruption cases.

[62] At [7(b)] and [7(c)]. See also FATF Recommendation 35. For a discussion on legal persons see Chapter 11.

[63] [2015] MWHC 492.

[64] Contrary to section 323 of the Malawi Penal Code.

initiative pleaded guilty and had actively assisted prosecutors. Turning to the aggravating feature of the case, Kapindu J referred to the negative impact on Malawian society and the dire economic consequences arising from the Cashgate case. He noted two previous money laundering cases[65] in which the High Court of Malawi had imposed sentences of three years' and five years' imprisonment respectively where sums of MWK63 and MWK24 million were involved but noted that these paled into insignificance in relation to the sums involved in the instant case. Turning to the sentence itself, he noted that the Money Laundering, Proceeds of Crime and Terrorist Financing Act provided a maximum sentence for money laundering of 10 years' imprisonment, and wondered why it was pitched so low. In view of this, he stated that 'given the gravity and aggravated form of money laundering in the present case, I would have proceeded to impose the maximum penalty' with the seriousness of the crime tending 'to otherwise eclipse most of the mitigating factors advanced, including that of being a first offender'.[66] However, he continued: 'the convict's co-operation with the State, which might help in the further fight and unearthing of the roles of others who might possibly be more culpable then the convict herein, deserves special credit. I have also discounted the convict's sentence on account of the efforts the convict has made in restituting the State ... and to a minor extent, his guilty plea.'[67] As a result a sentence of eight years' imprisonment was imposed. As regards the conspiracy count, Kapindu J imposed the maximum sentence of three years' imprisonment.[68] He noted that where a person is convicted of more than one offence, a court will normally order that sentences run concurrently. However, a court may depart from this general principle 'in order to ensure that a meaningful aggregate sentence results'.[69] Taking into account the exceptional gravity of the offences committed and the 'weakness of the sentencing regime which seems not to have envisaged the level of magnitude of the fraud and money laundering witnessed in the present case', the sentences were ordered to run consecutively.

In *Karonga*, the convicted person was a PEP who had taken a prominent role in embezzling the government funds and then laundering them. He was charged with conspiracy to defraud as well as two counts of money laundering. Again mitigating factors were considered. Mwale J in the High Court of Malawi considered the plea of guilty to be the most significant mitigating

---

65 *Republic v Namathanga*, 2013, unreported and *Republic v Kasamba, 2013*, unreported.

66 *Lutepo*, at [132].

67 Ibid, at [133].

68 Again, a remarkably low maximum for what is (as demonstrated in the instant case) a potentially grave offence.

69 *Lutepo*, at [142] applying *Maseya v Republic* [1993] 16(2) MLR 588 (SCA).

factor in such cases with a reduction of up to a third of the possible sentence. Here the stage at which the plea of guilty was made and the circumstances in which it was given were factors to be taken into account with consideration also being given to Article 37(2) of the UNCAC.[70]

Mwale J then set out the determining factors in order to qualify for a reduction in sentence:

(a) The defendant must have admitted the offences and pleaded guilty. In this case Karonga had signed a full confession.
(b) The defendant must offer substantial assistance of quality and quantity. In this case Karonga had revealed the scope and intricacies of the complex and sophisticated 'Cashgate' scheme.
(c) The defendant must bring to the attention of the authorities the names of criminals who were previously outside police intelligence. In this case Karonga had revealed information that was previously unknown to the state including the names of PEPs and others both inside and outside the key ministries who were implicated in the embezzlement scheme.
(d) The information supplied by the defendant must be accurate and he or she must display willingness to testify or otherwise confront other criminals. This was not disputed.[71]

As regards other possible mitigating circumstances Mwale J took the view (1) that domestic matters were not matters a court took into account unless there were exceptional or unusual circumstances; and (2) loss of employment and attendant benefits was only a minimal consideration; but (3) remorse could be considered in addition to a guilty plea.

He then referred with approval to the three-tier analysis as to the level of culpability in money laundering cases applied by the court in *Lutepo*. Here Kapindu J set out three levels of culpability:

A. High culpability factors:

(a) a leading role where offending is part of a group activity;
(b) involvement of others through pressure or influence;
(c) abuse of position of power or trust or responsibility;
(d) sophisticated nature of the offence/significant planning;
(e) criminal activity conducted over a period of time; and
(f) shockingly high sums of money involved.[72]

---

70 See Section 9.3 above.

71 *Karonga*, at pp. 22–4.

72 The final factor was added by Mwale J in *Karonga* at p. 17.

B. Medium culpability factors:

(a) other cases where characteristics for categories A and C are not present; and
(b) a significant role where offending is part of a group activity.

C. Lesser culpability factors:

(a) performed limited function under direction;
(b) involved coercion, intimidation of exploitation;
(c) not motivated by personal gain;
(d) opportunistic 'one-off' offence; very little or no planning; and
(e) limited awareness or understanding of extent of criminal activity.[73]

In Karonga, Mwale J regarded the facilitating money laundering charge as a 'High Culpability' case, although somewhat surprisingly, he took as a starting point a sentence of four years' imprisonment. The mitigating factors of remorse, loss and employment and career and an offer of restitution then led him to impose a sentence of two years' imprisonment. On the second charge of money laundering, the judge took nine years' imprisonment as a starting point. Taking into account the mitigating circumstances, a reduction of one and a half years was applied. In contrast to the approach in Lutepo, in view of the guilty plea, the sentences were ordered to run concurrently.

The principles enunciated in the two cases provide an excellent basis for judges to apply in other African countries when determining sentences in money laundering cases involving PEPs and their associates. In addition, the cases highlight the need for legislators to review the adequacy of the sentencing provisions in domestic money laundering legislation to ensure they are 'effective, proportionate and dissuasive'.

9.7 FUTURE DEVELOPMENTS IN PROSECUTING MONEY LAUNDERING BY PEPs

Despite the continent-wide strengthening in investigative and prosecutorial AML provisions, the fact remains that these have resulted in very few successful prosecutions of PEPs in African states. Arguably, part of the reason for this situation arises due to the ability of PEPs to 'control the controls'. Lesotho provides a case in point. Here a series of AML laws have been enacted which have largely brought the country into line with the FATF Recommendations.[74] In

[73] *Lutepo*, at [61].

[74] For example, Money Laundering and Proceeds of Crime Act 2008, Money Laundering and Proceeds of Crime (Amendment) Act 2016 and the Mutual Legal Assistance in Criminal Matters Act 2018.

addition, an AML/CFT National Coordination Committee housed within the FIU is designed to coordinate AML activities. Corruption is the most prevalent predicate offence. Yet no money laundering case has ever been prosecuted. The stated reasons for this unsatisfactory position are a lack of understanding of the crime, poor implementation of the AML laws through lack of resources and poor allocation of existing resources.[75]

The Lesotho experience is in sharp contrast to that in Malawi where, as noted earlier, a highly effective investigation led by the Anti-Corruption Bureau in the Cashgate scandal resulted in numerous corrupt PEPs and their accomplices being convicted of money laundering.

The strategies explored in this chapter are designed to provide prosecutors and judges in Africa with additional practical tools with which to address money laundering cases involving PEPs more effectively. They do not require any new legislation nor impose any new burdens. Rather, they can facilitate money laundering investigations and prosecutions and thus help to bring more PEPs to justice and help recover the stolen assets.

A further extremely promising development is the willingness of other countries to prosecute African PEPs for money laundering. The Thiam case is an excellent example in which the former Minister of Mines in Guinea was convicted in a United States District Court of money laundering and sentenced to seven years' imprisonment together with a criminal forfeiture order of US$8.5 million.[76] The case of Teodorin Obiang provides another example. In 2020, Obiang, the son of the President of Equatorial Guinea lost his appeal before the Paris Court of Appeal against a 2017 conviction for embezzlement and money laundering of at least US$174 million from public funds. The court in Paris sentenced him to a suspended prison term of three years, a US$32.75 million fine and the seizure of his assets in France.[77] It is hoped that other countries will follow this lead.

---

[75] Namibia has recorded very few successful AML investigations and prosecutions.

[76] See Section 2.9 above.

[77] Significantly, the complainants in the case were two French-based CSOs, Transparency International France and SHERPA. See further Section 10.2.

10. Asset recovery in the African context

Asset recovery is a fundamental principle of the UNCAC.[1] In *National Director of Public Prosecutions v Mohamed NO*, the Constitutional Court of South Africa noted that 'it is now widely accepted in the international community that criminals should be stripped of the proceeds of their crimes, the purpose being to remove the incentive for crime, not to punish them'.[2]

This includes the forfeiture of the 'instrumentalities' of corruption or money laundering offences. In *National Director of Public Prosecutions v R O Cook Properties (Pty) Ltd* the Supreme Court of Appeal of South Africa considered that for property to be an 'instrumentality of an offence' within the meaning of the Prevention of Organised Crime Act 1998 'the determining question is whether there is a sufficiently close link between the property and its criminal use, and whether the property has a close enough relationship to the actual commission of the offence to render it an instrumentality. Every case will of course have to be decided on its own facts.'[3]

10.1 FREEZING THE ASSETS

Asset recovery depends upon the ability of AML authorities to freeze the suspected proceeds of crime both domestically and transnationally. This is reflected in FATF Recommendations 4 and 32 that require countries to adopt measures to enable their competent authorities to 'freeze or seize and confiscate ... (a) property laundered, (b) proceeds from, or instrumentalities used in or intended for use in money laundering or predicate offences, ... or (d) property of corresponding value'. This includes the confiscation of funds carried by cash couriers.

Such measures must include the authority to:

> (a) identify, trace and evaluate property that is subject to confiscation; (b) carry out provisional measures, such as freezing and seizing, to prevent any dealing, transfer

---

1 Article 51. Chapter V of UNCAC is devoted to 'Asset Recovery'. See also Article 16 of the AU Convention although this contains less detailed provisions relating to asset recovery.

2 2002 (4) SA 843 [15], per Ackermann J.

3 [2004] ZASCA 36, at [32]. For an example, see Section 8.4.2 above.

or disposal of such property; (c) take steps that will prevent or void actions that prejudice the country's ability to freeze or seize or recover property that is subject to confiscation; and (d) take any appropriate investigative measures.

The operation of freezing orders involving PEPs is usefully illustrated in the Kenyan case of *Asset Recovery Agency v Aboo.*[4] Section 82 of the Proceeds of Crime and Anti-Money Laundering Act 2009 permits the Director of the Asset Recovery Agency to make an ex parte application to a court for a preservation (freezing) order. The court must make the order if there are reasonable grounds to believe the property concerned is the proceeds of crime. This has the effect of prohibiting any person from dealing with the property.[5] Section 89 of the 2009 Act empowers the court to vary or rescind the order where the party seeking to do so satisfies the court that the order will deprive them of the means to provide for reasonable daily living expenses and that the hardship suffered outweighs the risk that the property will be concealed or transferred.

In the Aboo case itself, Mrs Aboo's husband, Alex Khisa, was a senior officer in the Kenya Revenue Authority (and therefore both were PEPs). It was suspected that he had made unauthorised deposits of almost KShs20 million into three bank accounts held in the name of Mrs Aboo. Preservation orders were therefore made in respect of the funds.

Given the constitutional implications, freezing orders should be granted by a court. This makes Presidential Executive Order 6 of 2018 on the 'Preservation of Assets Connected with Corruption and Order Related Offences' (EO6) in Nigeria of interest. Whilst the power of a court to make freezing orders is well established in Nigeria, section 1(c) of EO6 empowers the Attorney General of Nigeria to freeze assets suspected of being the proceeds of crime as an interim measures i.e. without a court order. In *Barr Ikenga Imo & Anor v President of the Federal Republic of Nigeria & Anor*,[6] the constitutionality of EO6 was challenged, in particular that it breached the plaintiff's right to a fair hearing[7] and right to acquire and own property anywhere in Nigeria.[8] Whilst upholding the constitutionality of EO6 itself, the court took the view that the Attorney General should first obtain a court order in all circumstances before blocking

---

4 [2018] eKLR.

5 The evidential facts 'need not answer to description of any specific offences of corrupt conduct provided they point to that probability': *Ethics and Anti-Corruption Commission v National Bank of Kenya* [2017] eKLR [40].

6 2018, Suit No.: FHC/ABJ/CS/740/2018, Federal High Court in Abuja.

7 Article 36(1) of the Constitution of Nigeria provides that 'In the determination of his civil rights and obligations, including any question or determination by or against any government or authority, a person shall be entitled to a fair hearing within a reasonable time by a court ...'.

8 Ibid, Article 43.

or freezing or confiscating such funds or assets pending the conclusion of an investigation or legal action. The application could be made ex parte and if the Court was satisfied by the averments or information contained in the application, the order may be granted. This would circumvent any allegation of a breach of the constitutional right to a fair hearing.[9] This is surely correct as it ensures that the separation of powers is maintained.[10]

Having frozen the suspect assets, the challenge then is to recover them. There are several approaches for doing so:

- conviction-based asset forfeiture;
- non-conviction-based asset forfeiture;
- civil recovery/private civil claims brought by states; and
- recovery via taxation.

In practice, a combination of criminal sanctions and civil remedies is often the most effective strategy for seeking to recover the proceeds of crime.

10.2 CONVICTION-BASED ASSET FORFEITURE

Article 31 of the UNCAC requires each State Party to take 'to the greatest extent possible within its legal system' the necessary measures to enable it to confiscate the proceeds of corruption and instrumentalities. Conviction-based asset forfeiture is one such measure. Here an order for the confiscation of the proceeds of corruption is made as part of the sentence following a criminal conviction. Depending on the statutory framework, the forfeiture order is either made against specific property (object-based) or the offender is ordered to pay a sum equal to the benefit derived from the corrupt conduct (value-based). As the issue of forfeiture arises post-conviction, the constitutional right to a fair trial and other protections for accused persons are not applicable and the complex rules of the admissibility of evidence in criminal cases in common law/Roman-Dutch law countries do not apply.[11]

---

[9] For a useful analysis of the judgment see Commentary by Unini Chioma, Recent decision in *Barr Ikenga Imo v The President* and the constitutionality of Order 6 of 2018, (18 October 2018) *The Nigerian Lawyer*.

[10] The court rejected that there was a breach of Article 43 as EO6 did not abrogate the right of a person to seek redress before a court.

[11] See *McIntosh v Lord Advocate* [2001] 3 WLR 107 at 114 and the discussion in *Walsh v Director of Asset Recovery Agency* [2005] NICA 6.

For example, in the *Karonga* case, following his conviction for money laundering, the prosecution obtained a confiscation order against two houses and five motor vehicles with a combined value of over MK76 million.[12]

Similarly, following the conviction for money laundering of Teodorin Obiang, in addition to a suspended prison sentence and fine, the French court also ordered the forfeiture of his assets in France. These included a mansion in Paris reputedly worth over US$100 million, numerous expensive vehicles, and jewellery and furniture worth over $US49 million. It remains to be seen whether any of these assets are returned to the people of Equatorial Guinea.

The need for a criminal conviction to bring such forfeiture proceedings into play emphasises the importance that in a 'corruption-related' case prosecutors must select the appropriate charge(s) which is most likely to lead to a conviction. Hence the inclusion of a parallel money laundering charge against a PEP is commendable.[13]

Even when this is done, the challenge of obtaining convictions in corruption/ AML-related cases discussed in earlier chapters means that the conviction route is not always a viable option. In addition, a prosecution becomes impossible where it is time-barred or the suspect has died, disappeared or has fled to a country that is not prepared and/or able to extradite him/her.[14]

10.3 NON-CONVICTION-BASED ASSET FORFEITURE

10.3.1 The Basics

The power of PEPs to undermine the criminal justice process coupled with the other practical challenges in conviction-based asset forfeiture creates the need to adopt alternative approaches. Introducing a system of non-conviction-based

[12] The application was filed under section 48 of the Money Laundering, Proceeds of Serious Crime and Terrorist Financing Act 2006. Following his conviction for money laundering in 2012, James Ibori was sentenced to 13 years' imprisonment but in addition the UK authorities brought confiscation proceedings for the recovery of the proceeds of corruption amounting to some £50 million.

[13] Alternatively a charge of failing to disclose assets and income against a PEP may be more realistic than seeking to prove that s/he accepted a bribe. This will also overcome double jeopardy arguments in systemic corruption cases: see *Kazinda v Attorney General of Uganda* (unreported, 2020).

[14] Although FATF Recommendation 39 states that countries must 'constructively and effectively execute extradition requests in relation to money laundering'.

asset forfeiture (NCBAF) is therefore of immense importance. This is reflected in FATF Recommendation 4, which states:

> Countries should [must] consider adopting measures that allow [laundered proceeds] to be confiscated without requiring a criminal conviction (non-conviction-based confiscation) or require an offender to demonstrate the lawful origin of property alleged to be liable to confiscation ...[15]

This is one of the few FATF Recommendations that is not binding and perhaps reflects the reluctance of some states to introduce such a provision.[16]

Here the proceedings are directed against specific property (*in rem*) that is believed to be the proceeds (or instrumentalities) of crime.[17]

The advantages of such an action are as follows:

- the proceedings are civil in nature and only the civil rules of evidence are applicable;
- a criminal conviction is not required before seeking the forfeiture of the proceeds of corruption;[18]
- a NCBAF order is available regardless of the outcome of any criminal proceedings, or indeed whether criminal proceedings have started;[19]
- the double jeopardy rule does not apply and therefore an action for a NCBAF order is available where an earlier criminal prosecution has been unsuccessful;
- retrospective NCBAF legislation does not contravene the right to a fair trial as it does not involve the 'determination of any criminal charge';[20]
- proof that the property constitutes the proceeds of corruption is established on a balance of probabilities;

---

15 Article 54(1) of the UNCAC also provides that each State Party shall 'Consider taking such measures as may be necessary to allow confiscation of property without a criminal conviction in cases in which the offender cannot be prosecuted by reason of death, flight or absence in appropriate cases'.

16 See Article 54(1)(c) of the UNCAC above. Article 16(1) of the AU Convention requires State Parties to introduce legislation to enable the 'confiscation of proceeds or property, the value of which corresponds to that of such proceeds' derived from convention offences.

17 This means that the 'defendant' in the action is the property sought to be forfeited: see the Obiang case in Section 10.3.4 below and the Jammeh case in Section 15.3.

18 *Lameck v President of Namibia* 2012(1) NR 255 (HC).

19 Ibid.

20 *Dassa Foundation v Liechtenstein*, ECHR, Judgment of 10 July 2007.

- any immunity from criminal prosecution enjoyed by a public official is not effective in a civil forfeiture action;[21] and
- NCBAF can be applied to the property of PEPs, their family members and close associates as well as PMLs who may well have fled the country thus making it impractical to prosecute them.

Countries must be able to respond to requests for assistance in NCBAF proceedings unless this is inconsistent with fundamental principles of domestic law. At a minimum this must be provided in circumstances where a perpetrator is unavailable by reason of death, flight, absence, or the perpetrator is unknown.[22]

Such cases are usually entrusted to a government prosecutorial agency, for example the National Director of Public Prosecutions in South Africa, or to an asset recovery agency.

10.3.2 NCBAF Orders in African Countries

An increasing number of African states have introduced provisions for the making of such orders into their domestic law.[23] Their potential impact is highlighted in a 2019 ESAAMLG report where four countries reported that assets worth over US$4 million were recovered.

The Financial Crimes Act 2017 (FICA) in Malawi neatly sets out the operation of such orders. Having traced the suspected proceeds of crime, a 'competent authority'[24] may apply ex parte to a court for a preservation order (often referred to as a freezing order).[25] The order is made if there are reasonable grounds to believe that the property constitutes proceeds of crime (or instrumentalities).[26] The competent authority must then give notice of the order to those with an interest within 21 days.[27] The order expires after 90 days unless there is an application for a forfeiture order or the order is rescinded.[28]

Upon giving notice of 14 days to those with an interest in the property, the competent authority may apply to a court for a forfeiture order relating to the property. An order for the transfer of the property is made if the court finds,

---

21 In some civil law states, the prosecution of the offence may be time-barred.

22 FATF Recommendation 38 and the Interpretive Note.

23 For example Eswatini, Malawi, Namibia, Seychelles, Zambia.

24 Widely defined to include law enforcement agencies, the Anti-Corruption Bureau and the Director of Public Prosecutions: see section 2(1) FICA.

25 FICA, section 65(1).

26 Ibid, section 65(2).

27 Ibid, section 66(1).

28 Ibid, section 67.

on the balance of probability, that it constitutes the proceeds of crime.[29] The property is then forfeited to the government and an Administrator appointed to oversee its disposal.[30]

10.3.3 NCBAF Orders: A Kenyan Case Study

Having secured a preservation/freezing order in the Aboo case, the Assets Recovery Agency then applied to the High Court of Kenya for a NCBAF order.[31] Section 92(1) of the Proceeds of Crime and Anti-Money Laundering Act 2009 permits the High Court to make a civil asset forfeiture order:

> if it finds on a balance of probabilities that the property concerned
> (a) has been used or is intended for use in the commission of an offence or;
> (b) is proceeds of crime.

In the case, Ong'udi J made a number of rulings of general importance:

- NCBAF proceedings are civil in nature.
- There is no need for the applicant to allege the commission of any specific offence but they must set out the matters that are alleged to constitute the particular kind or kinds of unlawful conduct by or in return for which the property was obtained.[32]
- Civil recovery proceedings are directed at the seizure of property and not convicting any individual and thus there is no reason to apply the criminal standard of proof.[33]
- The constitutional protection of property does not extend to any property found to have been unlawfully acquired.[34]

On the facts of the case, the court entered judgment in favour of the applicant and ordered that the funds be forfeited to the Government of Kenya.

A similar order was made in the case of *Asset Recovery Agency v Quorandum Limited and 2 others*, a case where the company had allegedly been used by a PEP to launder proceeds of crime from a government account.

---

[29] Ibid, section 74.

[30] Ibid, section 81.

[31] Under section 92 of the Proceeds of Crime and Anti-Money Laundering Act 2009.

[32] Approving the views of the court in *Director of Asset Recovery v Green* [2005] EWHC 3168.

[33] Applying the decision of the Court of Appeal of Kenya in *Asset Recovery Agency v Rowe*, unreported, Case 2012 HCV 02120.

[34] *Asset Recovery Agency v Aboo* [2017] eKLR [65] at [65]. See also *Lameck v President of Namibia* 2012(1) NR 255 (HC).

In making the order, Ong'undi J highlighted that such an order was designed to 'deprive criminals of [their] ill-gotten wealth and to act as a deterrence and prevention of crime (*sic*)'.[35]

10.3.4 Using NCBAF Orders Against PEPs Outside Africa

The fact that NCBAF orders can be made against the assets of PEPs in other countries is helpful particularly in circumstances where there is no political will to take action in the home state of the PEP. In addition the individual need not be in the jurisdiction.

An outstanding example comes from the United States where NCBAF proceedings were launched to recover assets worth more than US$32 million belonging to Teodorin Nguema Obiang, the son of the President of Equatorial Guinea and Vice-President. Given his status it was inconceivable that he would face prosecution in his home state.[36] In 2014 his criminal activities were described in a United States DoJ press release as follows:

> Through relentless embezzlement and extortion, Vice-President Nguema Obiang shamelessly looted his government and shook down businesses in his country to support his lavish life-style, while many of his fellow citizens lived in extreme poverty ... After raking in millions in bribes and kickbacks, Nguema Obiang embarked on a corruption-fueled spending spree in the United States.[37]

The Obiang case highlights the importance of states having the political will to deal with the laundering of the proceeds of crime by foreign PEPs. Thus even if the criminal prosecution/forfeiture route is not available,[38] the power to take

---

[35] [2018] eKLR, at [102]. See also *Shaik v State* [2008] ZACC 7 and *Uganda v Byandala* [2018] UGHCACD 1.

[36] The case bore the memorable title *United States v One Michael Jackson Signed Thriller Jacket and Other Michael Jackson Memorabilia; Real Property located on Sweetwater Mesu Road in Malibu, California; and One 2011 Ferrari 599GTO.* Obiang later entered into a settlement with the US Department of Justice to hand over these assets: see https://www.justice.gov/sites/default/files/press-releases/attachments/2014/10/10/obiang_settlement_agreement.pdf (accessed 4 June 2020). This point does not apply to other countries: see the discussion in Section 9.7 above.

[37] US Department of Justice Press Release, 10 October 2014. Available at https://www.justice.gov/opa/pr/second-vice-president-equatorial-guinea-agrees-relinquish-more-30-million-assets-purchased (accessed 29 November 2016). In a deal reached with the Swiss authorities, Obiang also agreed to the sale of his collection of 25 luxury cars. These were auctioned in October 2019 and realised a total of almost £22 million.

[38] As discussed in Chapter 9, the development of new strategies by prosecutors and judges may increase the chances of successful prosecutions of PEPs. In addition, note the successful prosecution of Obiang in a French court on money laundering charges: see Section 9.7.

away the profit from a PEP represents a powerful weapon in the armoury of those seeking to combat corruption and money laundering.

In 2012 civil forfeiture proceedings were launched in the United States, not against Obiang himself but against his assets located there which were suspected of being proceeds of crime.[39] This resulted in a civil forfeiture settlement with the DoJ in which Obiang agreed to sell his $30 million mansion located in Malibu, California, a Ferrari automobile and various items of Michael Jackson memorabilia purchased with the proceeds of corruption. Some of these proceeds of crime were to be returned to the people of Equatorial Guinea.[40]

Given the extent and impact of his corruption and money laundering activities over such a long period of time, effective action against a kleptocrat such as Obiang is essential. The civil forfeiture proceedings in the United States illustrate what can be done given the political will and the availability of effective legal tools to carry out the task.

10.4 UNEXPLAINED WEALTH ORDERS (UWOs)

10.4.1 Basic Principles

An UWO requires a person who has 'unexplained wealth' that is reasonably suspected of being the proceeds of crime to establish, on a balance of probabilities, that such property is not unexplained wealth. The order is designed to address doubtful sources of wealth by applying the maxim: 'You fail to satisfactorily explain the lawful source of your assets, you forfeit it.'[41]

An application for an UWO constitutes a civil proceeding against property. Accordingly, constitutional fair trial protections do not apply. They are a useful complement to NCBAF orders and are particularly useful in cases involving PEPs where their 'life-style' and assets appear disproportionate to their known income. Laws providing for UWOs are found in countries around

---

[39] See *United States v One Michael Jackson Signed Thriller Jacket and Other Michael Jackson Memorabilia; Real Property Located on Sweetwater Mesa Road in Malibu, California; One 2011 Ferrari 599 GTO*. The Stipulation and Settlement Agreement is available at https://www.justice.gov/sites/default/files/press-releases/attachments/2014/10/10/obiang_settlement_agreement.pdf (accessed 7 June 2020).

[40] The 10 October 2014 press release, above, explains that 'Of those proceeds, $20 million will be given to a charitable organization to be used for the benefit of the people of Equatorial Guinea. Another $10.3 million will be forfeited to the United States and will be used for the benefit of the people of Equatorial Guinea to the extent permitted by law.'

[41] See *Amuti v Kenya Anti-Corruption Commission*, [2019] eKLR at [2]. I am grateful to Philip Kagucia of the Kenyan Ethics and Anti-Corruption Commission for drawing my attention to the case.

the world with Australia and Ireland being notable examples. In fact, Kenya is one of the first countries to introduce such orders and the application of the relevant legislation provides a useful case study. More recently, Mauritius has also enacted legislation providing for UWOs and this is considered below.

10.4.2 Unexplained Assets: A Kenyan Case Study

The Anti-Corruption and Economic Crimes Act 2003 (the ACECA) in Kenya provides a court with the power to confiscate 'unexplained assets' (a power akin to an UWO). These refer to the assets of a person:

> (a) acquired at or around the time the person was reasonably suspected on corruption or economic crime; and
> (b) whose value is disproportionate to [their] known income at or around that time and for which there is no reasonable explanation.[42]

In *Amuti v Kenya Anti-Corruption Commission*[43] the appellant, Mr Amuti, challenged an order made by the High Court of Kenya for the forfeiture of unexplained assets held by him. The decision of the Court of Appeal provides a useful overview of the process.

The Kenya ACC (now the Ethics and Anti-Corruption Commission of Kenya)[44] (the Commission) is empowered by notice in writing to require a person who is reasonably suspected of corruption or economic crime to provide information regarding unexplained assets. As the Court noted, this is a civil recovery mechanism and the information obtained cannot be used in criminal proceedings against the person.[45] If after an investigation the Commission is satisfied that the person has unexplained assets and that the person has been afforded a reasonable opportunity to explain the disproportion between the assets concerned and their known legitimate sources of income and the Commission is not satisfied that they have provided an adequate explanation it may commence proceedings against the person by way of an originating summons.[46] The Commission bears the evidential burden of satisfying the court that the person has unexplained assets. The person is then required

---

[42] Section 2.

[43] [2019] eKLR.

[44] The Kenya Anti-Corruption Commission was replaced pursuant to Article 79 of the Constitution of Kenya 2010.

[45] Amuti, at [5] and referring to section 30 ACECA.

[46] See section 55 ACECA.

to satisfy the court that the assets were acquired otherwise than as a result of corrupt conduct or economic crime.[47]

The court noted that Mr Amuti had been given an opportunity to explain the source of the assets and thus his right to a fair hearing under Article 50 of the Constitution of Kenya had not been violated.[48] On the facts, the court was not satisfied with his explanation, and therefore upheld the order of the lower court that required Mr Amuti to pay to the Kenyan government the value of the unexplained assets.

In its ruling, the Court of Appeal noted that the Kenyan legislation was akin to section 362A of the UK Proceeds of Crime Act 2002 in that it also focused on assets being disproportionate to an individual's known legitimate sources of income.[49] The court then considered the argument of Mr Amuti that the process violated his presumption of innocence. This was rejected, the court holding that only the evidential burden was placed on Mr Amuti and then only after the Commission had satisfied the court that he had unexplained assets. In reality, it is surprising that the court addressed this point at all. As it noted, the 'unexplained assets' procedure was a species of NCBAF and was an *in rem* action i.e. aimed at the property itself.[50] There was therefore no 'accused person' whose constitutional rights were in issue. Perhaps a more useful argument might focus on the fact that the seriousness of the allegation required the Commission to produce more 'cogent evidence' to support its case.[51]

Another argument raised by Mr Amuti that the order contravened his constitutional protection of the right to property was rejected, the Court noting that there was no such violation if an individual is requested to explain the source of any income disproportionate to the legitimate source of income. Further the right did not extend to any property 'found to have been unlawfully acquired' and, in any event, such interference was proportionate in that it struck a 'fair balance'.[52]

The Amuti case is an excellent illustration of the importance of unexplained wealth/assets orders and the legislation provides a model for other African countries.[53]

---

47 I.e. 'conduct that constitutes corruption or economic crime': section 55(1)(a) ACECA.

48 See the comment below on this point.

49 *Amuti*, at [71].

50 Ibid, at [78].

51 See for example, the views of Lord Carswell in *In re Doherty* [2008] 1 WLR 1499 at [26].

52 At [73] noting the decision of the England and Wales High Court in *National Crime Agency v A [Aliyeva]*, [2018] EWHC 2354.

53 See also Chapter IIIA of the Money Laundering and Proceeds of Crime (Amendment) Act 2019 (Zimbabwe) which contains similar provisions.

10.4.3 UWOs in Mauritius

In Mauritius, UWOs are provided for in the Good Governance and Integrity Reporting Act 2015. The Act establishes a powerful Integrity Reporting Services Agency (the Agency) which can require a person (the respondent) to establish that any property is not 'unexplained wealth'. This is defined as including any property:

> (a) under the ownership of a person to an extent which is disproportionate to [their] emoluments and other income;
> (b) the ownership, possession custody or control of which cannot be satisfactorily accounted for by the person who owns, possesses, has custody or control of the property; or
> (c) held by a person for another person to an extent which is disproportionate to the emoluments or other income of that other person.

As well as carrying out its own investigations, other government agencies, such as the Mauritius FIU, Independent Commission Against Corruption and the Mauritius Revenue Authority, have a duty to report to the Agency when there are reasonable grounds to suspect a person has acquired unexplained wealth.[54] The matter is then referred to the Integrity Reporting Board which makes the decision as to whether to seek an UWO. If so, an application is made to a judge in chambers. This is a civil proceeding with the onus on the respondent to establish, on a balance of probabilities, that any property is not unexplained wealth. If granted, and the order is not the subject of an appeal, the property in question is confiscated and vests in the Agency.[55]

The statute goes further than the Kenyan equivalent in that the UWO is made on the ground that the respondent cannot 'satisfactorily account' for their 'ownership, custody or control'. There is no requirement for 'reasonable grounds to suspect' that the property in question constitutes unexplained wealth. Indeed the Constitution of Mauritius was also amended to specifically permit the confiscation of property by way of an UWO in such circumstances.[56]

The 2015 Act provides another example of the tension between providing adequate powers to take away the proceeds of crime of PEPs and their enjoyment of constitutional rights. Whilst the introduction of UWOs is com-

---

54 Section 9 Good Governance and Integrity Reporting Act 2015.

55 Ibid, section 16.

56 Constitution (Amendment) Act No. 30 of 2015 introduced a new Article 8(4)(aa).

mendable, there is a concern that the Mauritian approach provides inadequate protection for PEPs.[57]

10.4.4 Overview

UWOs are a relatively new mechanism for attacking the proceeds of crime of PEPs, albeit that Kenya was one of the first to introduce such orders. As with NCBAF orders, by focusing on the assets, they can provide AML authorities with an effective and efficient means to recover the proceeds of crime, particularly as no predicate offence needs to be established. However, a word of caution is necessary. Proving that the assets are 'disproportionate to an individual's known legitimate sources of income' (as required in Kenya) or are under the 'ownership, custody or control' of a specific PEP (as in Mauritius) may well be challenging. This is because of the ability of PEPs to conceal 'unexplained wealth' both through establishing complex off-shore companies and the misuse of beneficial ownership. This means that domestic investigating authorities may still face significant legal challenges in seeking to link the proceeds of crime with a PEP.[58] This emphasises the urgent need for transparency in the beneficial ownership of off-shore companies, trusts and foundations.[59]

10.5 CIVIL LAW ACTIONS

10.5.1 Bringing a Civil Action in a Foreign Jurisdiction: The Chiluba Case[60]

Article 53 of the UNCAC requires State Parties to take the necessary measures 'to permit another State Party to initiate civil action in its courts to establish title to or ownership of property acquired' through the commission of a convention offence, including money laundering. Thus the object of a civil

---

[57] For a helpful critique of the Act see Shalini Soopramanien, Explaining the unexplained wealth orders: (Mauritius) Good Governance and Integrity Reporting Act 2015, (2018) 39(1) *Statute Law Review* 46.

[58] For a disturbing example of such challenges see *National Crime Agency v Baker* [2020] EWHC Civ (Admin) 822. The case involved high-value real estate in London registered in the name of a Panamanian foundation named the Villa Magna Foundation and which was registered under the Private Interest Foundation Law of Panama. Here the beneficial ownership of the property was particularly opaque: indeed sufficient for the court to find the evidence of ownership submitted by the National Crime Agency unreliable and accordingly to discharge the unexplained wealth order.

[59] See further the discussion in Chapter 12.

[60] The case is reported as *Attorney-General for Zambia v Meer Care & Desai* [2007] EWHC 952 (hereinafter 'Meer Care').

recovery claim is to recover illegally obtained funds, no matter where in the world they are located with the action being brought against all those allegedly involved in the misconduct.[61] The Chiluba case neatly illustrates the operation of such actions.

In 2003 the Attorney General of Zambia (AGZ) commenced proceedings in the England and Wales High Court alleging that former President Frederick Chiluba had conspired with senior Zambian public officials and others to misappropriate government funds and launder them through a London bank. The case demonstrates several significant procedural features of civil recovery claims.

Firstly, the plaintiff is generally able to choose the jurisdiction in which to bring the action.[62] Thus the AGZ chose to bring the case in the England and Wales High Court because some of the 'significant defendants' were based in the United Kingdom and 'due to the close nexus [of the case] with London[63] as well as the advantage of having orders that could be enforced because they were made in an English court rather than a Zambian court'.[64] Secondly, the action can be brought against a range of defendants. Thus in the Chiluba case the defendants included the former Zambian President, senior Zambian public officials, two firms of London solicitors together with individual partners therein, a number of companies registered in the BVI and Luxembourg, as well as Boutique Basile, a tailoring business in Geneva.[65]

Thirdly, the defendants do not need to be in the jurisdiction. For example, in the Chiluba case several of the defendants were facing criminal charges in Zambia and, as part of their bail conditions, had been required to surrender their passports. It was therefore not possible for them to attend the civil trial in London. Here the trial judge, Peter Smith J, adopted the imaginative approach of offering to go to Zambia to hear their evidence live in court as a 'special examiner' as well as having the rest of the proceedings take place by way of a live video link. Fourthly, such proceedings can also run parallel to criminal proceedings. This was the position in the Chiluba case and raised concerns over the privilege against self-incrimination. In a significant ruling, the trial judge directed that the civil proceedings be 'ring fenced' so that the 'material deployed in the civil trial and the evidence given and the arguments arising

---

[61] For a detailed examination of civil forfeiture, see Colin Nicholls et al., *Corruption and Misuse of Public Office*, 2nd edn., Oxford University Press 2011, chapter 7.

[62] The key test is which jurisdiction has the most and substantial connection with the dispute: see Nicholls et al., *Corruption and Misuse*, para 8.101.

[63] Large amounts of the allegedly stolen monies were passed through accounts held by them onward to other destinations both in Europe and elsewhere.

[64] Meer Care at pp. 15–16.

[65] Boutique Basile supplied Chiluba with clothing worth over US$1 million.

out of it would not be disclosed to any other person or used by AGZ for any purpose in the criminal or other proceedings without permission'.[66] The procedure adopted to find and secure the assets is also of considerable interest. As the system of MLA only operates as regards criminal matters, the ability to track down the proceeds of crime in a civil case is a major undertaking, particularly where the assets are located in a number of different jurisdictions. In the Chiluba case, the AGZ retained a specialist firm of chartered accountants to assist in tracing the monies paid into the London bank account and its subsequent disbursement abroad. Whilst an expensive and, as the court noted, an extremely difficult and complicated exercise,[67] as a result, stolen assets were located in numerous jurisdictions around the world.

In order to secure the defendants' assets, the next step is often to seek a freezing order which secures the defendant's assets and will usually be declared to be worldwide in serious cases.[68] This is facilitated by the power of the court to make search and seizure orders via the use of Anton Piller orders (or equivalent)[69] as well as pre-action disclosure under the principles developed in *Norwich Pharmacal v Customs and Excise Commissioners*[70] and *Bankers Trust v Shapiro*.[71] In appropriate cases, an application may also be made to the court using the *Shapiro* procedure for an order that the police disclose to the plaintiffs all relevant evidence obtained by means of MLA in connection with their criminal investigations.[72]

[66] Meer Care at [21]. See also the views of the Constitutional Court of South Africa in *Prophet v National Director of Public Prosecutions* [2006] ZACC 17; 2007 (2) BCLR 140 (CC); 2006 (2) SACR 525 (CC); 2007 (6) SA 169.

[67] Meer Care at [54].

[68] Thus as regards England and Wales, Rule 25.1(1)(f) of the Civil Procedure Rules states that a court may grant a 'freezing injunction' (1) restraining a party removing from the jurisdiction assets located there; or (2) restraining a party from dealing with any assets whether located within the jurisdiction or not. The freezing injunction is also widely known elsewhere as a *Mareva* injunction (see *Mareva Compania Naviera SA v International Bulk Carriers SA*, [1980] 1 All ER 21).

[69] The conditions for the making of such orders were set out by Ackermann J in *National Director of Public Prosecutions v Mohamed NO* [2003] ZACC 843 as the following: '(1) That he, the applicant, has a cause of action against the respondent which he intends to pursue; (2) that the respondent has in his possession specific (and specified) documents or things which constitute vital evidence in substantiation of applicant's cause of action (but in respect of which applicant cannot claim a real or personal right); and (3) that there is a real and well-founded apprehension that this evidence may be hidden or destroyed or in some manner be spirited away by the time the case comes to trial or to the stage of discovery' at [30].

[70] [1974] AC 175.

[71] [1980] 1 WLR 1274.

[72] This was not necessary in the Chiluba case. However, it was vital in the case of Alamieyeseigha for it enabled Nigeria to secure and recover the proceeds of corruption via civil proceedings, see Section 11.1 below.

The final step is to seek the recovery of the assets themselves. In the Chiluba case, the trial judge found that Chiluba and six of his associates all actively participated in a series of conspiracies against the Republic of Zambia and a judgment was entered against them ordering them to pay back the misappropriated funds.

10.5.2 Civil Actions in the Domestic Setting

Under Article 35 of UNCAC, States Parties are required to take such measures as may be necessary

> to ensure that entities or persons who have suffered damage as a result of an act of corruption have the right to initiate legal proceedings against those responsible for that damage in order to obtain compensation.

In practice there are a range of civil remedies that can be employed by both the state and individuals[73] against PEPs who are involved in corruption and money laundering. For example, any bribes moneys which are received are, technically, held in trust for the state. This enables the state to sue the official for the full amount of the value of the bribes that he or she has received. It can also make an equitable claim for compensation for breach of fiduciary duty.[74]

Civil remedies offer a range of advantages, including, firstly, that they require a lower standard of proof; secondly, there are less onerous rules relating to the admissibility of evidence; thirdly, that a range of persons and corporate entities can be targeted as defendants; and finally, that they are relatively easy to start and can be brought by individuals, companies and the state.

10.6 RECOVERY VIA TAXATION

Some states also have legislation providing for the non-conviction-based power to secure the tax on an individual's or company's income, profits or gains where there are reasonable grounds to suspect these were accrued from criminal conduct on the part of that person. This is a strategy that African coun-

---

[73] The wording of Article 35 of UNCAC includes states as well as legal and natural persons: see UN, *Report of the* Ad Hoc *Committee for the Negotiation of a Convention against Corruption on the work of its first to seventh sessions* 2003 [37].

[74] For a full discussion on private civil recovery mechanisms see Nicholls et al., *Corruption and Misuse*, at [9.01] et seq. See also Simon N M Young, Why civil actions against corruption? (2009) *Journal of Financial Crime* 144.

tries may wish to adopt as it enables the tax authority to make the assessment simply on the grounds that it cannot ascertain the source of the PEP's income.[75]

10.7 GIVE US BACK OUR MONEY: RETURNING THE PROCEEDS OF CRIME

The return of the assets looted by PEPs to the victim country is a vital final step in the recovery process. Article 57(3)(c) of the UNCAC specifically provides that as a general principle 'priority consideration should be given to returning the confiscated property to the requesting States party, returning the property to its prior legitimate owners or compensating the victims of the crime'. The various asset recovery mechanisms discussed earlier should now help facilitate this process.[76]

Given the vast assets held by corrupt African PEPs in facilitating and safe haven states, their return is a matter of the highest priority. As the Nigerian President, Muhammadu Buhari, neatly put it at an anti-corruption conference in London in 2016: 'Give us back our money'. There is certainly some merit in the argument that as these assets belong to a sovereign state, it alone is entitled to determine how they are utilised. Yet returning such assets unconditionally raises concerns that they may be looted again by the very PEPs who originally laundered them or who may use them to otherwise benefit themselves and their families. This raises the sensitive issue of whether there is a need to provide for a 'responsible' or 'accountable' return process in which the returning country requires transparency (or even a decision-making/oversight role) in the way in which the assets are to be utilised in the victim country. The Obiang case highlights the point. The 'deal' struck by Obiang with the Swiss authorities involved an agreement that the proceeds from the sale of his luxury cars would be repatriated to Equatorial Guinea via donations to charity. A similar agreement was reached with the US Department of Justice regarding his assets located in the United States. Yet given the fact that Obiang's father is the long-time President of the country, it remains unclear as to whether and, if so, how in practice these assets will be used for the benefit of the people of Equatorial Guinea.

It follows that there is a strong argument that the 'Give us back our money' approach must be accompanied by transparency and accountability in order to counter any further corrupt acts and money laundering by PEPs. This requires negotiations between the returning and victim countries as to how the assets

---

75 See for example, sections 317 and 319 Proceeds of Crime Act 2002 (UK).

76 This is supported by the UNODC/World Bank 'Stolen Assets Recovery (StAR) Initiative' which is designed to assist victim states in their recovery efforts.

are to be returned and how they are to be used for the benefit of the people. Such negotiations must be transparent and inclusive and thus involve representatives of the returning state as well as the widest range of representatives of government, political leaders, civil society and the media from the victim country. Ideally any resultant agreement must provide that the assets are held in a trust fund or foundation for the benefit of the people of the country. At least when significant sums are involved, it is advisable that such an agreement should include a requirement for outside and ongoing monitoring of the use of the funds. This might be undertaken by representatives of the returning state or the World Bank or similar institution.[77]

10.8 TOWARDS A COMMON AFRICAN POSITION ON ASSET RECOVERY

In recent years the AU has taken significant steps to strengthen asset recovery. Following the 2015 Report of the High Level Panel on Illicit Financial Flows, headed by Thabo Mbeki, in the AU Assembly *Special Declaration on Illicit Financial Flows*, African countries resolved to enhance asset recovery mechanisms with a view to ensuring the return of the laundered funds to the member states. The work is on-going. It is supported by the adoption of the *Nouakchott Declaration on the African Anti-Corruption Year* in 2018, in which member states committed to 'progressively' abolish bank secrecy jurisdictions, establish public beneficial ownership registers and declare their assets. This work has led to the convening of the 3rd edition of the AU African Anti-Corruption Dialogue on the theme 'Towards a Common African Position on Asset Recovery'.[78] This will bring together all sections of society, both private and public, to address the issue. Clearly, the discussion in this chapter can make a significant contribution to the debate.

---

[77] A useful example of a structured return process is set out in the Swiss Federal Act on the Freezing and the Restitution of Illicit Assets held by Foreign Politically Exposed Persons (Foreign Illicit Assets Act) (Law No. 196.1). The Act is helpfully reviewed by François Membrez and Matthieu Hösli in *How to Return Stolen Assets: The Swiss Policy Pathway* 2020, Centre for Civil and Political Rights.

[78] See African Union Advisory Board on Corruption, *Concept note of the 3rd Edition of the African Anti-Corruption Dialogue on the Theme 'Towards a Common African Position on Asset Recovery'*, Arusha, 2019.

11. PEPs and the use and abuse of the constitutional power of pardon

11.1 INTRODUCTION[1]

In 2013 the then President of Nigeria, Goodluck Jonathan, granted a pardon to the former Bayelsa State governor, Diepriye Alamieyeseigha, who had been convicted of a series of corruption and money laundering-related offences. The ostensible reason given was that the pardon was in the 'public interest' and for the welfare of the people of the Niger delta. Others took a very different view, arguing that, amongst others, the pardon was granted for purely political gain.[2]

The presidential power of pardon (which forms part of the prerogative of mercy) is enshrined in the constitutions of all Anglophone African states.

Its exercise is often controversial and one that can have very serious constitutional and political implications. As the Alamieyeseigha case highlights, this arises especially in cases involving PEPs who have been convicted (or are accused) of corruption and/or money laundering.

This chapter explores the scope of the presidential power of pardon and its use and potential abuse by PEPs. In doing so, it reviews the provisions in the African Constitutions.[3] It then critically analyses the adequacy of the constitutional post-convictions safeguards as well as the problem of pre-emptive pardons.

---

[1] This chapter is based on a chapter in Charles Fombad and Nico Steytler (eds), *Corruption and Constitutionalism in Africa: Revisiting Control Measures and Strategies*, Oxford University Press, 2020. Reproduced with the permission of the publisher.

[2] Jonathan had previously been deputy to Alamieyeseigha when the latter was serving as Governor of Bayelsa State: see, for example, the critical comment 'Alamieyeseigha: Unpardonable Pardon' in *Vanguard* 23 March 2013. For a more detailed analysis of the case see Z Adangor, The Presidential Pardon granted to Chief DSP Alamieyeseigha, (2015) 39 *Journal of Law, Policy and Globalization* 178.

[3] These are mostly based on the Westminster export model constitution and, although much amended or replaced, still share a similar structure. Examples are drawn from Ghana, Kenya, Malawi, Namibia, Nigeria, South Africa, Uganda, Zambia and Zimbabwe. However, the chapter does not consider the constitutional position in each state: see further Section 6.2 above.

11.2 RATIONALE FOR THE PRESIDENTIAL POWER OF PARDON

In *President of the Republic of South Africa v Hugo*[4] Goldstone J in the Constitutional Court of South Africa noted with approval the words of Holmes J in *Biddle v Perovich*:[5]

> A pardon in our days is not a private act of grace from an individual happening to possess power. *It is part of the Constitutional scheme.* When granted it is the determination of the ultimate authority that the public welfare will be better served by inflicting less than what the judgment fixed. (emphasis added)[6]

In his authoritative work *Commonwealth and Colonial Law*, Roberts-Wray states that the

> essence of the Prerogative [of Mercy] is that it enables justice to be done by giving due weight to factors which have not been taken into account by the Courts, because they are not relevant to the legal issues, or not admissible in evidence or have come to light after legal proceedings have terminated.[7]

This echoes the well-known words of Taft CJ in *Ex p Grossman* who emphasised that such a power exists: 'to afford relief from undue harshness or evident mistake in the operation or the enforcement of the criminal law. The administration of justice by the courts is not necessarily always wise or certainly considerate of circumstances which may properly mitigate guilt'. Accordingly 'it has always been thought essential ... to vest in some authority other than the courts the power to ameliorate or avoid particular criminal judgments'.[8]

The power to grant a full pardon is thus seen as being designed to provide a 'safety net' for those convicted of criminal offences in a wide range of circumstances especially where some error or oversight by the courts or other miscarriage of justice has occurred or on humanitarian grounds. It is an essential constitutional tool and, as Duker notes, it provides the head of the executive with the gift of 'benevolence'.[9] However, this 'apparently benign gift'[10]

---

4 [1997] ZACC 4; 1997 (6) BCLR 708; 1997 (4) SA 1 at [24].

5 (1927) 274 US 480.

6 Ibid, at p. 486.

7 Sir Kenneth Roberts-Wray, *Commonwealth and Colonial Law*, Sweet & Maxwell, 1966, p. 341.

8 (1925) 267 US 87, 120.

9 William F Duker, The President's power to pardon: a constitutional history, (1977) 18 *William and Mary Law Review* 475.

10 Ibid, at p. 475.

has the potential to be a tool for the abuse of power where it is utilised to protect corrupt PEPs for political motives and accordingly undermines the criminal justice process.

11.3 DEVELOPMENT OF THE PRESIDENTIAL POWER OF PARDON: ISSUES OF USE AND ABUSE

11.3.1 Use of the Power

The power itself is an ancient one going back at least to the Code of Hammurabi. For common law countries, it has an ancient English heritage with the prerogative of mercy being traceable back to Anglo-Saxon times. It was then used extensively over the centuries by English monarchs and as the colonial Empire expanded, so the pardoning power followed.[11] During the colonial period the prerogative of mercy was exercisable by the governor of the territory in the name, and on behalf, of the British monarch. In the exercise of this power the governor was obliged to consider the advice of the Executive Council, which comprised a majority of government officers,[12] but was to 'make his decision according to his own deliberate judgment'.[13]

It was the practice in colonial legislation to specify the various forms of clemency.[14] Thus the colonial governor had the discretion to:

(a) grant to any person concerned in the commission of any offence for which *he may be tried* in the [territory] or to any person convicted of an offence in any court in the territory a pardon, either free or subject to lawful conditions;
(b) grant to any person a respite ... of the execution of any sentence ...;
(c) substitute a less severe form of punishment;

---

[11] For a helpful historical overview, see Andrew Novak, *Comparative Executive Clemency: The Constitutional Pardon Power and the Prerogative of Mercy in Global Perspective*, Routledge, 2016, especially chapter 2.

[12] The Executive Council was presided over by the Governor with the majority being government officers as *ex officio* and nominated official members: see further Roberts-Wray, *Commonwealth and Colonial Law*, pp. 317–18.

[13] See Roberts-Wray, *Commonwealth and Colonial Law*, p. 343. There were no female Governors.

[14] As Sebba points out, a 'pardon' can cover a free pardon; full pardon; conditional pardon; commutation, remission, reprieve, respite, amnesty; clemency; or mercy. Leslie Sebba, The pardoning power: a world survey, (1977) 68 *Journal of Criminal Law and Criminology* 83, at 116.

(d) remit the *whole or part of any sentence or any penalty or forfeiture* otherwise due to Her Majesty on account of any offence in respect of which a person has been convicted (emphasis added).[15]

The italicised words highlight the fact that the power extended not only to post-conviction pardons but also to pre-emptive pardons, i.e. where criminal proceedings have not yet commenced or been concluded, and also to the return of property forfeited as part of the sentence.

11.3.2 Abuse of the Power

There are numerous modern examples of cases where the power has been utilised to benefit PEPs, allegedly for improper purposes. The case of Marcellino Pipite (hereafter the Pipite case) in Vanuatu provides a striking example of several issues involving PEPs which are of direct relevance to African states.

Section 38 of the Constitution of Vanuatu provides that the President of the Republic 'may pardon, commute or reduce a sentence imposed on a person convicted of an offence'. In October 2015 Mr Pipite, the then Speaker of Parliament, and 14 other MPs (each of whom were members of the government) were convicted of corruption and the bribery of officials,[16] the Supreme Court of Vanuatu having found that they had accepted bribes from the opposition to support a vote of no confidence. At the time, the State President was out of the country and in his absence Mr Pipite was appointed Acting President until his return. In this capacity he proceeded to grant a presidential pardon to himself and 10 of the other parliamentarians claiming it was to 'maintain stability in the Government of the Republic of Vanuatu'.[17] Upon his return, the President immediately rescinded the pardons.

The case highlights the potential for abuse and the need for effective constitutional and judicial constraints on the exercise of the power of pardon. In particular, firstly, whether once granted a pardon can validly be revoked; secondly, whether a President can grant him/herself a pardon; and thirdly, whether, and if so in what the circumstances, a court can review the exercise of the power of pardon.[18]

---

15 See The Gambia Royal Instructions, 1962, cl 12.

16 Contrary to section 73 of the Penal Code.

17 Pardon dated 10 October 2015 (*Gazette* No. 87).

18 The saga is set out in *Pipite and Others v Public Prosecutor* Court of Appeal of the Republic of Vanuatu decision dated 7 April 2017. Available at https://courts.gov.vu/bi/services/downloads/file/79-criminal-appeal-case-583-of-2017-pipite-v-public-prosecutor (accessed 7 June 2020). For a background to the case, see Miranda Forsyth, 'Fourteen Jailed: Politics and Justice in Vanuatu' ANU Briefing Paper, 2015/65.

How the current constitutional constraints operate in practice in Anglophone African states now needs to be considered.

11.4 CONSTITUTIONAL CONSTRAINTS ON THE EXERCISE OF THE PRESIDENTIAL POWER: THE POSITION POST-CONVICTION

The granting of a pardon to a convicted person strikes at the independence of the judiciary, for the criminal justice system is nullified when that person is freed by presidential order and the legislature is powerless to reverse the decision. Thus it is always an extraordinary process.

This highlights the need for effective constitutional safeguards on the exercise of the power for otherwise it becomes a significant weapon in the hands of the President. In fact the issue of the need for a check on its exercise was a hotly debated topic at the Philadelphia Convention in 1797. However, a motion that any pardon required the approval of the Senate failed[19] and as a result Article II s 2(1) of the Constitution of the United States simply provides that '[t]he President ... shall have Power to grant Reprieves and Pardons for Offenses against the United States, except in Cases of Impeachment'. Thus the power of the United States President to grant a pardon is a rare example of the failure in the United States Constitution to incorporate any check or balance on the exercise of executive power. Further it appears that the power may be exercised before, during or after any criminal proceedings, i.e. providing for both a pre-emptive pardon and a post-conviction pardon. This was highlighted in 1974 with the granting to former President Richard Nixon by the US President Gerald R Ford of a 'full, free and absolute' pardon ... for all offences against the United States which he, Richard Nixon, has committed or may have committed or taken part in ...'.[20] Further, it raises the possibility of a 'blanket' or open pardon for PEPs and this is considered in Section 11.9 below.

Available at http://bellschool.anu.edu.au/sites/default/files/publications/attachments/2016-07/ib2015.65_forsyth.pdf (accessed 7 June 2020).

[19] The discussion on the issue is neatly summarised by Duker, The President's power to pardon, at 501 et seq.

[20] Presidential Proclamation 4311, 1974, 39 Fed Reg 32601-02. According to President Ford, the reason for doing so was to 'change our national focus ... to shift attention from the pursuit of a fallen President to the pursuit of the urgent needs of a rising nation': referred to by Duker, The President's power to pardon, at 531.

The African Constitutions all vest the prerogative of mercy in the President. Section 53 of the Constitution of Botswana provides a typical example. The President may:

> (a) grant to any person convicted of any offence a pardon, either free or subject to lawful conditions;
> (b) grant to any person a respite, either indefinite or for a specified period, of the execution of any punishment imposed on that person for any offence;
> (c) substitute a less severe form of punishment for any punishment imposed on any person for any offence; and
> (d) remit the whole or part of any punishment imposed on any person for any offence or of any penalty or forfeiture otherwise due to the Government on account of any offence.

The powers in section 53 are almost identical to those enjoyed by colonial governors save for one key exception: the granting of a pardon is limited to those convicted of a criminal offence. A virtually identical provision to section 53 appears in most of the African Constitutions.[21] Seemingly, constitutional drafters have been content to retain the original colonial provisions minus the pre-emptive pardon power, although even this is included in the Constitution of Nigeria.[22]

In practice, whilst the powers under paragraphs (b), and (c) are frequently used by Presidents for a range of purposes and a range of individuals,[23] the following discussion will focus on the exercise of the power in paragraph (a), i.e. to grant a full/free pardon and the power to remit any penalty or forfeiture to a PEP found in paragraph (d).

---

[21] Section 89(2) of the Constitution of Malawi contains a much shorter formulation: 'The President may pardon convicted offenders, grant stays of execution of sentence, reduce sentences, or remit sentences'. The Constitution of Kenya (Article 133(1)) and the Constitution of Zambia (Article 97(1)) contain slightly different formulations but are to the same effect as section 53.

[22] See section 175(1) Constitution of Nigeria. The Constitution of the Gambia omits any reference to the power to remit the forfeiture of property: see section 82(1).

[23] The prerogative of mercy is often utilised to release prisoners under an amnesty (for example, Independence Day or Africa Day) or where the beneficiaries have committed minor criminal offences. A pardon may be granted to individuals on humanitarian grounds: see for example, *R v Soko and Kapecha* [2010] MWHC 2 and Bradley Demone, LGBT rights in Malawi: one step back, two steps forward? The case of *R v Steven Monjeza Soko and Tiwonge Chimbalanga Kachepa*, (2016) 60(3) *Journal of African Law* 365.

11.5 REVIEWING THE EXERCISE OF THE PRESIDENTIAL PARDON: THE ROLE OF THE CONSTITUTIONAL REVIEW BODIES

Given the potential for an 'abuse of benevolence', there is an obvious need to introduce effective constraints on the exercise of the power based on the principles of transparency, administrative justice and accountability. All the African Constitutions provide for a review body although these vary widely both as regards composition and role.

11.5.1 Composition of the Review Body

The African Constitutions adopt one of two approaches to the review process. The minority require the involvement of the Cabinet or Council of State. In Zimbabwe the President may exercise the power 'after consultation with the Cabinet'[24] whilst in Nigeria and Ghana the President exercises his/her power after consultation with the Council of State.[25] In the case of Nigeria, the President is the Chair of the Council and the Vice-President is the deputy Chair.[26] In Ghana, members of the Council are appointed by the President in consultation with Parliament and comprise a range of serving and former senior public officials together with 11 'other members appointed by the President'.[27] Presidential influence means that this approach offers only a limited prospect of an independent review.

The majority of the African Constitutions provide for a separate Advisory Committee on the prerogative of mercy, although there is a wide variation as to its composition. In most constitutions the membership of the Committee is entirely a matter for President. For example in Uganda the Advisory Committee consists of the Attorney General and six 'prominent citizens of Uganda appointed by the President',[28] whilst in The Gambia the membership comprises three persons appointed by the President.[29] Remarkably, in Zambia

---

[24] Article 112(1) Constitution of Zimbabwe.

[25] See section 175(2) Constitution of Nigeria and Article 72(1) Constitution of Ghana.

[26] The other members comprise former Presidents of the Federation and all former Heads of the Government of the Federation; all former Chief Justices of Nigeria; the President of the Senate; the Speaker of the House of Representatives; all the Governors of the states of the Federation; and the Attorney General of the Federation: see Third Schedule, Part 1 para. 5 Constitution of Nigeria.

[27] Article 72(1) Constitution of Ghana.

[28] Article 121(1) Constitution of Uganda.

[29] Section 89(2) Constitution of The Gambia.

the Advisory Committee consists of members 'appointed by the President' who hold office at the pleasure of the President[30] but no details are released as to its membership.[31] In Botswana the composition of the Advisory Committee on the prerogative of mercy is something of a hybrid with the President presiding over the committee with its membership consisting of (a) the Vice-President or a minister appointed by the President by instrument in writing under his hand; (b) the Attorney General; and (c) a person qualified to practise in Botswana as a medical practitioner.[32]

Again, this approach holds out little realistic prospect of an independent and transparent review body.

In Malawi[33] and Kenya a statute sets out the composition of the Advisory Committee. The most detailed consideration on the matter comes from Kenya, which is the only jurisdiction under review where the constitutional drafters have sought to provide for an effective review mechanism. Article 133 of the Constitution of Kenya provides for an Advisory Committee on the Power of Mercy comprising the Attorney General, the Cabinet Secretary responsible for correctional services and at least five other members as prescribed by a statute. In addition, Parliament is required to pass legislation to provide for the tenure of the members of the Committee, its procedure and the criteria to be applied in formulating its advice. These provisions are enshrined in the Power of Mercy Act 2011 (the 2011 Act).[34]

The 2011 Act is notable for its detailed provisions relating to the appointment and tenure of members of the Committee, and its power and functions. Section 5 sets out its composition and provides that in addition to those prescribed in the Constitution, the Committee is to consist of seven other members representing a cross-section of society. A member must be a citizen of Kenya, possess a recognised university degree, have 'had a distinguished career in their respective field' and at least 10 years' proven experience in one of a range of fields including law, human rights, governance and religion.[35]

---

[30] Article 96(1)(3) Constitution of Zambia.

[31] This was highlighted by a telephone conversation between the author (then on the Faculty of Law at the University of Zambia) and a very senior Zambian judge. When a gentle enquiry was made as to the membership of the Advisory Committee, the response was that this was a state secret and the conversation came to an abrupt end.

[32] Section 54(1) Constitution of Botswana.

[33] Advisory Committee on the Granting of Pardons Act.

[34] For a brief overview of the Act see Jane Muhia, 'Key Legal Provisions in the Exercise of the Presidential Power of Mercy in Kenya' 2016. Available at http://www.dlm-advocates.com/index.php/2016/11/07/key-legal-considerations-in-the-exercise-of-the-presidential-power-of-mercy-n-kenya/ (accessed 7 June 2020).

[35] Section 6 Power of Mercy Act 2011.

With the exception of the Attorney General and Cabinet Secretary, members hold office for a single term of five years.[36]

The procedure for appointment is also noteworthy. A selection panel is established comprising both public officials and representatives of civil society. Applications for membership of the Committee are then invited from members of the public via advertisements in the national press. The names of those shortlisted for interview are also published. The selection panel then recommends to the President ten suitably qualified persons for appointment. Section 9(3) then provides that '[t]he President shall ... appoint seven members from among the persons recommended by the panel'.

The Kenyan model is a fresh approach that provides for transparency and independence within the membership of the review committee and stands in stark contrast to the 'state secrecy' approach in Zambia. It provides an excellent model for other African states.

11.5.2 Role of the Advisory Committee

The role of the review body is of crucial importance. Once again, the African Constitutions demonstrate a variety of approaches. In the majority of states, the President is merely required to consult with the Advisory Committee (or Council of State or Cabinet) before reaching a decision. For example, in Uganda the President may pardon convicted offenders provided the decision is taken 'in consultation with the Advisory Committee on the Granting of Pardon...'.[37] Similarly, Article 72(1) of the Constitution of Ghana states that the President may 'acting in consultation with the Council of State' grant a pardon to those convicted of a criminal offence.[38] There is no specific requirement to provide the reasons for the decision.

What constitutes a 'consultative' role is unclear. For example, in the Alamieyeseigha case, it was alleged that members of the Council of State 'were not availed of any information relating to [his] application for pardon until the meeting of March 12, 2013, and that the presentation of the matter by the President was "done in a manner that left no room for discussion"'.[39]

---

[36] Ibid, section 13.

[37] Constitution of Uganda, Article 121(1).

[38] Curiously, the Independence Constitution of 1957 simply vested the power of mercy in the President: see Article 48. In Nigeria the President is required to consult the Council of State except as regards military offences where s/he is required to act on the advice of the Council of State (section 175(2) and (3)): a provision which perhaps reflects the fact that the document was drafted at the end of a lengthy period of military rule.

[39] See Adangor, The Presidential Pardon, at 189.

In any event, even if a 'consultation' takes place, the President is under no obligation to follow the advice. In effect, there is no constitutional restriction on the presidential power to grant a pardon to a PEP or indeed to whoever s/he chooses and for whatever reason. The need for an Advisory Committee in such circumstances is dubious indeed.

However, in *Chantunya v The State*,[40] a somewhat different view on the consultative role was expressed by Kgoele J:

> The Presidential Pardon is regulated by section 89(2) of the Malawian Constitution, which states that the President may pardon convicted offenders, but such decision shall only be taken in consultation with an advisory committee on the granting of pardon. It thus stands to reason that the President does not have the prerogative alone and is not the ultimate authority with respect to the granting of pardon.

This view is difficult to understand. Arguably, so long as there is appropriate 'consultation' with the Advisory Committee, the decision is entirely one for the President.

A different formulation provides the committee with an advisory function. For example, Article 97(1) of the Constitution of Zambia states that the President '*may on the advice* of the Advisory Committee on the Prerogative of Mercy … remit the whole or part of a fine, penalty or forfeiture' (emphasis added). Article 133(1) of the Constitution of Kenya provides a stronger formulation. Here the President '*may* exercise a power of mercy *in accordance with the advice* of the Advisory Committee' (emphasis added). This raises the issue as to whether under such formulations the President may grant a pardon but *only* if advised to do so by the Advisory Committee.

In *Law Society of Botswana and Motumise v President*[41] the Court of Appeal of Botswana considered the meaning of the phrase 'acting in accordance with the advice of' albeit in the context of a judicial appointment. Here the Judicial Service Commission had recommended the appointment of the second appellant as a judge of the High Court. Section 96(1) of the Constitution of Botswana provides that '[t]he Chief Justice shall be appointed by the President'. Section 96(2) provides that '[t]he other judges of the High Court *shall be* appointed by the President, *acting in accordance with* the advice of the Judicial Service Commission' (emphasis added). The President declined to appoint the second appellant as a judge of the High Court. It was accepted by both parties that section 96(1) gave the President the sole power to appoint the Chief Justice. The question for the Court of Appeal was whether 'it was peremptory under

40 [2013] AANWHC 45 at [13]. This was a case involving an extradition request from Malawi heard by the North West High Court in South Africa.

41 [2017] 3 LRC 472.

[section 96(2)] for the president not to decline or to refuse to appoint a judge recommended for appointment by the Judicial Service Commission'.[42]

Crucially, the Court held that the expression 'shall, acting on the advice of' required the person advised to follow the advice and act upon it. The Court paid particular attention to principles of constitutional interpretation. In his judgment, Lesetedi JA referred to the well-established principles on constitutional interpretation developed by courts in several Commonwealth countries[43] and emphasised the importance of considering the context in which any such construction should be undertaken.[44] He concluded:

> At the end of the day the duty of the Court in trying to ascertain the meaning of a provision of the Constitution is to look at the totality of the various considerations that come into play in the interpretation; this being the wording of the provision in the context of other provisions of the Constitution having regard to the mores and values of the society as a contextual setting, being mindful that a constitution is not a static document but one that lives with the times and evolves for the better good of the society within the limits of its language.

The analysis of the Court of Appeal as to the interpretation of the phrase 'acting on the advice of' provides invaluable assistance in considering the scope of the presidential power of pardon. The wording in the Kenyan provision substitutes 'may' for 'shall'. Arguably, whilst this means that the President is not required to act on the advice of the Advisory Committee, crucially, s/he is unable to act *against* the advice of the Committee. Arguably, this also applies to the position in Zambia. Provided there is an element of independence amongst the membership of the Committee, this represents a key element to enhance transparency and accountability.

11.6 PEPs AND POST-CONVICTION PARDONS

The Kenyan approach regarding the role of the Advisory Committee is praiseworthy in respect of those convicted of 'ordinary' criminal offences. Yet there remains the problem of dealing with the pardoning of corrupt PEPs where political and/or national security considerations may influence the decision. In such cases, the traditional reasons for pardoning offenders as being designed to 'afford relief from undue harshness or evident mistake' or on humanitarian grounds are often inapplicable.

---

42 Ibid, at [25].

43 See for example, *R v Big M Drug Mart Ltd* [1985] 1 SCR 295; *Dow v A-G* [1992] LRC (Const) 623 and *e.tv v Minister of Communications* [2016] ZASCA 85: see Section 6.2.1 above.

44 [2017] 3 LRC 472, at [40].

This poses something of a conundrum in that the pardoning of a PEP may be perceived in very different ways. On the one hand, some may see it as an act of benevolence on the basis that the conviction was politically motivated. On the other hand, others may view the same pardon as an abuse of benevolence in that a PEP, who was convicted of corruption or money laundering, has now been pardoned for purely political motives. The differing views on the Alamieyeseigha case noted earlier highlight the point. Another possible (and potentially highly controversial) scenario is the granting of a pardon to a former President or PEPs convicted of a corruption-related offence where this is considered necessary by the incoming President for the sake of 'national unity', or as part of a pre-election 'bargain',[45] or following a period of intense political uncertainty and/or violence or as part of some other political arrangement. This might apply to the case of Jacob Zuma, the former President of South Africa, following any criminal conviction on corruption/money laundering-related charges.

Given this reality, there is considerable merit in placing PEPs in a special category. There are several possibilities.

1. *An untrammelled presidential decision*

One approach is to recognise that this is essentially a political decision and therefore the pardoning of a PEP is solely in the hands of the President. Thus whilst the strengthening of the role of the Advisory Committees is advisable for 'ordinary' pardons, they should play no role in cases involving PEPs. In essence, this is to adopt the approach in the Constitution of the United States of providing the President with the unrestricted power to grant a pardon.[46]

This is an extremely dangerous approach for it provides the President with excessive and unrestrained power. It is potentially highly controversial and any (alleged) abuse of benevolence can undermine national anti-corruption/AML efforts. It is unsupportable.

2. *The 'no pardon for PEPs' approach*

A second approach is to recognise that the danger of an abuse of benevolence is so strong that a PEP convicted of corruption and/or money laundering

---

[45] Ensuring a full royal pardon for Anwar Ibrahim, a key political opposition figure who had been convicted of sodomy and corruption, was a key part of the agreement between the former prime minister of Malaysia, Mahathir Mohamed, and the opposition when it was decided in January 2018 he would swap sides and run as their leader in the election. This led to the May 2018 election victory for Mahathir and the opposition and the immediate pardoning and release from prison of Anwar Ibrahim.

[46] See Section 10.4 above.

is never entitled to a pardon. This approach was suggested by the Malawi Law Commission report on the *Development of Legislation on Sentencing Guidelines*. This recommended that any person who commits an offence that causes public harm should not be eligible for a pardon. This was on the basis that 'public anger is stirred whenever perpetrators are pardoned'.[47] Based on the unsatisfactory and controversial pardoning of Alamieyeseigha, Adangor has also advocated this approach, arguing strongly that 'the enormity of the danger posed to Nigerian society by corrupt practices demands an immediate [constitutional] amendment ... by prohibiting the President from exercising the pardoning powers in respect of any person concerned with or convicted of corrupt practices [and money laundering]... This will make it impossible for the President to jeopardise the fight against such criminality ... .'[48]

This is unrealistic for it fails to take into account the variety of situations that can arise with the pardoning of PEPs and unnecessarily restricts presidential power. There is therefore no room for this 'one-fit-all' approach.

3. *The legislature as a safeguard*

The power of the legislature to review the merits of the decision is seemingly found in the Constitution of Namibia, a document not based on the Westminster export model. Article 32(3)(d) provides that the President may 'pardon or reprieve offenders, either unconditionally or subject to such conditions as the President may deem fit'. There is no constitutional provision for a separate review body but Article 32(9) provides that such a decision:

> shall be capable of being reviewed, reversed or corrected on such terms as are deemed expedient and proper should there be a resolution proposed by at least one-third of all the members of the National Assembly and passed by a two-thirds majority of all the members of the National Assembly disapproving any such action and resolving to review, reverse or correct it.

Whilst obtaining the required majorities may well cause problems in practice, such an approach has the advantages of requiring the President to provide the grounds for the decision to pardon and providing a platform for public debate on the matter.

---

47 See report in *The Nyasa Times* 26 September 2016.

48 Adangor, The Presidential Pardon, at 189.

11.7 REVIEWING THE EXERCISE OF THE PRESIDENTIAL POWER: THE ROLE OF THE COURTS

Given that the constitutional power to grant a pardon is vested in the President, the decision is not justiciable on its merits but the lawfulness of the process by which it was made is open to judicial review. As Chan Sek Keong CJ in the Court of Appeal of Singapore in *Yong Vui Kong v Attorney General*,[49] neatly put it:

> no legal power, including a constitutional power, ... is beyond the reach of the supervisory jurisdiction of the courts if it is exercised beyond its legal limits (i.e. *ultra vires* the enabling law) or if it is exercised *mala fide* (i.e. for an extraneous purpose).

In *Maru Ram v Union of India*,[50] the Supreme Court of India also observed:

> Pardon, using this expression in the amplest connotation, ordains fair exercise .... Political vendetta or party favoritism cannot but be interlopers and will vitiate the exercise...

The court added that the pardoning power 'can be subject to a review where an executive decision [involved] grounds such as discrimination on the basis of religion, caste, colour or political loyalty'.[51]

The requirement for administrative justice is specifically enshrined in several African Constitutions. The fundamental principle is that executive power must be exercised in a manner that is consistent with the constitution. For example, Article 47(1) of the Constitution of Kenya states that '[e]very person has the right to administrative action that is expeditious, efficient, lawful, reasonable and procedurally fair'. Similarly, Article 68 of the Constitution of Zimbabwe provides a justiciable 'right to administrative conduct that is lawful, prompt, efficient, reasonable, proportionate, impartial and both substantively and procedurally fair'. This provides the 'infrastructure within which official power of all sorts affecting individuals must be exercised'.[52]

---

49 [2011] SGCA 9; [2012] LRC 439 at [77]. This was a case where the appellant sought judicial review of a presidential decision, acting on the advice of the Cabinet, to deny a grant of clemency.

50 1981(1) SCC 107.

51 For a useful analysis of the relevant Indian jurisprudence, see J P Rai, Exercise of the pardoning power in India: emerging challenges, (2014) XII(2) *NEHU Journal* 1–26.

52 Per Mathonsi J in *Telecel Zimbabwe (Pvt) Ltd v Postal and Telecommunications Regulatory Authority of Zimbabwe* (HH/446/15, 2015, unreported). See also section 43(1) Constitution of Malawi.

The Pipite case, noted earlier, neatly illustrates the effectiveness of judicial review as a potential check on the exercise of a presidential pardon. Two particular issues were in question: firstly whether a President can pardon him/herself and secondly, whether a pardon once granted can be revoked.

11.7.1 A Presidential Self-pardon?

The constitutional power of the President to grant a pardon to 'any person' convicted of a criminal offence suggests that this can also include a 'self-pardon'. In *Natuman v President of the Republic of Vanuatu*[53] the three applicants who were all members of Parliament sought a declaration that the granting of a pardon to himself by Mr Pipite, the Acting President of Vanuatu, was unconstitutional. The Supreme Court held that it had jurisdiction in the matter[54] with Saksak J emphasising that:

> Within any country which is committed to the rule of law, notwithstanding the general terms of the [pardon] article, [this] is not a power which can be exercised except in a way which is consistent with the entire constitutional framework. It is not a power which is beyond the purview of the Court to review and assess its exercise for legality.[55]

He also held that the applicants had *locus standi* on the basis both as members of Parliament and as citizens of Vanuatu.[56]

As regards the factual issue, the applicants claimed that the conduct of Mr Pipite in granting a pardon to himself and other government officials had breached his constitutional duties, amongst others, to act with integrity and avoid conflicts of interest.[57] Saksak J agreed, holding that Mr Pipite, as Acting President, had exercised his powers of pardon 'wrongly and unlawfully' and his action was therefore *ultra vires* section 38 of the Constitution. The pardon was therefore 'unconstitutional, invalid and of no force or effect'.[58]

---

[53] [2015] VUSC 148.

[54] See further, Lee-Anne Sackett, Vanuatu Constitutional Cases Nos 6 and 7 of 2015: Article 38 pardons and multilingual legal interpretation principles, [2015] (2) *Journal of South Pacific Law* 1, at 4.

[55] [2015] VUSC 148, at [18.13] and adopting the words of the Court of Appeal of Vanuatu in *Public Prosecutor v Willie* [2014] VUCA 4.

[56] This suggests that the *locus standi* for judicial review in such cases applies widely. The basis was that they had demonstrated that their constitutional rights to protection of the law and equal treatment under the law had been infringed or were being infringed: para. 17.5. See also the discussion regarding the judicial review of decisions relating to the Auditor General in Section 7.5.1 above.

[57] As enshrined in section 66 of the Constitution of Vanuatu.

[58] Above, 'Conclusions'.

The Court Appeal of Vanuatu in *Vohor v President of the Republic of Vanuatu*[59] upheld the decision of the lower court, Lunabek CJ, giving the judgment of the court, emphasising that the then Acting President:

> had a duty to conduct himself so as not to place himself in a position in which he had or could have had a conflict of interest, or in which the fair exercise of his public duties might be compromised.[60]

The *Wednesbury* principles therefore applied[61] and the ostensible reason for the pardon, i.e. to maintain the stability in the Government of Vanuatu, was 'plainly an irrelevant consideration'. The decision to pardon was also a clear misuse of public power and was 'so outrageous in its defiance of logic [and] accepted moral standards that no sensible person who had applied his mind to the question to be decided could have arrived at it'.[62] He added that '[i]t is difficult to imagine a more serious and obvious conflict of interest, and a more palpable failure of a leader to recognise his responsibilities to Parliament and his nation'.

In essence, a self-pardon is a constitutional impossibility. Whilst the President has the power to grant a pardon to 'any person' convicted of a criminal offence, the act is clearly open to judicial review and must be ruled unlawful. Arguably, the action falls foul of the *nemo judex in sua causa* rule, for here the President is acting as a judge in his own case. Further arguments can be based on bad faith, irrationality and a conflict of interest.[63]

11.7.2 Revoking the Pardon

There is no specific constitutional mechanism empowering a President to revoke a pardon once granted and therefore the basis for doing so, if one indeed exists, is uncertain. The issue was considered in *Natuman v President of*

---

[59] [2015] VUSC 40.

[60] Ibid, at [23].

[61] *Associated Provincial Picture Houses v Wednesbury Corporation* [1948] 1 KB 223.

[62] [2015] VUSC 40 at [31] applying the words of Lord Diplock in *Council of Civil Service Unions v Minister for the Civil Service* [1985] AC 374 (the CCSU case). In a different context, Lestedi JA in the Court of Appeal in Botswana in *Law Society of Botswana v President* (above at [27]) noted that a presidential refusal to appoint a judge contrary to the recommendation of the Judicial Service Commission was amenable to judicial review on the ground of irrationality as explained in the CCSU case.

[63] For a helpful discussion in the South African context, see Piet Olivier, 'Crime and Punishment (and Presidential Pardons): Does the Constitution Permit the Pardoning of the Corrupt?', Helen Suzman Foundation, 2016.

the Republic of Vanuatu (above). Upon his return, the President had purported to revoke the pardons issued by Mr Pipite via the Pardon (Revocation) Order No. 14 of 2015. In the Supreme Court of Vanuatu, the applicants argued that once a pardon was granted under Article 38 of the Constitution of Vanuatu the President had no power to revoke it. Saksak J firmly rejected this argument:

> 20.2 It is common knowledge that Article 38 does not expressly provide a power of revocation. But the absence thereof does not mean the President seeing the legal and constitutional wrong and error done by a person he appointed as Acting President ... [should] sit back and not do the right thing he ought and should do to undo the legal and constitutional wrong. That would be absurd and unacceptable in my view.

Saksak J noted that the Interpretation Act provided that the power to appoint included the power to remove and by analogy reasoned that Article 38 'must be accorded the same interpretation as having that implied power'. The validity of the Revocation Order was accordingly upheld. On appeal, the Court of Appeal in *Vohor v President of the Republic of Vanuatu*[64] upheld the revocation of the pardon on other grounds (see above) and dismissed the appeal concerning the presidential revocation power without considering its merits.

The basis for the decision seems to focus more on political realism than any firm constitutional basis. The principles of interpretation of a constitution are far more complex and detailed than merely prescribed in a statute. However, whilst a constitution is not a static document and one which moves with the times, it is dubious that a constitutional 'granting power' of this nature can include a constitutional 'revoking power'. The true position surely is that the act is final and irrevocable albeit that it is subject to judicial review.

11.8 PEPs, PARDONS AND COLLATERAL CONSEQUENCES

A criminal conviction may also lead to 'collateral consequences' that can significantly adversely affect ex-offenders such as the ability to obtain employment or gain access to financial services. A pardoning power is therefore a useful mechanism for removing the stigma of past conviction(s)[65] and the issue of collateral consequences has received much attention elsewhere.[66]

---

64 [2015] VUCA 40.

65 Other strategies for removing the stigma attached to the ex-offender include non-disclosure of a criminal record after a specified period and rules limiting or preventing the disclosure of evidence of 'bad character' at the accused's trial.

66 For example, in the United States a number of states have passed legislation addressing the issue: for details see Collateral Issues Resource Center: http://ccresourcecenter.org/ (accessed 7 June 2020).

There has been relatively little attention paid to the issue in Anglophone African states but as a general principle Pinard's view has much merit, i.e. that a 'dignity-based approach' is required so that only those consequences are imposed 'that directly relate to the underlying criminal conduct and are therefore necessary to minimize the risk of further harm'.[67]

The issue of collateral consequences is of considerable importance as regards PEPs, particularly in relation to two issues: firstly, as regards a possible return to political office, and secondly, as regards the forfeiture/confiscation of the proceeds of corruption.

11.8.1 A Return to Public Office?

The first issue concerns the effect of a pardon on a constitutional provision that bars persons convicted of a serious criminal offence(s) from political office either permanently or for a specified period. Such a provision has significant implications for corrupt PEPs as it denies them access to political power at least for a significant period. This is a potentially significant deterrent and is an important part of an anti-corruption/AML strategy.

There are two main views as to the consequences of a pardon.[68] One is that it 'wipes out'/erases both conviction and guilt and places the offender in a position as if he or she had not committed the offence. As was stated in *Ex parte Garland*:[69]

> when the pardon is full, it releases the punishment and blots out of existence the guilt, so that in the eye of the law the offender is as innocent as if he had never committed the offence.[70]

This view was echoed in the Nigerian case of *Falae v Obasanjo (No. 2)* where Musdapher JCA emphasised that '[t]he effect of a pardon is to make the

---

[67] Michael Pinard, Collateral consequences of criminal convictions: Confronting issues of race and dignity, (2010) 85 *New York University Law Journal* 457, at 529.

[68] These are usefully considered, albeit in a mainly US context, by Vivian Chu, 'The President's Pardon and Legal Effect on Collateral Consequences', 26 July 2016. Available at https://www.everycrsreport.com/reports/R44571.html (accessed 7 June 2020).

[69] (1866) 71 U.S. (4 Wall.) 333, 380–1.

[70] Thompson also notes that the Federal Courts in the United States continue to take the approach that 'a pardon should generally remove any collateral consequences that may legally attach to a person as a result of the commission or conviction of the pardoned offense'. See Richard M Thompson II, 'The President's Pardon Power and Legal Effects on Collateral Consequences', Congressional Research Service, 2016.

offender a new man (*novus homo*) … His civil rights and liberties are fully restored.'[71]

A similar view was taken by the Constitutional Court of South Africa in *The Citizen 1978 (Pty) Ltd v McBride*,[72] a case that focused on the issue of the 'expungement' of a criminal record in the context of an amnesty granted under the Reconciliation Act to an individual previously convicted of murder. Here the court ruled that:

> Expungement entitles the grantee of amnesty to full civic status. All civil disabilities are lifted. He is entitled to stand for Parliament. Should he ever be convicted of another crime, he will for sentencing purposes be deemed to be a first offender.[73]

The removal of collateral consequences thus leads to the restoration of the full constitutional rights of the individual including eligibility to return to public office. Indeed Article 47(1)(a) of the Constitution of Ghana specifically provides that a disqualification from eligibility for membership of the legislature ends with the granting of a free pardon.[74]

An alternative view is that whilst the criminal conviction is expunged, this is not equivalent to an acquittal. This is the position in Kenya, where the Power of Mercy Act 2011 states that a presidential pardon is not to be construed as an acquittal.[75] This means that 'guilt remains' and this precludes a return to public office at least for the period specified in the Constitution.[76]

The other African Constitutions are seemingly silent on the collateral consequences issue although most provide the President with the power to grant a pardon 'either free or subject to lawful conditions'. In the case of a PEP, a lawful condition might well include a prohibition on a return to public office. In the absence of any other constitutional or statutory provision, it is likely to be a matter for the courts to determine.

---

[71] [1999] 4 NWLR (Pt 599) 476 at 495.

[72] [2011] ZACC 11.

[73] Ibid, at [64].

[74] This does not apply to a candidate for the office of President: Article 62(c). In a parliamentary system, this seemingly means that following a pardon, a PEP convicted of corruption can seek re-election to the legislature and, as a member, be eligible for appointment as a Minister.

[75] Section 25(1) provides that the exercise of a pardon under Article 133(1)(a) of the Constitution 'shall not be construed to be an acquittal'.

[76] This 'hybrid' approach reflects the view of several courts in the United States when dealing with pardons granted to PEPs convicted of corruption-related offences: see Chu, 'The President's Pardon', at 6–8. Sebba notes that civil law systems generally emphasise that a pardon affects only the penalty and does not affect other consequences of a conviction: Sebba, The pardoning power, at 119–20.

The different approaches reflect the tension between the gift of 'benevolence' and the 'abuse of benevolence' discussed earlier. Where the pardon is acting as a 'safety net', for example to remedy a miscarriage of justice, it is appropriate that it is deemed to wipe away collateral consequences. This is not the case with an 'abuse of benevolence'. As the Alamieyeseigha case illustrates, the 'wiping away of guilt' approach is unsatisfactory as it provides a route for a potential return to public office for corrupt PEPs.

Arguably the wiping clean/erasure approach is acceptable for all ex-offenders except PEPs convicted of corruption or money laundering offences. They fall into a special category because of the circumstances in which their conviction took place. Here providing the reasons for the pardon are crucial, especially as the decision is subject to judicial review. In cases where the PEP was the victim of a miscarriage of justice, the *novus homo* approach is appropriate. In other cases, the Kenyan approach is appropriate i.e. that the pardon does not amount to an acquittal and guilt remains, thus precluding a return to public office for the appropriate period of time.

11.8.2 PEPs and the Confiscation/Forfeiture of the Proceeds of Corruption

The second question concerns the fate of the laundered proceeds. The power of confiscation/forfeiture is a fundamental tool for taking the profit out of corruption and money laundering.[77] In practice, most states now have legislation providing a court with the power, following a conviction for a corruption-related/money laundering offence, to order the forfeiture of assets as part of the sentence.[78]

However, with the exception of The Gambia, Malawi and Kenya, the African Constitutions each provide that the President may remit any 'penalty or forfeiture on account of any offence in respect of which a person has been convicted'.[79] This is a separate power and is therefore not dependent upon the granting of a pardon.

Such constitutional provisions override any asset recovery legislation and arguably a President can order the return of forfeited assets to a corrupt PEP. This is a matter of concern as it undermines a key anti-corruption/AML strat-

---

[77] See Article 51 UNCAC.

[78] See Section 10.2 above.

[79] Interestingly, Article 133(1) of the Constitution of Kenya simply provides that the President may remit 'all or part of a punishment'. Section 89(2) of the Constitution of Malawi refers to the power to 'remit sentences'. Presumably, the omission of a specific power to remit any 'forfeiture' was designed to restrict the presidential power in this respect.

egy for the forfeiture of the proceeds of corruption is in line with public policy and the interests of victims of crime. This is further supported by the need for criminals to 'be stripped of the proceeds of their crimes, the purpose being to remove the incentive for crime, not to punish them'.[80]

The reality is that the continued inclusion of the colonial-era provision is entirely unsuited to modern constitutions. The forfeiture of the proceeds of corruption of PEPs is too important to be undermined by such a provision. It is therefore necessary to remove the power entirely as part of a constitutional amendment package. Given the importance of asset recovery in anti-corruption/ AML strategies the present provision places an unacceptable amount of power in the hands of the President that is always susceptible to abuse.

Of course the presidential power only applies to criminal cases. This raises the possibility of making use of NCBAF. Here the action is brought against property as being 'proceeds of crime' and there is no requirement to prove any criminal offence. This is also a very useful approach where a possible prosecution of a PEP suspected of corruption and/or money laundering is undermined by political considerations.[81]

11.9 PEPs AND PRE-EMPTIVE PARDONS

The power of the President to issue a pre-emptive pardon i.e. one where criminal proceedings have not yet been commenced or concluded is less clear. Its attraction was noted by Alexander Hamilton in *The Federalist Papers: No. 74*, where he argued that:

> there are often critical moments, when a well-timed offer of pardon to the insurgents or rebels may restore the tranquillity of the commonwealth; and which, if suffered to pass unimproved, it may never be possible afterwards to recall. The dilatory process of convening the legislature, or one of its branches, for the purpose of obtaining its sanction to the measure, would frequently be the occasion of letting slip the golden opportunity. The loss of a week, a day, an hour, may sometimes be fatal.

In the African context, there are a number of examples of such arrangements. For example, in 1983 in Kenya, President Moi announced that he had decided to extend executive clemency to some 412 ex-servicemen and 61 university students who had been accused (but never tried) of involvement in the 1982 coup attempt. The basis for such 'clemency' is not clear as there was (and still is) no constitutional pre-emptive presidential pardoning power in

---

[80] Per Ackermann J in *National Director of Prosecutions v Mohamed NO* [2003] ZACC 843 at [15].

[81] See Section 10.3.

Kenya. A pre-emptive pardon was also granted by the President of Nigeria to Odumegwu Ojukwu, the former Biafra leader and other political detainees. The point is of particular contemporary significance where a President wishes to pardon a PEP, such as a former President, who is facing corruption/money laundering-related charges. The case of former South African President, Jacob Zuma, springs to mind.

The issue becomes more complex where a pre-emptive pardon is offered to a PEP (including close family members) in exchange for the return of assets representing the proceeds of corruption. For example, in 2004 the then President of Zambia, Levy Mwanawasa, reportedly offered a pardon to former President Frederick Chiluba if he returned 75 per cent of the money he had allegedly looted whilst in office. Similarly, the then President of Nigeria, Olusegun Obasanjo, ordered negotiations with the Abacha family over the release of Mohammed Abacha, who was being held in prison on multiple money laundering and corruption charges in exchange for the return by the Abacha family of over US$1 billion to the government that had been looted by General Sani Abacha when head of a military government in Nigeria.[82]

For the state, such a 'deal' is attractive in that it allows for the swift return of the proceeds of corruption. This is especially so given the reality that such proceeds are often concealed in jurisdictions around the world and recovering them through the judicial process is frequently a long, expensive and often fruitless exercise. Whatever the morality of the arrangement, the deal ensures the return of a significant percentage of the proceeds of corruption to the victim state and, reinforces the primary aim of asset recovery: that of taking the profit out of corruption.

Assuming that a pre-emptive pardoning power is desirable in relation to PEPs, the question arises as to the constitutional basis (if any) for its exercise.

1. *A specific constitutional power*

In Nigeria, the Constitution specifically provides for such a power. Section 175(1) states that '[t]he President may (a) grant any person *concerned with* or convicted of any offence … a pardon either free or subject to lawful conditions' (emphasis added). Incorporating the power into the Constitution recognises that the decision is a political one and it is the President who is best placed to determine the matter. Of course, judicial review is available to challenge the legality of the decision.

---

82 For a helpful discussion of the case, see David U Enweremadu, Nigeria's quest to recover looted assets: The Abacha Affair, (2013) 48(2) *Africa Spectrum* 51.

2. *A residual constitutional power*

No such comparable provision is found in the other African Constitutions. This raises the question as to the legality of any such presidential action for only the courts can determine the guilt of an accused and the President seemingly has no express power to grant a pardon for 'offences' that have not yet been judicially determined.

If the power does not reside in the Constitution, the question arises as to whether there is a residual prerogative power available to the President, especially in that the pre-emptive power of pardon was exercised as part of the royal prerogative and was reflected in the powers of colonial governors. Some guidance on such powers is provided from two cases from Botswana.

In the *Law Society of Botswana* case (above) the respondents argued that the President had the prerogative power to refuse to appoint a candidate recommended by the Judicial Service Commission. This was on the basis that such power 'involves a consideration and balance of high policy considerations, for example factors of security and socio-political factors'.[83] The Court of Appeal impliedly accepted that the President enjoyed prerogative powers although the argument was rejected on the ground that 'once a power is conferred by statute or by the Constitution expressly, it ceases to be a prerogative power'.[84] However, as the constitutional provisions on the power of pardon fail to address the 'no prosecution deal' scenario, there is an argument the President continues to enjoy the prerogative power to issue a pardon in such cases.

In *Patson v A-G*[85] Kirby J considered the exercise of the prerogative in the context of the issuing of a passport. He noted that:

> the prerogative power still applies, exercised in the name of the President. By s 47(1) of the Constitution the executive power of Botswana is vested in the President. This provides that: 'The executive power of Botswana shall vest in the President and, subject to the provisions of this Constitution, shall be exercised by him or her either directly or through officers subordinate to him or her.' In practice he exercises his powers, both statutory and non-statutory (or prerogative) powers, through the relevant ministers of state and their departments.

He then added:

> Many of these principles and concepts have been re-defined and specifically included in the Constitution, such as the prerogative of mercy, but others remain as

83 *Law Society of Botswana* case, above, at [19].
84 Ibid, at [44].
85 [2008] BLR 66 (High Court of Botswana).

> part of the common law of Botswana, such as the non-statutory prerogative powers of the state ...

As noted earlier, the prerogative of mercy contained in the Constitution of Botswana (and, with the exception of Nigeria, the other African Constitutions) applies only to the post-conviction scenario. Arguably, the granting of a pre-emptive pardon remains part of the 'non-statutory prerogative powers of the state', albeit that this is subject to any provision to the contrary.

3. *No pre-emptive power*

Given the 'abuse of benevolence' concern, it may be argued that a pre-emptive pardon is, and should remain, a constitutional impossibility in the absence of a specific power to the contrary.

The practical scenarios suggest that there is no easy answer. The 'clemency' shown by President Moi in the case of the coup plotters may well have been necessary for the sake of national unity and national security: any future pardon of Jacob Zuma might fall into a very different category. Perhaps the most satisfactory approach is to retain the no pre-emptive pardon policy whilst ensuring that there is a constitutional/statutory power to pass an amnesty Act on a case-by-case basis.

One other approach is to utilise the power of the Attorney General to terminate a prosecution by entering a *nolle prosequi* albeit with the decision being subject to judicial review. In addition the common law tradition has always provided prosecutors with the discretion as to whether or not to prosecute a particular case and this enables a decision not to prosecute a case as it is not in the public interest. Of course, the danger of the state capture of the prosecution process may rule out an objective assessment of the case and undermine the independence of prosecutors.

11.10 CONCLUSION AND OVERVIEW

A notable feature of many of the African Constitutions, old and new, is the retention of the various forms of clemency derived from the powers of the colonial governors. These include the power to grant a pardon to those convicted of a criminal offence as well as the power to remit any penalty or forfeiture imposed as part of the sentence of the court. Invariably the pardoning decision is exercised by the President and is often surrounded by opaqueness and as Clark neatly puts it '[if] the history of civilisation proves nothing else, it proves that where secrecy cloaks the use of power it also clocks the abuse of power'.[86]

As Head of State, the President is the appropriate pardoning 'agent' but the danger of an abuse of benevolence towards PEPs requires constitutional drafters to re-visit the question of putting in place effective and appropriate safeguards on its use.

11.10.1 Post-conviction Pardons

The discussion has focused largely on post-conviction pardons. As an 'act of benevolence' designed to provide a safety net for those subject to a miscarriage of justice or on humanitarian grounds, the power of pardon enjoys an important place in every constitution. Yet this chapter has highlighted that it also provides an avenue for the 'abuse of benevolence', particularly as regards PEPs convicted of corruption and money laundering offences. It has been argued that this calls for a re-examination of the pardoning powers. Two strategies have been identified. Firstly, to strengthen the existing provisions so as to provide for more effective constitutional constraints based on the principles of transparency, administrative justice and accountability. Secondly, to recognise that due to their political importance, the pardoning of corrupt PEPs demands separate provisions.

11.10.1.1 Reviewing the review mechanisms

All the African Constitutions provide for a formal review mechanism. Thus on the face of it the granting of a pardon is not an act of benevolence entirely within the gift of the President. It is at this point that the constitutions vary widely both as regards the membership of the review body and its role.

Whilst the majority of constitutions provide for an Advisory Committee on the Prerogative of Mercy, there is no agreement as to its membership. In most states the President appoints the members and can remove them at will. This approach holds out little prospect of an independent review body. A similar comment applies to those states where the review role is undertaken by the Cabinet or Council of State.[87]

This calls for a membership of the committee that can provide the President with an independent review of each case. Here Kenya provides the leading example with the members of the Advisory Committee on the Power of Mercy

---

[86] Naeemah Clark, The impact of mass communications in America, (1968) *Annals* 68, at 73 referred to by Duker, The President's power to pardon, at 504.

[87] In essence, reflecting the colonial relationship between the Governor and Executive Council.

being appointed via an open and transparent process with each enjoying security of tenure.

The role of the Advisory Committee is also a matter of concern. At present, in the majority of the constitutions the President is merely obliged to 'consult' with it. This is an extremely weak formulation that provides no real possibility of an independent review of cases. It is not suggested that the power of pardon is removed from the President: rather that the incumbent be required either to 'act on the advice' of the Committee or at least be unable to act against the advice of the Committee. A constitutional amendment will be required.

The chapter has also highlighted the fact that in practice it is the courts that hold out the prospect of an effective safeguard on the exercise of the pardoning decision by way of judicial review.

11.10.1.2 The position of PEPs

It has been noted that PEPs are unlike other convicted offenders in that they are often high-profile individuals whose cases often raise important constitutional and political issues. An abuse of benevolence can result in corrupt PEPs being pardoned on purely partisan political grounds. However, there may be circumstances where the pardoning of a PEP is necessary in the public interest. Given this reality, PEPs fall into a different category to 'ordinary' convicted offenders and should be subject to a different constitutional regime. This is the only way to address the variety of situations that can arise with the pardoning of PEPs.

The chapter has also explored the difficult issue of collateral consequences. In the case of corrupt PEPs, a criminal conviction leads to two key consequences, i.e. a bar on the holding of public office and the confiscation/forfeiture of the proceeds of corruption as part of the sentence. As regards the former, the majority of the African Constitutions are silent as to whether a pardon wipes clean/erases the conviction. If this is the case, then the PEP is entitled to return to public office, thus removing a key deterrent in the fight against corruption. It follows that the Kenyan approach is appropriate, i.e. that an acquittal does not erase the conviction. This would preclude an automatic right of a PEP to return to public office. However, the variety of reasons for the pardoning of a PEP prevents a 'one-fit-all' approach. Thus the prohibition of a return to public office could be overturned with the approval of the legislature.

As regards the return of assets, the scope of the power to remit 'any penalty or forfeiture' suggests that a presidential pardon will overturn a criminal forfeiture order, certainly prior to the order being enforced. As yet, this point does not seem to have arisen but its potential importance in the fight against corruption is such that it must be reviewed. With asset forfeiture being an international priority in the fight against corruption and money laundering, the presidential power to overturn a forfeiture order is no longer appropriate. This is another area for constitutional reform.

11.10.2 Pre-emptive Pardons

The only significant difference between the pardoning power of the colonial governor and that contained in most of the African Constitutions is the absence of the power to grant a pre-emptive pardon. The sole exception is that of Nigeria, where the Constitution specifically provides for such a power.

On the face of it, a pre-emptive pardoning power provides the President with a degree of flexibility to deal with any situation where national security/national interests or the like demands his/her intervention. The extending of 'presidential clemency' by President Moi to those involved in the 1982 coup attempt in Kenya is a good case in point. The point takes on an even greater importance in view of the development of 'deals' in which PEPs (and/or their family members) agree to return their proceeds of corruption in exchange for a non-prosecution agreement.

At present, in the absence of a residual prerogative power, it is not constitutionally possible for the President to grant a pre-emptive pardon. This would require a constitutional amendment following the Nigerian provision. An alternative is to utilise the power of the Attorney General (or Director of Public Prosecutions) to discontinue a prosecution at any stage prior to judgment.[88] Certainly not an ideal situation given the executive influence over the judicial process, but one that is perhaps justified on public interest grounds.

Overall, there are three key conclusions.

1. There is an urgent need for African states to undertake a review of their constitutional provisions relating to the granting of pardons and remitting of sentences, particularly as they relate to PEPs. It is remarkable that the current provisions in the African Constitutions still largely reflect the powers of the colonial governors and in many jurisdictions have seemingly not been subject to any critical review or analysis since independence.
2. The exercise of the presidential power of pardon requires effective constitutional safeguards.
3. There is a need for special provisions relating to the pardoning of PEPs. These are required to address situations covering an 'act of benevolence', an 'abuse of benevolence' or one where there are very different views about the pardoning decision.

---

[88] This may also prove problematic in that in some jurisdictions the permission of the court is required to discontinue a prosecution: see for example, Article 157(8) Constitution of Kenya. It remains to be seen whether a presidential 'deal' is viewed as a justifiable reason to do so.

PART IV

PEPs and transnational AML initiatives

12. 'Know your beneficial owner': PEPs and beneficial ownership transparency

12.1 INTRODUCTION

The misuse of beneficial ownership by PEPs in order to facilitate the laundering of the proceeds of crime is now the focus of considerable international attention, not least because of the revelations from the Panama Papers and the Luanda Papers. In this context the term beneficial owner 'refers to the natural person(s) who ultimately owns or controls a customer and/or the natural person on whose behalf a transaction is being conducted. It also includes those persons who exercise ultimate effective control over a legal person or arrangement.'[1]

Reflecting the often complex ownership and control structures of companies, the FATF Recommendations add that: 'Reference to "ultimately owns or controls" and "ultimate effective control" refer to situations in which ownership/control is exercised through a chain of ownership or by means of control other than direct control.'[2]

Inevitably the last tier of control is a natural person(s).

The FATF has categorised the misuse of beneficial ownership into three broad methods:

- generating complex ownership and control structures through the use of legal persons and legal arrangements, particularly when established across multiple jurisdictions;
- using individuals and financial instruments to obscure the relationship between the beneficial owner and the asset, including bearer shares, nominees and professional intermediaries; and
- falsifying activities through the use of false loans, false invoices and misleading naming conventions.[3]

This chapter reviews the work of the FATF and G20 in setting international standards designed to enhance beneficial ownership transparency. The posi-

1 FATF Recommendations General Glossary.
2 Ibid.
3 FATF/Egmont, *Concealment of Beneficial ownership*, 2018, Paris, at [53].

tion in African states is then considered and this is followed by a case study of the UK and its 'secrecy jurisdictions'.

12.2 INTERNATIONAL EFFORTS TO ADDRESS BENEFICIAL OWNERSHIP TRANSPARENCY: 'KNOW YOUR BENEFICIAL OWNER'

The FATF has highlighted that the 'lack of accurate information on the ultimate owner of legal persons and arrangements on a timely basis is a significant vulnerability' for money laundering.[4] This has led to increasing international efforts, particularly by the FATF and G20, to improve the transparency and availability of beneficial ownership information.[5]

12.2.1 FATF

FATF Recommendation 24 states that:

> Countries should [must] ensure that there is adequate, accurate and timely information on the beneficial ownership and control of legal persons that can be obtained or accessed in a timely fashion by competent authorities...[6]

These are 'all public authorities with designated responsibilities for combating money laundering'.[7] Such authorities must be able to 'obtain, or have access in a timely fashion to, adequate, accurate and current information on the beneficial ownership and control of companies and other legal persons (beneficial ownership information) that are created in the country'.[8] At a minimum this must include information about the legal ownership and control structure of the company, its shareholders and directors. All companies created in a country must be registered in a company registry. Accurate and up-to-date information

---

4 FATF, *Report to G20 Finance Ministers and Central Bank Governors*, 2018, at [16].

5 Another key player is the Global Forum on Transparency and Exchange of Information for Tax Purposes, which is 'an international body for ensuring the implementation of the internationally agreed standards on tax transparency and exchange of information in the tax area'.

6 The 5th European Union (EU) Money Laundering Directive was published in 2015 and reflects the additional AML obligations contained in the FATF Recommendations.

7 See FATF Recommendations General Glossary. This includes the FIU, investigative and prosecutorial authorities and authorities with AML supervisory or monitoring responsibilities.

8 Interpretive Note to FATF Recommendation 24 [1]. A note adds that 'References to creating a legal person, include incorporation of companies or to any other mechanism that is used'.

on the beneficial ownership must be held by that company or mechanisms be in place to enable a competent authority to determine the beneficial ownership in a timely manner.

In addition, countries must take steps to prevent the misuse of nominee directors and nominee shareholders, for example by requiring them to disclose the identity of their 'nominator' and for this information to be included in the company register.[9] To reflect the development of new entities, this now applies to virtual asset service providers (VASPs).[10]

FATF Recommendation 25 further requires countries to 'ensure that there is adequate, accurate and timely information on express trusts, including information on the settlor, trustee and beneficiaries that can be obtained or accessed in a timely fashion by competent authorities'.[11] Similar provisions apply to foundations, Anstalt, and limited liability partnerships.

As regards international co-operation, the FATF requires countries to 'rapidly, constructively and effectively' provide basic and beneficial ownership information. This may include facilitating access by foreign competent authorities to basic information held by company registries and using their domestic powers to obtain beneficial ownership information on behalf of foreign counterparts.[12]

Improving the transparency and availability of beneficial ownership information of all these legal entities remains a high priority, especially as few countries, including G20 countries, have effective co-operation mechanisms in place.[13] Clearly, this remains work in progress. It is also useful to note that the

---

9 Interpretive Note to FATF Recommendation 24 [15].

10 Defined in the FATF Recommendations General Glossary as meaning 'any natural or legal person ... and as a business conducts ... operations for or on behalf of another natural or legal persons: i) exchange between virtual assets and fiat currencies; ii) exchange between one or more forms of virtual currencies; iii) transfer of virtual assets; iv) safekeeping and/or administration of virtual assets or instruments enabling control over virtual assets; and v) participation in and provision of financial services related to an issuer's offer and/or sale of a virtual asset'. See generally FATF Guidance, *Virtual Assets and Virtual Asset Service Providers*, Paris, 2019.

11 In 2014 the FATF published its *Guidance on Transparency and Beneficial Ownership*. This requires states to ensure that measures are in place to: prevent legal persons or arrangements from being used for criminal purposes; make legal persons/arrangements sufficiently transparent; and ensure that accurate and up-to-date basic and beneficial ownership information is available on a timely basis.

12 Interpretive Note to FATF Recommendation 24 [19].

13 The FATF has reported that 'few countries have demonstrated that information is available to competent authorities on the beneficial owner of legal persons and arrangements, or that these persons and arrangements are prevented from being misused'. FATF, *Report to the G20 Finance Minister and Central Bank Governors*, Paris, 2018, at [23].

focus of the FATF is on law enforcement co-operation and there is no mention in the FATF Recommendations of the need for countries to establish a public register of beneficial ownership of companies and trusts.

12.2.2 The G20

The G20 is an informal group of 19 countries and the European Union that addresses issues relating to international economic co-operation. Reducing corruption remains a high priority and at its 2014 meeting in Australia the G20 *High-Level Principles on Beneficial Transparency Ownership* (the Principles) were agreed. These are a set of 'core principles on the transparency of beneficial ownership of legal persons and arrangements and are built on existing international instruments and standards'. The Principles include the following:

> 1. Countries should have a definition of 'beneficial ownership' that captures the natural person(s) who ultimately own or control the legal person or legal arrangement;...
> 3. Countries should ensure that legal persons maintain beneficial ownership information onshore and that information is adequate, accurate and current;
> 4. Countries should ensure that competent authorities (including law enforcement and prosecutorial authorities, supervisory authorities, tax authorities and FIUs) have timely access to adequate, accurate and current information regarding the beneficial ownership of legal persons and legal arrangements.

Again, there is no reference to a requirement for states to introduce a public register of beneficial ownership.

12.3 PEPs AND BENEFICIAL OWNERSHIP TRANSPARENCY IN AFRICAN STATES

In the domestic African context, PEPs use a range of strategies to conceal their beneficial ownership of property. As noted in Section 2.6 they are often assisted by PMLs. Companies and trusts are used both to conceal the involvement of PEPs in a corrupt public procurement process and/or to facilitate the laundering of the proceeds of corruption. In the Cashgate scandal in Malawi, for example, businesses and companies were registered just a few months or days before being used by the PEPs to launder their stolen proceeds.[14]

With many African countries having largely cash-based economies, there are numerous opportunities for money laundering activity. Car dealers are used as a front for PEPs and it 'remains very difficult to identify the beneficial

---

[14] See also Zambia Financial Intelligence Centre, *Money Laundering Trends and Terrorist Financing Trends Report 2018*, Lusaka, 2018, section 5.

ownership of the businesses thus posing a very high threat to money laundering'.[15] The use of microfinance banks through which to conceal the beneficial ownership of funds lodged with commercial banks is also a likely vehicle for money laundering. Real estate remains a particularly vulnerable sector because the legal ownership of land registered in a company register may be used to conceal beneficial ownership.[16]

Access to beneficial ownership information in African countries remains very limited and many seemingly do not satisfy their FATF Recommendations 24 and 25 obligations. For example a 2018 study by the Tax Justice Network found that of the eight African states studied only Ghana had beneficial ownership laws in place,[17] i.e. where bearer shares posed no risk and all types of companies were required to register and update their beneficial ownership information.[18] However, there are some positive recent developments elsewhere. For example in Kenya a 2017 statutory amendment now requires every company to 'keep a register of its members which shall include information relating to beneficial owners of the company, if any'.[19] Companies risk a fine of KShs500,000 for failure to update their registers. Information on the beneficial ownership of companies registered under the Companies Act 2015 can be accessed on-line on the e-Citizen platform.[20] Similarly, in Zambia the Companies Act 2017 contains extensive provisions regarding beneficial ownership transparency including requiring the disclosure of beneficial ownership in the public company registry to a Registrar of Beneficial Ownership.[21] There is a now a proposal that this is extended to other forms of business entities such

---

[15] *Report of Nigeria National Risk Assessment on Money Laundering and Terrorism Financing 2016*, Abuja, 2016, p. 30.

[16] See Section 4.6 for a full discussion on PEPs and money laundering techniques.

[17] Those with no beneficial ownership registration laws were Botswana, The Gambia, Kenya, Liberia, Mauritius, Seychelles and Mauritius. But see the Kenyan Companies (Amendment) Act 2017 discussed below.

[18] Of course, the problem is not Africa-specific for only 18 of the 112 jurisdictions covered in the study had effective beneficial ownership registration provisions.

[19] Section 8 Companies (Amendment) Act 2017 amending section 93 Companies Act 2015.

[20] The main challenge to this requirement is that companies' records at Companies Registry are notoriously out of date and there is no mechanism by which the Company can compel shareholders to reveal the beneficial ownership of shares being held: see Daly and Imander Legal Alert, 'Impact of the new Companies (Amendment) Act 2017'. Available at http://www.dalyinamdar.com/wp-content/uploads/2017/10/impact-of-the-new-companies-amendment-act-2017.pdf (accessed 7 June 2020). See also Section 8.2.3 above.

[21] As at March 2020 regulations to implement the provisions of the Act were still awaited. Tunisia is also establishing a register of beneficial ownership.

as trusts and cooperatives 'to ensure transparency across the regime'.[22] These provide excellent models for other African states to follow.

A related issue that African states, amongst others, have not yet addressed fully, or at all, concerns the threshold for reporting beneficial ownership. The 25 per cent 'control' threshold in many countries is seen as being an 'Achilles heel' due to the ability of PEPs to avoid being identified.[23] A wider definition is therefore desirable.[24]

As regards trusts, in most countries there is no legal requirement to register trusts or at least to identify the beneficial owner of the trust although both the Seychelles and South Africa require the registration of express trusts.[25]

Overall, enhancing transparency of legal persons and arrangements is work in progress. This is emphasised by GIABA, which has noted the significant shortcomings, with most of the company registries in the region failing to have a comprehensive understanding of their FATF obligations and thus failing to implement effectively beneficial ownership requirements at the national level.[26]

12.4 TOWARDS BENEFICIAL OWNERSHIP TRANSPARENCY IN FACILITATING STATES

The Panama Papers and the Luanda Papers have highlighted the role played TCSPs in assisting African PEPs to establish off-shore companies based in 'secrecy jurisdictions'/facilitating states through which to launder their proceeds of crime. Shell companies remain key players in schemes designed to conceal or disguise beneficial ownership.[27] These are defined by the OECD as: 'entities established not to pursue legitimate business activity but solely to obscure the identity of their beneficial owners and controllers' and

---

22 Zambia Financial Intelligence, *Centre Money Laundering and Terrorist Financing Trends Report 2018*, Lusaka, 2018, p. 13.

23 See Andres Knobel, 'The Achilles heel of effective beneficial ownership registration: Why is everyone fixed on 25%?' Tax Justice Network, 2017. Available at www.taxjustice.net/2017/05/11/achilles-heel-effective-beneficial-ownership-registration-everyone-fixed-25/ (accessed 6 June 2020).

24 See for example, the definition of 'control' in section 3 Companies Act 2017 in Zambia.

25 For a scathing report about the lack of registration requirements for both trusts and foundations see Tax Justice Network, *Financial Secrecy Index: Key Financial Secrecy Indicator 2: Trust and Foundation Register*, 2020. Available at https://fsi.taxjustice.net/PDF/2-Trusts-Foundations-Register.pdf (accessed 7 June 2020).

26 See GIABA press release, 'GIABA organizes Regional Workshop on Beneficial Ownership Requirements' December 2019 and GIABA 2018 report, at [284].

27 FATF/Egmont Group, *Concealment of Beneficial Ownership*, Paris, 2018, p. 5.

which function as a corporate veil, providing an effective screen separating criminals from illicit financial activities.[28] As Findlay has observed: 'Shell companies that cannot be linked back to the real individuals in control create near-insuperable obstacles for regulators and law enforcement officials.'[29] A 'shelf company' is an incorporated company that has inactive shareholders, directors, and secretary and is left dormant for a longer period even if a customer relationship has already been established'.[30] They also pose a particular money laundering challenge as they enable the PEPs who ultimately own or control the company to remain concealed behind a nominee director(s) and nominee shareholder(s).[31]

In some countries bearer shares pose a money laundering risk. These are 'negotiable instruments that accord ownership in a legal person to the person who possesses the bearer share certificate'.[32]

The use of facilitating states through which PEPs are able to launder their proceeds of crime is noted by Nicholls et al., who point out that there has been 'persistent criticism of the off-shore financial sector ... since there exist jurisdictions in which legal frameworks and practices [deliberately] obscure the identity of beneficial owners by, for example, placing ownership in the hands of nominee directors and shareholders'.[33]

The Panama Papers also highlight their importance, with the BVI, a British overseas territory, being the jurisdiction of choice for Mossack Fonseca for the incorporation of off-shore companies. African PEPs such as James Ibori have used BVI incorporated companies through which to launder their proceeds of

---

[28] OECD Steering Committee on Corporate Governance, *Behind the Corporate Veil: Using Corporate Entities for Illicit Purposes*, Paris, 2001, 17. The FATF/Egmont Group consider shell companies as 'companies that are incorporated but which have no independent operations, significant assets, ongoing business activities, or employees', ibid, p. 11.

[29] Michael Findlay, Daniel Neilson and Jason Sharman, 'Global Shell Games: Testing Money Launderers' and Terrorist Financiers' Access to Shell Companies', Centre for Governance and Public Policy, 2012, at 5. Available at http://www.gfintegrity.org/wp-content/uploads/2014/05/Global-Shell-Games-2012.pdf (accessed 20 July 2018).

[30] FATF/Egmont Group, *Concealment of Beneficial Ownership*, 2018, at [65–7].

[31] The Conference of State Parties to the United Nations Convention Against Corruption, *Report of the International Group Meeting on Beneficial Ownership* (CAC/COSP/2017/CRP.5) [32], also notes that corruption schemes increasingly use new sophisticated types of corporate vehicles with so-called 'tax havens or secrecy jurisdictions' being used to facilitate the criminality.

[32] FATF Recommendations General Glossary.

[33] Colin Nicholls et al., *Corruption and Misuse of Public Office*, 3rd edn., Oxford University Press, 2017, [23.04].

corruption, with much of the money being used to purchase real estate and other high-end goods in the 'safe haven' of the UK.

The use of such companies to purchase high-end real estate for PEPs in safe haven states is highlighted in a 2018 study by Global Witness which found that '[o]ver 87,000 properties in England and Wales valued at an excess of US$132.4 billion are owned by anonymous companies registered in tax havens'.[34] This reflects the findings of a 2014 study by Transparency International that 9.3 per cent of properties in the City of Westminster, 7.3 per cent in Kensington and Chelsea, and 4.5 per cent in the City of London were owned by shell companies registered in an off-shore 'secrecy' jurisdiction.[35] The study further revealed that 36,342 London properties were held by off-shore companies, with the vast majority being registered in the British Overseas Territories and Crown Dependencies.[36] Not surprisingly, the use of off-shore companies for the purchase and sale of property for PEPs in London has been described as 'prolific'.[37]

Of course, the use of such entities through which to purchase real estate and other property is perfectly legal. However, given the danger that they can be used to facilitate money laundering by PEPs, it is not surprising that the need to identify the beneficial ownership of companies (and not just shell and shelf companies) is now of international and national significance in the fight against money laundering by PEPs.

---

[34] Global Witness press release, 17 March 2017.

[35] Transparency International, *Corruption on your doorstep: How corrupt capital is used to buy property in the UK*, London, 2014, p. 16.

[36] Ibid, 5. More than one-third of all foreign companies holding London property were incorporated in the British Virgin Islands (13,831 properties), Jersey 14% (5,960 properties), the Isle of Man 8.5% (3,472 properties) and Guernsey 8% (3,280 properties).

[37] See *Solicitors Regulation Authority v Sharif*, 2019, unreported, Solicitors Disciplinary Tribunal, at [21]. Mr Sharif, a senior London solicitor provided this information in mitigation when faced with a charge of failing to comply with AML KYC regulations in relation to the proposed purchase of high-end property in London by two foreign PEPs. For a comment see John Hatchard, Legal practitioners as potential money launderers: Beneficial ownership transparency and PEPs: *Solicitors Regulation Authority v Sharif*, (2019) 31(1) *Denning Law Journal* 189.

12.5 THE UNITED KINGDOM, BRITISH OVERSEAS TERRITORIES AND CROWN DEPENDENCIES AND BENEFICIAL OWNERSHIP TRANSPARENCY: A CASE STUDY

The UK National Crime Agency has calculated that £90 billion is laundered through the UK each year and that 'this laundering can only be done, by and large, through British Overseas Territories, which are central to this nefarious activity'.[38] This makes a case study of moves to enhance beneficial ownership in the British Overseas Territories all the more significant. Recent developments are therefore of great significance.

12.5.1 The Constitutional Relationship

There are 14 British Overseas Territories including Anguilla, Bermuda, the BVI, Cayman Islands, Gibraltar, Montserrat and the Turks and Caicos Islands,[39] whilst the Crown Dependencies comprises the Bailiwick of Guernsey, the Bailiwick of Jersey and the Isle of Man.[40] All are of international significance as off-shore financial centres and potential facilitating states. Examining their constitutional relationship with the UK is fundamental to an understanding of recent developments concerning beneficial ownership transparency.

According to a 2012 UK Government White Paper entitled *Overseas Territories: Security, Success and Sustainability* (the White Paper):

> The UK, the [British] Overseas Territories and the Crown Dependencies form one undivided Realm ... Each Territory has its own Constitution and its own Government and has its own local laws. *As a matter of constitutional law the UK Parliament has unlimited power to legislate for the Territories.* (emphasis added).

The italicised words emphasise that the Crown retains a residual power to legislate for the British Overseas Territories with the exercise of this power normally being undertaken by an Order in Council.

As regards the Crown Dependencies, they are self-governing dependencies of the Crown with their own directly elected legislative assemblies, admin-

---

[38] Andrew Mitchell MP in the House of Commons debate of the Report Stage of the Sanctions and Anti-Money Laundering Bill, Hansard, 1 May 2018, p. 42.

[39] The full list is set out in the British Nationality Act 1981, sch 6.

[40] Within the Bailiwick of Guernsey there are three separate jurisdictions: Guernsey (which includes the islands of Herm and Jethou), Alderney and Sark (which includes the island of Brecqhou).

istrative, fiscal and legal systems and law courts.[41] UK legislation does not normally extend to them and in any event requires prior consultation with, and consent from, each of them.[42]

12.5.2 Law Enforcement Co-operation between the UK, British Overseas Territories and Crown Dependencies

In 2016 the then British Prime Minister, David Cameron, proposed greater compliance by the British Overseas Territories and Crown Dependencies to provide UK tax and law enforcement authorities with access to company ownership records. The proposal was made having regard to the FATF and G20 initiatives noted earlier and the UK Government's decision to introduce a public central register of beneficial ownership.[43]

This resulted in an Exchange of Notes between the UK Government and each of the key British Overseas Territories and the Crown Dependencies. In each Note, the UK and respective government (referred to as the 'Participants') recognised:

> the importance of the provision of beneficial ownership information for the prevention and detection of corruption, money laundering, terrorism financing, financing of the proliferation of weapons of mass destruction and other serious and organised crime.[44]

Each individual Note focuses on three key commitments by each of the Participants:

(i) To provide the law enforcement authorities of the other Participant with beneficial ownership information for corporate and legal entities incorporated in their respective jurisdiction;
(ii) To hold adequate, accurate and current beneficial ownership information for corporate and legal entities incorporated in their own jurisdictions; and

---

[41] For an illuminating background see the judgment of Lady Hale in *R (Barclay) v Secretary of State for Justice* [2014] UKSC 54, [2015] AC 276.

[42] UK Ministry of Justice 'Factsheet on the UK's relationship with the Crown Dependencies' (2014). This reflects the position set out, for example in the States of Jersey Law 2005, Article 31. See further Michael Birt, The power of the UK to legislate for the Crown Dependencies without consent: Fact or fiction? (2017) 21(2) *Jersey and Guernsey Law Review* 152.

[43] See Technical Protocol, at [3].

[44] See *Exchange of Notes between the Government of the United Kingdom and the Government of the Cayman Islands in respect of the sharing of beneficial ownership information*, at [2].

(iii) To give law enforcement authorities of the Participants the 'automatic' right to the provision of unrestricted and timely (within 24 hours or, where urgently required, within an hour) beneficial ownership information held in the other jurisdiction.[45]

This is a significant development, especially given the fact that previously, as each British Overseas Territory and Crown Dependency is a separate jurisdiction for the purposes of international co-operation, such information could only be requested by the UK via the potentially lengthy and complex MLA process.

The Exchange of Notes therefore provides for the 'timely, safe and secure access for law enforcement [and tax] authorities to beneficial ownership information', with the security of the request and information being specifically provided for in each Note.[46] The Notes are a neat example of the manner in which the political will can bring about a fundamental improvement in AML action. Perhaps not surprisingly, the new arrangements did not meet with universal approval, with accusations that the UK Government had 'managed to strong-arm the Crown Dependencies and a number of Overseas Territories into signing [the Exchange of Notes]'.[47]

Since then, the British Overseas Territories and Crown Dependencies have reportedly made 'significant progress in implementing the commitments by introducing legislation and establishing, where they did not already exist, central registers or similar effective systems'.[48] This represents a major step forward in assisting law enforcement agencies and tax authorities to identify the ultimate beneficial ownership of companies registered in the British Overseas Territories and Crown Dependencies.

12.5.3 Towards a Public Registry of Beneficial Ownership: the United Kingdom, British Overseas Territories and Crown Dependencies

Whilst making beneficial ownership information available to law enforcement authorities is a major step forward, the Panama Papers and the Luanda Papers disclosures have increased pressure on countries to introduce a public

[45] A Technical Protocol is attached to each *Exchange of Notes* setting out the practicalities of the arrangements (Technical Protocol).

[46] See Technical Protocol, at [7(vi)].

[47] See Fillipo Noseda, Too much information: When the UK gets it wrong, (2017) 21(2) *Jersey and Guernsey Law Review* 182, at 193–4.

[48] See statement to the House of Commons by Sir Alan Duncan, Minister for Europe and the Americas, HC Deb 1 May 2018, vol 640.

registry of beneficial ownership. As noted above, this is not a FATF or a G20 requirement.

The UK is the first G20 country to introduce such a register. Section 81 of the Small Business, Enterprise and Employment Act 2015 amended the Companies Act 2006 and requires companies to keep a 'register of people who have significant control over the company'. The annual returns by companies (known as 'confirmation statements') must contain beneficial ownership details. The register is accessible to the public free of charge.

At that point, the UK Government resisted the idea of imposing similar provisions on the British Overseas Territories or Crown Dependencies, although Bermuda (1981) and Jersey (2018) had already established central registers of beneficial ownership with Montserrat having committed to doing so. However, all-party parliamentary pressure led to the UK Government agreeing to require all British Overseas Territories to introduce a public beneficial register. Section 51 of the Sanctions and Anti-Money Laundering Act 2018 is headed 'Public registers of beneficial ownership of companies registered in British Overseas Territories' and provides as follows:

> (1) For the purposes of the detection, investigation or prevention of money laundering, the Secretary of State must provide all reasonable assistance to the governments of the British Overseas Territories to enable each of those governments to establish a publicly accessible register of the beneficial ownership of companies registered in each government's jurisdiction.[49]

The register must be broadly in line with the UK provisions, noted earlier.[50]

Not surprisingly, the reaction from some Overseas Territories was very critical, arguing in particular that beneficial ownership registers should only be introduced if and when they become a global standard.[51] However, in October 2019 the Government of the Cayman Islands announced its commitment to introduce a public beneficial ownership register by 2023[52] and others are likely to follow suit.

During the parliamentary debate on the Act, a clause requiring the introduction of a similar provision for the Crown Dependencies was withdrawn. This

---

[49] Section 49(3) provides that 'Money laundering' has the meaning given by the Proceeds of Crime Act 2002, section 340(11).

[50] Section 22(7) provides that 'a 'publicly accessible register of the beneficial ownership of companies' means a register which, in the opinion of the Secretary of State, provides information broadly equivalent to that available in accordance with the provisions of Part 21A of the Companies Act 2006.

[51] See D S Smith, 'Statement by Premier on the Royal Assent of the Sanctions and Anti-Money Laundering Bill', 23 May 2018, Government of the Virgin Islands.

[52] Statement by the Government of the Cayman Islands dated 9 October 2019.

was in recognition of the very different constitutional relationship between the UK and the Crown Dependencies. However, in June 2019 the Crown Dependencies made a joint commitment to establish a public beneficial ownership register.[53]

12.6 FUTURE DEVELOPMENTS

The introduction of public beneficial registers in the UK, British Overseas Territories and Crown Dependencies is extremely welcome and is part of an international move towards beneficial ownership transparency. This is reinforced by the introduction of the 5th EU Anti-Money Laundering Directive, which entered into force on 9 July 2018. The Directive (which was partly influenced by the publication of the Panama Papers) requires all states to allow 'any member of the general public' access to beneficial ownership registers to obtain information concerning the beneficial owner's month and year of birth, country of residence, and nationality, as well as the nature and extent of the beneficial interest held. It means that there is a clear shift towards a global commitment to address the vulnerability of beneficial ownership as a money laundering tool.[54]

It is encouraging that African states are starting to take active steps to comply with their FATF obligations for such transparency. Providing AML investigative authorities with access to up-to-date and accurate information about the beneficial ownership of real estate, corporate entities, trusts, foundations and Anstalt must be a priority. This might be achieved in a number of ways. For example, by establishing a central register of beneficial ownership with access limited to law enforcement authorities; placing a legal obligation on companies and trustees to report such information to a FIU; or requiring financial institutions and DNFBPs to obtain the information when carrying out their KYC and other relevant AML obligations and to provide this to AML authorities when required. However, the key to addressing the abuse of the off-shore sector for laundering purposes by PEPs is by establishing a central register of beneficial ownership that is freely accessible to members of the public. Here Kenya provides a model for all other African countries.

---

[53] 'Joint Commitment by Guernsey, Jersey and the Isle of Man: Registers of beneficial ownership of companies', Press release dated June 2019. This action is designed to bring the Crown Dependencies into line with the requirements of the EU 5th Anti-Money Laundering Directive.

[54] In another example of the challenge of obtaining the political will to comply with AML obligations, by March 2020 just five of the 27 EU member countries had established publicly available centralised registers of beneficial ownership. These were Bulgaria, Denmark, Latvia, Luxembourg and Slovenia.

In reality, the introduction of public beneficial ownership registers is only the start of a process. The idea that such a register will immediately disclose corrupt PEPs and their proceeds of crime is unsound, for by the very nature of the illegal activity PEPs and their PMLs are extremely likely to provide false information. This draws attention to the operation of the company registries themselves. Without an effective and constant review of company records, the effectiveness of the registers is likely to be considerably diminished: as the study by Global Witness has highlighted. This illustrates the watchdog role of CSOs by overseeing the records and highlighting those companies where the beneficial ownership record is opaque or missing.[55]

[55] For a review of the operation of the register see Global Witness, *In Pursuit of Hidden Owners Behind Companies*, London, 2018. See also Andres Knobel, Moran Harari and Markus Meinzer, 'The state of play of beneficial ownership registration: A visual overview', Tax Justice Network, 2018. Available at https://www.taxjustice.net/wp-content/uploads/2018/06/TJN2018-BeneficialOwnershipRegistration-StateOfPlay-FSI.pdf (accessed 7 June 2020).

13. Combating money laundering by PEPs: the private sector and the 'reveal all' approach

13.1 TRAINS AND PLANES: THE PRIVATE SECTOR AND THE 'ART OF PERSUASION'

This book has argued that combating money laundering by PEPs requires a three prong approach. The first is to have in place effective AML laws and institutions at the national level. The second is the need for effective AML investigation, prosecution and asset recovery laws and institutions. The third is to address the bribe-payers.

In particular, this means 'persuading' even the most powerful private sector entities[1] to 'reveal all' concerning their bribery and money laundering activities involving PEPs in international business transactions. Given their economic muscle and influence, 'persuading' them to do so is potentially extremely challenging.[2] This is especially problematic when, as in the Thiam case, PEPs are only too willing to accept bribes and the assistance provided in the laundering of their proceeds of crime. In practice the challenge is to 'persuade' private sector entities, *whether they want to or not*, to:

1. take effective steps to prevent the bribery of PEPs in their business activities; and
2. 'reveal all' about any past involvement in bribery and money laundering, including identifying the PEPs to whom the bribes were paid.

---

1 This term covers a wide range of entities. The FATF Recommendations General Glossary refers to 'Legal persons' as a term that includes companies, bodies corporate, foundations, *anstalt*, partnerships, or associations. Article 11 of the AU Convention refers to the 'private sector' but also requires State Parties to adopt such measures 'as may be necessary to prevent companies paying bribes to win tenders'. In this chapter, the term 'corporate entities' is also used where this is a more accurate reflection of the entity.

2 KPMG, *Anti-Bribery and Corruption: Rising to the Challenge in the Age of Globalization*, 2015, p. 7 (KPMG report).

This chapter explores these challenges using two case studies involving the bribery of African PEPs: one concerning the French engineering and train-manufacturing firm Alstom S.A. and the second concerning the giant aircraft manufacturer Airbus S.E. In particular it considers the impact of the 'reveal all' approach for African states and the resultant lessons and strategies that they can put into practice.

13.2 ALSTOM: A CASE STUDY

Alstom S.A. is headquartered in France and operates in some 70 countries. It operates via a series of subsidiaries through which it bids to secure contracts on projects around the world, some of which are funded by the World Bank and other international financial institutions.[3] In 2014, the United States Department of Justice (DoJ) announced that investigations had revealed that Alstom had paid more than US$75 million in bribes to PEPs in Africa and indeed globally in order to secure US$4 billion in projects with a profit to the company of approximately US$300 million.[4]

On 22 December 2014 under a Plea Agreement,[5] Alstom pleaded guilty to charges of violating the United States FCPA by falsifying its books and records and failing to implement adequate internal controls. Alstom then issued a brief press release:

> Alstom S.A. has agreed to plead guilty to violating the books and records and internal controls provisions of the FCPA and to pay a fine of approximately US$772 million.

The fine was then the largest ever levied for FCPA offences.[6]

This admission of guilt is of considerable importance for it demonstrates that even one of the most powerful private sector global entities was open to 'persuasion' to 'reveal all' about its criminal conduct. This included agreeing to provide detailed information about the bribe payments to PEPs and the alleged role of individual Alstom executives, employees and 'consultants'. In exchange prosecutors allowed Alstom to plead guilty to a *non-bribery offence*,

---

[3] The information is drawn from the Statement of Facts contained in Alstom's Plea Agreement with the US Department of Justice in 2014: see *United States v Alstom SA*, Case 3:14-cr-00246-JBA.

[4] DoJ Press Release, 13 November 2015.

[5] The full details of the Plea Agreement are set out in *United States v Alstom SA*, Case 3:14-cr-00246-JBA.

[6] In March 2020 it was the 7th largest with the Airbus settlement (below) now topping the list.

a matter of great significance as regards possible debarment proceedings (see below).

There are two strategies for dealing with the bribe-payers: prosecution and or doing 'deals'.

13.3 PROSECUTING PRIVATE LEGAL ENTITIES

13.3.1 Prosecutions in African Victim States

In common law jurisdictions, corporate entities are subject to the criminal law in the same way as natural persons. Thus in Anglophone African states (including those with a Roman-Dutch law tradition),[7] corporate entities involved in bribing PEPs and/or assisting in the laundering of the proceeds of crime can face prosecution. In practice, few such prosecutions have occurred: perhaps due to the influence of those PEPs who were the beneficiaries of the bribes.[8]

It has therefore been left to other states to prosecute the bribe-payers. This has opened up new opportunities for African states to identify and to take effective action against both the bribe-payers, the corrupt PEPs and the launderers.

13.3.2 Prosecutions in other States: Alstom and the FCPA

The Commission for Africa has rightly demanded that: 'rich nations should put in place a series of measures to ... deter their own companies from paying bribes in the first place'.[9] This is reflected in the OECD Anti-Bribery Convention, which requires each State Party to establish an offence of the bribery of a foreign public official.[10] All OECD member states have ratified the Convention as well as several non-members including South Africa. Each has complied with this requirement. In practice, the key issue remains as to the effective enforcement of such laws.

The US has led the way in doing so. Indeed it was the passing of the FCPA that was the catalyst for the adoption of the OECD Convention itself. The Act makes it an offence for US persons to make a corrupt payment to a foreign

---

[7] I.e. Botswana, Eswatini, Lesotho, Namibia, South Africa and Zimbabwe.

[8] See Chapters 8 and 9 concerning investigation and prosecution challenges in money laundering cases. For an excellent example of the political will to prosecute the corporate bribe-payers see the Lesotho Highland Water Project cases in John Hatchard, *Combating Corruption: Legal Approaches to Supporting Good Governance and Integrity in Africa*, Edward Elgar, 2014, pp. 236 et seq.

[9] Commission for Africa, *Our Common Interest*, 2005, p. 31.

[10] See Section 3.7 above.

public official for the purpose of obtaining or retaining business for or with, or directing business to, any person.[11] Further, the Act requires companies to keep accurate books and records and to establish and maintain adequate internal controls. Failure to do so constitutes a criminal offence. What makes the FCPA especially powerful is that its provisions also apply to issuers of securities listed and traded on a US exchange.[12] Alstom's shares were listed on the New York Stock Exchange and accordingly it was an 'issuer' for the purposes of the FCPA.[13] Consequences for violations of the FCPA provisions can lead to the imposition of draconian fines on companies and lengthy prison terms and punitive fines for individuals.[14]

In recent years, the DoJ has actively used the FCPA to take action against offending companies, such as Alstom. This active commitment, coupled with the threat of debarment and the potentially dire economic consequences thereof, have 'persuaded' even the most powerful private sector entities, such as Alstom, to 'reveal all' about their criminal activities.

13.3.3 Persuasive Threats, Debarment and Self-reporting: the Alstom Experience

The threat of debarment following a conviction for a foreign bribery offence can *in itself* represent such a persuasive threat as to encourage private legal entities to self-report any wrongdoing and to seek a 'deal' or settlement with prosecutors. Debarment (also known as blacklisting or exclusion) is the mechanism whereby a private legal entity or an individual is prevented from tendering for, or participating in, a project(s) for a specific reason, such as previous involvement in corrupt practices.[15] Debarment is now widely regarded as an important procedure for combating foreign bribery, for it is fear of *economic loss* that drives the decision to self-report. Indeed an OECD study suggests

---

11 Curiously, the word 'bribe' does not appear in the Act itself.

12 See generally, US Department of Justice, *FCPA: A Resource Guide to the US Foreign Corrupt Practices Act*, DoJ, Washington DC, 2015.

13 For a full discussion on the FCPA see Colin Nicholls et al., *Corruption and Misuse of Public Office*, 3rd edn., Oxford University Press, 2017, chapter 20. For a useful discussion on FCPA enforcement cases involving energy issues in Africa see Sarah Banco et al., Anti-Corruption Initiatives in Africa, in Marc Hammerson and John C LaMaster (eds), *Oil and Gas in Africa: A Legal and Commercial Analysis of the Upstream Industry*, Globe Law and Business, 2015, pp. 157–63.

14 See Title 15 United States Code sections 76dd-2(g((1)(A) and ss 78dd-2(g)(2)(A).

15 See further John Hatchard, Recent Developments in combating the bribery of foreign public officials: A cause for optimism? (2007) 85 *University of Detroit-Mercy Law Review* 1, at 23–8.

that one in three foreign bribery cases were instigated by self-reporting by companies.[16]

Much of the funding for major projects in developing countries is provided by the five multilateral development banks.[17] In recent years, these institutions have paid increasing attention to combating fraud and corruption in the procurement process. The role of the World Bank Group (WBG) in this respect is illustrative.[18] The WBG Procurement Guidelines[19] include a strict requirement that those involved in WBG-financed projects 'observe the highest standard of ethics during the procurement and execution of Bank-financed contracts'.[20] A similar provision is found in the WBG Consultants Guidelines.

A violation of the guidelines renders a 'Respondent' (i.e. a company or individual) liable to sanctions. These include debarment for a fixed period. During this period the respondent is declared ineligible to tender for a WBG-funded project, either indefinitely or for a stated period of time. Further, under an *Agreement for Mutual Enforcement of Debarment Decisions* (the Mutual Enforcement Agreement) the five multilateral development banks together with the International Monetary Fund and European Investment Bank Group have agreed to mutually enforce debarment decisions.[21] This coordinated and comprehensive approach to debarment is a significant milestone as it provides a common framework for tackling transnational corruption.[22]

The Alstom case neatly illustrates the debarment and cross-debarment process, albeit involving different facts. In 2002 Alstom made an improper payment of €110,000 to an entity controlled by a former PEP for consultancy services in relation to the WBG-financed Zambia Power Rehabilitation

---

16 OECD, *Foreign Bribery Report: An Analysis of the Crime of Bribery of Foreign Public Officials*, Paris, 2014, p. 9 (OECD Foreign Bribery report).

17 The African Development Bank Group, the Asian Development Bank, the European Bank for Reconstruction and Development, the Inter-American Development Bank Group and the World Bank Group.

18 The World Bank Group comprises five agencies: the International Bank for Reconstruction and Development (IBRD); International Development Agency (IDA); International Finance Corporation (IFC); Multilateral Investment Guarantee Agency (MIGA); and the International Centre for Settlement of Investment Disputes (ICSID). The term 'World Bank' generally refers to the IBRD and the IDA.

19 World Bank Group, *Guidelines: Procurement of Goods, Works, and Non-Consulting Services under IBRD Loans and IDA Credits & Grants by World Bank Borrowers*, 2011, updated 2014.

20 Ibid, at [1.16].

21 This is subject to the criteria set out in paragraph 4 of the Agreement.

22 For a useful discussion on the 2010 Agreement see Lorenzo Nesti, The 2010 'Agreement on Mutual Enforcement of Debarment Decisions' and its impact for the fight against fraud and corruption in public procurement, (2014) 14(1) *Journal of Public Procurement* 62–95.

Project. Following Alstom's acknowledgement of misconduct in relation to the project, in 2012, Alstom Hydro France and Alstom Network Schweiz AG (Switzerland) and their affiliates were debarred by the World Bank for a period of three years. As a result, they were also subject to cross-debarment under the Mutual Enforcement Agreement. This was part of a negotiated resolution agreement between Alstom and the World Bank which also included a restitution payment by the two companies totalling some $9.5 million. In addition, Alstom itself and its other affiliates were conditionally non-debarred.[23]

13.3.4 The Political and Economic Dimension

The Alstom case highlights that a combination of the political will by governments to take action against the bribe-payers coupled with economic consequences faced by corporate entities can break through the secrecy surrounding the bribery of PEPs. These provide potentially new opportunities for African states to address the problem of corruption and money laundering by PEPs.

13.4 AIRBUS: A CASE STUDY

Airbus S.E. is a multi-national company registered in the Netherlands. Over a period of several years the company paid bribes to PEPs in 14 countries, including Ghana, in order to obtain or retain business.[24] During this time it had in place a compliance programme which had been awarded an anti-corruption compliance certificate whilst its Business Ethics Policy and Rules set out fundamental ethical principles for all employees and detailed the due diligence process to be undertaken as regards business partners.[25] The revelations of a whistleblower concerning the widespread bribery of foreign PEPs by the company and its agents in order to obtain orders for the purchase of aircraft, led to investigations in France, the UK and the USA.

A notable feature in the case was close international co-operation involved between the three countries. The investigation was undertaken by a Joint Investigation Team (JIT) involving the UK SFO and the French *Parquet National Financier* in parallel with an investigation by the US DoJ. Each took responsibility for a particular geographical area or customers. In the case of the UK this involved, amongst other things, investigating payments to PEPs

---

[23] World Bank Press Release, 22 February 2012.

[24] The discussion in this section is based on the judgment of Dame Victoria Sharpe P in *Director of the Serious Fraud Office v Airbus SE*, 2020, Case No. U20200108, Crown Court at Southwark. Available at www.judiciary.uk/wp-content/uploads/2020/01/Director-of-the-Serious-Fraud-Office-v-Airbus-SE-1.pdf (accessed 7 June 2020).

[25] Ibid, at [24].

in Ghana. This is the focus of the following discussion and is drawn from the resultant settlement between Airbus and the SFO. In January 2020 the transnational coordination led to a simultaneous resolution in all three jurisdictions by way of settlement agreements with the company.

The case neatly complements the Alstom case and illustrates the impact of the global approach to dealing with the bribe-payers.

13.4.1 'Turning Out Its Pockets': The Importance of 'Exemplary' Co-operation

Self-reporting by corporate entities remains a prime factor in settlement agreements. However, it is not the only factor, and in the UK the more flexible 'exemplary co-operation' test is used. As Dame Victoria Sharp P noted, whilst Airbus had not self-reported as such, it had identified 'conduct overseas ... which the SFO would otherwise not have known. Airbus has, to use a colloquial phrase, truly turned out its pockets ... .'[26] This included providing access to 30.7 million documents relevant to the JIT investigations, the waiving of LPP and providing a list of business partners possibly involved in the bribe payments. This exemplary co-operation by Airbus was taken into consideration by Dame Victoria when considering whether to approve a deferred prosecution order.

13.4.2 The Economic Factor and the Threat of Debarment

The threat of debarment following a criminal conviction was also a key factor in Airbus seeking a settlement. In the case of the UK, a criminal conviction could have resulted in Airbus being debarred from tendering for UK and EU public sector contracts as well as those funded by the multilateral lending agencies. It was also estimated that future revenue at risk from such debarment could exceed 200 billion euros and that it would have the collateral consequence of threatening the loss of thousands of jobs as well as having serious negative impact on national economies.[27]

13.4.3 The Political Will to Investigate

In the Alstom case, one reason the United States took action against the company was the apparent reluctance of France, its home state, to pursue investigations. The development of the JIT perhaps illustrates an increasing

---

[26] Ibid, at [87].

[27] Ibid, at [85–6].

willingness for countries to co-operate and to take action against their own corporate entities.[28]

13.4.4 Airbus and Ghana

As noted above, one of the victim countries named in the scandal was Ghana, with Airbus providing the SFO with detailed information about its corrupt payments. Here an Airbus defence company had engaged a close relative of a Ghanaian PEP as its business partner[29] in respect of the proposed sale of military transport aircraft to the government of Ghana. The PEP was a key decision-maker in respect of the proposed sale. The business partner was promised approximately 5 million euros 'to induce or reward "improper favour" by the [PEP] towards Airbus'.[30] When an external diligence report for Airbus raised the possibility of the business partner having a conflict of interest, a number of Airbus employees deliberately circumvented the proper compliance process in order to make the money available to the business partner.[31] In August 2011, the purchase agreement for the sale of two C-295 aircraft was signed by the Airbus subsidiary and the government of Ghana.[32]

It remains to be seen whether Ghana takes steps to investigate the matter. The scandal took place prior to the coming into power of the present government and it provides an interesting test of the political will to take action against the PEPs involved. Certainly the information provided by Airbus, including how and where the corrupt payments were made, would provide an excellent platform to do so. Given the threat of debarment, the revelations also raise the prospect of prosecuting (or doing a 'deal') in Ghana with Airbus itself.[33]

---

[28] This in compliance with Article 5 of the OECD Anti-Bribery Convention.

[29] Although the BP had no prior expertise in the aerospace industry: ibid, at [54].

[30] Ibid, at [53].

[31] Ibid, at [56].

[32] Amongst other things, it contained a declaration of compliance with the OECD Anti-Bribery Convention although the arrangements raised concerns that there was a risk of non-compliance with the Convention, ibid, at [55].

[33] An illustration of this approach comes from Lesotho. Here Lahmeyer International, a German company, was faced with corruption charges with the threat of possible debarment if convicted. The company opted to provide prosecutors with detailed documentation and other evidence which led to the successful prosecution of two local PEPs: see John Hatchard, *Combating Corruption*, pp. 340 et seq.

13.4.5 The Settlement

In the case of the UK, the case revolved around whether Airbus would be allowed to enter into a deferred prosecution agreement (DPA) rather than face criminal prosecution.[34] Dame Victoria Sharp P noted that whilst the seriousness hardly needed to be spelled out, given the exemplary co-operation provided by the company to investigators and the impact on the company employees and those involved with Airbus, the public interest factors against prosecution clearly outweighed those tending in favour of prosecution. She therefore approved a DPA for three years. Airbus was required to pay a total financial sanction of 990, 963,712 euros including costs, made up of the disgorgement of profits of 585, 939,740 euros and a penalty of 398, 034,571 euros.[35]

As a result of the joint investigations, in total Airbus agreed to pay in excess of 3.5 billion euros in settlement with the US, France and the UK.

13.5 AFRICAN STATES AND LESSONS FROM THE ALSTOM AND AIRBUS CASES

The Alstom and Airbus cases provide a series of vital lessons in the art of persuading private sector entities to disclose their involvement in foreign bribery and money laundering. It also provides investigators and prosecutors in the victim African states with another weapon through which to prevent corruption in procurement and to combat money laundering by PEPs and their associates.

13.5.1 The Importance of Self-reporting and Exemplary Co-operation

A significant factor in the massive fine levied against Alstom by the DoJ was its failure to self-report: i.e. to disclose voluntarily its misconduct.[36] In addition, Alstom initially failed to co-operate fully with the DoJ's investigation and this impeded the investigation of individuals involved in the bribery scheme.[37] However, as the Airbus case indicates, a settlement may be in order where the

---

[34] See Section 45 Crime and Courts Act 2013 and the extensive consideration given to them in *Serious Fraud Office v Standard Bank Plc*, [2015] 11 WLUK 804.

[35] *Airbus*, at [87–8].

[36] Another factor was the fact that Alstom's conduct spanned many years and a number of countries and business lines, and involved sophisticated high-level schemes to bribe government officials: Plea Agreement [14].

[37] Plea Agreement at [68].

corporate entity has provided 'exemplary co-operation', where Dame Victoria Sharp P stated:

> It would be wrong to look at the issue of self-reporting purely from the perspective of the first report of wrongdoing, however. Even if the prosecuting authorities became aware of the relevant conduct by the actions of a third party, if subsequent self-reporting or co-operation overall, is of a high quality and brings significant wrongdoing to light that would not otherwise have come to the attention of the authorities, this will be a significant factor in favour of a DPA: see [*Serious Fraud Office v Rolls Royce* [2017] 1 WLUK 189 at para 22 of the final judgment and *Serious Fraud Office v Sarclad Limited* [2016] 7 WLUK 211 at paras 37 to 38 of the preliminary judgment]. To that extent, there is no necessary bright line between self-reporting and co-operation.

What is clear is that a corporate entity cannot now simply adopt a 'wait and see' approach.

The 'reveal all'/exemplary co-operation approach also removes the secrecy surrounding the corrupt bargain itself and thus identifies the PEPs involved in the bribery scandal and details of any assistance provided in laundering the proceeds. This provides an opportunity for the investigation and prosecution of PEPs and their accomplices in the victim African states.

13.5.2 Recognising the Importance of Effective Corporate Codes of Ethics and Compliance Programmes

Both Alstom and Airbus had codes of ethics and compliance procedures in place throughout the period of their bribe-paying activities, yet these did not impact on the way in which the companies operated.

Today, such codes and programmes are far more significant, with the failure of Alstom to have in place an effective anti-corruption compliance programme being noted in both the agreement with the World Bank and the Plea Agreement with the DoJ. As part of the World Bank settlement, the World Bank's Integrity Compliance Office required Alstom to implement a corporate compliance programme in line with the World Bank's integrity compliance guidelines. An independent compliance monitor was appointed to oversee the process. This is another useful 'persuasive' technique, for by 2014 the Integrity Compliance Office was satisfied that this had been implemented and accordingly Alstom's subsidiaries were released from debarment. Based on the Integrity Compliance Office's findings, the DoJ settlement with Alstom did not include the imposition of a compliance monitor. However, the finding by the DoJ that Alstom lacked an effective compliance and ethics programme at the time of the offence was another key factor in determining the fine.[38]

In the past, such corporate codes and programmes may well have been ignored by directors, managers and shareholders alike. This is not the case today. Private sector entities must now have in place effective programmes.

13.5.3 Controlling the Activities of Sales Agents and other Third Parties

A particular challenge for many corporate entities is controlling the activities of their sales agents, subsidiaries and related third parties. This is emphasised in a KPMG International survey which found that an increasing number of companies were finding corporate anti-bribery and corruption compliance highly challenging, with their overriding concern relating to the auditing of third parties for compliance. This was due to the 'very high proportion of bribes now paid either by third parties to the ultimate recipient or to seemingly unrelated parties acting on behalf of the ultimate recipient'.[39] This is confirmed by the OECD Working Group on Bribery, which reported that three out of four cases analysed involved the use of intermediaries.[40] In the case of Alstom, the company had used external 'sales consultants' for many years, each of whom was compensated on a 'success fee' basis.[41] In the case of Airbus, this was as high as 5 per cent of the value of the contract.

In 2014 the danger of such a practice was highlighted by the US DoJ in its press release:

> In connection with the bidding on the power projects, ... Alstom retained Consultant I [whose] primary purpose was not to provide legitimate consulting services to Alstom and its subsidiaries but instead was to pay bribes [to a PEP] who had the ability to influence the award of power contracts.

It is noteworthy that the company later announced that 'in an effort to further reduce compliance risks to the Group and in line with Alstom achieving the highest ethical business standards, the company has decided to discontinue the hiring of such Sales Consultants'.[42] In the case of Airbus, the Legal and Compliance function was re-structured and given far greater prominence and

38 Similarly the existence of a code of ethics is an important factor in determining whether or not a 'commercial organisation' has 'adequate procedures' in place to prove it has a defence to a section 7 charge under the UK Bribery Act 2010.

39 KPMG report, at p. 7. As illustrated in the Airbus case.

40 OECD Foreign Bribery Report, p. 8.

41 Alstom Press Release, 17 January 2014.

42 Alstom Press Release, ibid.

authority under a newly appointed General Counsel.[43] Other private sector entities will need to follow suit.

13.5.4 Prosecuting Individuals within Private Sector Organisations

It is notoriously difficult to identify those individuals within large private sector entities who were responsible for authorising the payment of the bribes to PEPs and/or laundering of the proceeds. As Yates puts it:

> In large corporations, where responsibility can be diffuse and decisions are made at various levels, it can be difficult to determine if someone possessed the knowledge and criminal intent necessary to establish their guilt beyond a reasonable doubt. This is particularly true when determining the culpability of high-level executives, who may be insulated from the day-to-day activity in which the misconduct occurs.[44]

It is therefore necessary to 'persuade' such entities to disclose information about those of its officials and employees who were responsible for or involved in the acts of foreign bribery and money laundering. If successful, this can provide a most powerful deterrent as it now exposes even their most senior officials to criminal or civil liability. In practice, the US has been willing to prosecute such individuals. For example, between 2012 and 2014, four senior officials of Alstom subsidiaries pleaded guilty to FCPA violations in respect of the awarding of a US$118 million power contract in Indonesia known as the Tarahan project.[45]

To emphasise this commitment, in September 2015 the US Deputy Attorney General, Sally Yates issued an internal DoJ memorandum (the Yates Memo) entitled 'Individual Accountability for Corporate Wrongdoing'.[46] This states that:

> One of the most effective ways to combat corporate misconduct is by seeking accountability from the individuals who perpetrated the wrongdoing. Such accountability is important for several reasons: it deters future illegal activity, it incentivizes changes in corporate behavior, it ensures that the proper parties are held responsible for their actions, and it promotes the public's confidence in our justice system.[47]

---

43 *Airbus*, at [29].

44 See the Yates Memo, discussed below at p. 2.

45 See Department of Justice Press Release, 17 July 2014. Marubeni Corporation, Alstom's consortium partner on the Tarahan project also pleaded guilty to conspiracy to violate the FCPA and was sentenced to pay a criminal fine of US$88 million.

46 Available at https://www.justice.gov/dag/file/769036/download (accessed 7 June 2020).

47 Ibid, at [1].

The Yates Memo provides 'Guidance' which will apply to all future investigations of corporate wrongdoing. It makes it clear that, amongst other things:

1. to be eligible for *any* co-operation credit, corporations must provide to the Department (of Justice) all relevant facts about the individuals involved in corporate misconduct;[48]
2. both criminal and civil corporate investigations should focus on individuals from the inception of the investigation;[49] and
3. absent extraordinary circumstances, no corporate resolution will provide protection from criminal or civil liability for any individuals.[50]

Given the already significant financial penalties being imposed on corporate entities by the DoJ, this represents a most significant persuasive threat that puts further pressure on corporate entities to adopt a 'reveal all' approach.

The findings of the EY 14th Global Fraud Survey make the position quite clear:

> Boards need to be aware that regulators are enforcing anti-corruption legislation with vigor, and are increasingly focused on individual misconduct. Boards must respond and confirm that they are doing enough to protect their business from these risks, or both board members and their employees may be held personally responsible for misconduct under their watch.[51]

13.5.5 International Co-operation and Prosecuting in Multiple Jurisdictions

The adoption (i.e. being 'persuaded' to adopt) of the 'reveal all' approach, may open a private sector entity to enforcement actions in multiple jurisdictions or face debarment by international financial institutions based on the same or similar facts.

This is potentially enormously significant for African countries. The Bonny Island case provides a useful illustration of the point. This related to contracts for a natural gas project in Nigeria obtained by four foreign companies (the TSKL consortium) allegedly through bribery. The TSKL consortium later

---

48 Emphasis in the original.

49 Guidance, at [2]. The Yates Memo (at p. 2) states that the Guidance also applies to civil corporate matters as these 'serve to redress misconduct and deter future wrongdoing'.

50 Guidance, [4].

51 EY 14th Global Fraud Survey, *Corporate Misconduct: Individual Consequences*, 2016, 4 (EY Survey). The EY Survey also found that the majority of respondents supported the prosecution of individual executives with 83% of respondents viewing enforcement against management as an effective deterrent in combating corruption: 5.

agreed a FCPA-related settlement with the DoJ and Securities and Exchange Commission (SEC) and then, following an investigation in Nigeria, to a settlement with the Nigerian government. The consortium also agreed to pay penalties to the African Development Bank totalling US$22.7 million for bribes relating to the same contracts whilst an Italian court also fined one of the partner companies to the consortium some US$27.4 million.[52]

In the Alstom case itself, the settlement with the US DoJ was to resolve charges that it paid bribes to government officials in Egypt, Saudi Arabia, the Bahamas and Taiwan, whilst 14 countries were involved in the Airbus case. Even so, in neither case was there a 'global' settlement. This raises the prospect of a bribe-paying company also facing prosecution (or reaching a separate financial agreement with prosecutors) in 'victim' African states with significant additional financial penalties being imposed on it.

This is a developing area which raises two further issues.

13.5.5.1 Towards a global settlement approach?

In cases where more than one State Party has jurisdiction over the foreign bribery offence, Article 4(3) of the OECD Anti-Bribery Convention provides that 'the Parties involved shall, at the request of one of them, consult with a view to determining the most appropriate jurisdiction for prosecution'. The JIT in the Airbus case being a good example. However, there is no *obligation* to consult or to agree a global settlement. Further the provision only applies to parties to the Convention. The UNCAC takes a similar approach. Article 49 provides that 'States Parties shall consider concluding bilateral or multilateral agreements or arrangements in relation to matters that are subject to investigations, prosecution or judicial proceedings in one or more States'. Further, that in such proceedings, 'the competent authorities of those States Parties shall, as appropriate, consult one another with a view to coordinating the actions'. Again, there is no obligation on states to reach a global settlement.

This raises the possibility of carbon copy prosecutions[53] of, or other enforcement action against, the private sector organisation in multiple 'victim' states based on the same or similar conduct.[54] This is potentially of particular value for African 'victim' countries, which have an opportunity of using the

---

[52] For details and sources of the information see Jay Holtmeier, Cross-border corruption enforcement: a case for measured coordination among multiple enforcement authorities, (2015) 84 *Fordham LR* 493, at 498–9.

[53] A term coined in Andrew S Boutros and T Markus Frank, 'Carbon Copy' prosecutions: a Growing anti-corruption phenomenon in a shrinking world, [2012] *U Chicago Legal Forum* 259, 260.

[54] Alstom's plea agreement with the DoJ specifically states that it is only binding on the DoJ: see *United States v Alstom SA* 14-CR-236 (2014), at [3] (the Alstom set-

corporate disclosures to identify their own PEPs involved in the criminality and prosecute them along with the bribe-paying company.[55] This raises the question of whether investigators and prosecutors in the victim countries can gain access to the material, for example whether material gathered by the JIT in the Airbus case could be shared with investigators and prosecutors in Ghana. The practice as regards information exchange in such circumstances varies from country to country. However, in principle, such material should be made available, subject to any national security issues.

13.5.5.2 Double jeopardy and the sharing of information

The double jeopardy rule was developed by the common law to prevent a person being tried twice for the same crime and is widely recognised in both national laws and international human rights conventions. Yet the rule is potentially limited by the dual sovereignty principle, which provides that two sovereign states can each prosecute a person for the violation of their own domestic laws even if based on the same facts. As Colangelo asserts:

> A national prosecution applying and enforcing a national law does *not* erect a bar to successive prosecutions by other States with national jurisdiction over the crime in question.[56]

For example, in a case involving an employee of the German company Siemens, the defendant sought to have a corruption charge dismissed in an Argentinian court on the basis that he had previously been prosecuted for the same offence in Germany. The court refused to dismiss the case, ruling that the German court had focused on the private effects of the alleged bribery whilst

---

tlement). For a useful discussion on this area, see Holtmeier, Cross-border corruption enforcement, at 508–11.

[55] An excellent example of this is provided by the Lesotho Highlands Water case: see Hatchard, *Combating Corruption*, pp. 245 et seq.

[56] Anthony J Colangelo, Double jeopardy and multiple sovereigns: a jurisdictional theory, (2009) 86 *Washington University Law Review* 769, at 797. Emphasis in the original. The article provides a detailed examination of the issue: see especially 790–805.

the Argentine case involved potential harm to the public sector.[57] As Holtmeier comments:

> Thus, as conceived, the double jeopardy principle is narrow enough that if courts and enforcement agencies can find *some* way to distinguish the separate proceedings, and show they are not identical, it will rarely be a bar to prosecution.[58]

Again, this will assist prosecutors in African states in bringing (or threatening) separate criminal proceedings against the bribe-paying corporate entities.

13.6 CONCLUSION: THE ART OF PERSUASION

This chapter has explored the challenge of persuading even the most powerful private sector entities *whether they want to or not*, to:

1. take effective steps to prevent the bribery of foreign public officials in their business activities (the prevention strategy); and
2. reveal everything about any past involvement in bribery and money laundering including identifying the PEPs involved (the reveal all strategy).

The Alstom and Airbus cases have highlighted that there are a range of persuasive techniques that can meet this challenge and prevent the payment of bribes to obtain international business. As a result African 'victim' states can potentially obtain significant benefits not least from the identification of PEPs involved in corruption and money laundering.

As regards the prevention strategy, the moral persuasion approach, i.e. persuading private sector entities to publicly commit to corporate good governance through putting in place codes of ethics and compliance programmes, may seem of limited value. As Transparency International points out, at worst such programmes are 'mere window dressing' exercises, a point emphasised by the fact that Alstom and Airbus had code of ethics and compliance programmes in place during their diverse foreign bribery activities. Yet today, the development of corporate codes of conduct and compliance programmes goes beyond moral persuasion and mere window dressing. There is now real pressure on all private sector entities to commit to a 'rigorous anti-corruption compliance programme that includes policies and procedures designed to detect and deter violations' of anti-bribery laws. Coupled with the threat of

---

57 This information is drawn from Lucio Fabiani Larranga, 'Double Jeopardy? Siemens Defendant Loses Argentina Dismissal Motion', The FCPA blog, 21 July 2015. Available at http://www.fcpablog.com/blog/2015/7/21/double-jeopardy-siemens-defendant-loses-argentina-dismissal.html (accessed 7 June 2020).

58 Colangelo, above, 515. Emphasis in the original.

whistleblowers, as in the Airbus case, the hope is that private sector entities will indeed take the necessary steps to prevent the bribery of foreign public officials in their business activities.

As regards the 'reveal all' strategy, a combination of forceful persuasion and persuasive threats led to Alstom and Airbus disclosing their global bribery activities. Yet many State Parties to the OECD Anti-Bribery Convention remain reluctant to comply with their convention obligations. The failure of France to take any action against Alstom, a company that has its headquarters in that country, epitomises the point. Here there is progress. In 2016, France enacted Law 2016-1691 (known as 'Sapin 2') which allows magistrates to enter into DPAs with companies with the maximum fine being 30 per cent of the company's annual turnover. To ensure transparency, the agreement requires the approval of a judge at a public hearing. This was applied in the Airbus case, where the company entered into a DPA (known as a Judicial Public Interest Agreement (CJIP)).

The active enforcement of the OECD Anti-Bribery Convention by all State Parties remains essential and this will not only act as an important deterrent but should also facilitate the development of more effective multi-jurisdictional coordination in combating foreign bribery, including encouraging and facilitating a 'global settlement' approach. Only time will tell as to whether the Airbus-type settlement will now become the norm.

Both cases also highlight that the *threat* of debarment and with it the resultant dire economic consequences for the company, as well as the serious collateral effects, play the key role in the 'reveal all' strategy. Once again, it is the political will on the part of countries to take action against even the most powerful corporate entities coupled with the economic threat that produces real results.

The Yates Memo is highly significant. By making eligibility for a settlement dependent upon the private legal entity providing the DoJ with 'all the relevant facts about the individuals involved in corporate misconduct', it enhances the prospect of making accountable those PEPs involved in authorising and/or undertaking the illegal activity as well as those in the highest echelons of the organisation who turn a 'blind eye' to corporate wrongdoing. It also acts as an important deterrent on any future illegal activity and provides a further incentive for senior officials of private sector entities to ensure that their compliance programmes are effectively implemented. This approach should be adopted elsewhere. The Yates Memo has drawn some criticism. One commentator describes it as rhetoric because the reality is that few DoJ corporate enforcement actions result in any related charges against company employees.[59] However, only time will tell whether this remains the case. What is important is that the policy is in place. As Yates herself has noted: 'Our goal is to get to the bottom of who did what and if there are culpable individuals, hold them accountable … Our goal is to uncover the truth.'[60]

These are exciting times. Just a few years ago, the idea that even the most powerful corporate entities could be persuaded *whether they wanted to or not* to take effective steps to prevent foreign bribery in their operations, would have seemed highly unlikely. This chapter has demonstrated that through the Art of Persuasion, good corporate governance and transparent management corporate conduct can be developed and that this can be of significant benefit in tackling corruption and money laundering by African PEPs. This remains work in progress.[61] In particular, China is not a party to the OECD Convention and, as a Transparency International report has noted, whilst there are reports of the alleged bribery of PEPs in several African states, there are no known foreign bribery cases or investigations brought by Chinese companies.[62] There is also no indication that the Chinese consortium responsible for bribing Mahmoud Thiam and laundering the proceeds of crime was ever prosecuted.[63]

Overall, the chapter has demonstrated the importance of the third AML 'prong': i.e. to prevent the future payment of bribes to PEPs and to persuade the past bribe-payers to 'reveal all', i.e. to identify the PEPs to whom the payments were made and how the proceeds of crime were laundered on their behalf. Breaking through the secrecy that has so long protected PEPs can make a major contribution to AML efforts in African states.

---

59 See FCPA Professor blog http://fcpaprofessor.com/the-yates-memo/ (accessed 7 June 2020). It is further asserted in the blog that between '2008 and 2014 75% of DOJ corporate enforcement actions have not (at least yet) resulted in *any* DOJ charges against company employees' (emphasis in the original).

60 Speech given by Sally Q Yates at the New York City Bar Association, White Collar Crime Conference, 17 May 2016, p. 5.

61 For example, the results of the EY Survey show that 'a significant minority of global executives [are] willing to justify unethical conduct' with the report concluding that 'individuals, including some senior executives entrusted with the guardianship of their firms, cannot be assumed to act with integrity if the end might seem to justify the means': pp. 20 and 41.

62 Transparency International, *Exporting Corruption: Progress report: Assessing enforcement of the OECD Anti-Bribery Convention*, 2018, pp. 93–7. The states named are Ethiopia, Kenya and Zambia.

63 See Section 2.1 above.

14. PEPs, money laundering and the African Court of Justice and Human and Peoples' Rights

14.1 BACKGROUND TO THE COURT

It was noted in earlier chapters that, with notable exceptions, there have been few (and even fewer successful) prosecutions of PEPs for money laundering offences in national courts or the recovery of their proceeds of crime.[1] This raises the question as to whether a pan-African court might provide an effective alternative approach to addressing money laundering by PEPs. This chapter critically explores the potential role of the International Criminal Law section of the African Court of Justice and Human and Peoples' Rights (the Court) in doing so.

At their June 2014 summit in Malabo, Equatorial Guinea, AU leaders adopted the Protocol on Amendments to the Protocol on the Statute of the African Court of Justice and Human Rights (the Malabo Protocol). This added a new international criminal law section (ICL Section) with an original and appellate jurisdiction to the General Affairs section and the Human and Peoples' Rights section.[2]

As a result, when in operation, the ICL Section will be competent to try both natural and legal persons in respect of 14 crimes which are 'of serious concern to African states'.[3] As Jalloh has noted, these cover a somewhat eclectic mix of crimes, including money laundering.[4]

---

1 The Cashgate and Amuti cases being notable exceptions: see Sections 2.1 and 10.4.2.

2 Article 3.1. All references to Articles in this chapter refer to the Malabo Protocol.

3 The Assembly of the Heads of State and Government of the African Union (the Assembly), upon the consensus of all States Parties, may also incorporate additional crimes to reflect developments in international law: Article 28A.2.

4 Charles Jalloh, A classification of the crimes in the Malabo Protocol, in Charles Jalloh, Kamari Clarke and Vincent Nmehielle (eds), *The African Court of Justice and Human and Peoples' Rights in Context: Development and Challenges*, Cambridge University Press, 2019, pp. 225 and 239. Other crimes include genocide, crimes against humanity and war crimes.

Some have criticised the Malabo Protocol as simply being a response to decisions of the International Criminal Court, which are seen as an abuse of universal jurisdiction by Western states for crimes committed in Africa, whilst others are more positive and regard it as a genuine attempt to tackle a series of serious crimes that have long bedevilled the African continent.[5] Whatever the merits of the discussion, arguably the key question is whether, in practice, such a court can play an effective role in addressing these serious crimes. The discussion on money laundering offences in this chapter will provide some assistance in answering this general question. Regrettably there are no *travaux preparatoires* available, thus making it difficult to clarify some of the more obscure provisions.

14.2 THE MONEY LAUNDERING OFFENCES

The offence of Money Laundering in Article 28I *Bis*.1 is based on Article 6 of the Palermo Convention albeit with significant differences.[6]

Firstly, unlike the Palermo Convention and the requirement in FATF Recommendation 3 that the crime of money laundering must apply to 'all serious offences', the Malabo Protocol restricts the predicate offence to corruption and related offences.[7]

Secondly, the Palermo Convention requires states to criminalise money laundering 'when committed intentionally'. This requirement is absent in the Malabo Protocol. The reason for this is not known although, in practice, it is likely that the Court will follow the approach in the Palermo Convention.[8]

Thirdly, the Palermo Convention requires that the concealment or disguise of property is an offence when undertaken 'knowing that such property is the

[5] See for example, the contrasting views of M Sirleaf, The African Justice Cascade and the Malabo Protocol, (2019) 11(1) *International Journal of Transitional Justice* 71, and C Bhoke Murungu, Towards a criminal chamber in the African Court of Justice and Human Rights, (2011) 9(5) *Journal of International Criminal Justice* 1067, at 1077–9.

[6] See the discussion on Article 6 in Section 2.2 above. FATF Recommendation 3 requires all countries to criminalise money laundering on the basis of the Palermo Convention.

[7] See further Section 14.3 below.

[8] Rose suggests that the use of the words 'knowing' and 'with the knowledge of' in other Articles of the Malabo Protocol could enable the Court to infer intention as the *mens rea* of the offence: see Cecily Rose, Money laundering and the African Court of Justice and Human and Peoples' Rights, in Jalloh Charles, Clarke Kamari and Nmehielle Vincent (eds), *The African Court of Justice and Human and Peoples' Rights in Context: Development and Challenges*, Cambridge University Press, 2019, p. 505, at p. 515.

proceeds of crime'.[9] The final words are missing from the Malabo Protocol. This was seemingly an oversight on the part of the drafters, especially as a money laundering offence can also involve the 'Acquisition, possession or use of property *with the knowledge at the time of receipt*, that such property is the proceeds of corruption or related offences' (emphasis added).[10]

Fourthly, Article 28I *Bis*.2 provides that '[n]othing in this article shall be interpreted as prejudicing the power of the Court to make a determination as to the seriousness of any act or offence'. The purpose and meaning of this provision is not immediately clear.

14.3 THE PREDICATE OFFENCES

The money laundering offence applies only to the predicate offence of corruption or related offences. There is no clear rationale for this restriction especially as PEPs may be involved in laundering the proceeds of crime from other Protocol offences.[11] In any event, it is not clear as to the meaning of the phrase 'or other offences'. Article 28I is headed 'Corruption' but contains no definition of the word, rather instead referring to a series of individual 'acts of corruption' which are largely based on those found in the UNCAC and the AU Convention. Whether one is to read the phrase 'or other offences' as referring to 'acts of corruption' is uncertain and the matter is bound to cause confusion for prosecutors and the Court alike.

14.4 WHO CAN COMMIT THE OFFENCES?

The ICL Section is competent to try both natural and legal persons.

With the exception of bribery in the private sector, corruption offences require the involvement of a 'public official'. The term is not defined but in practice the requirement that the act of corruption is of a 'serious nature' will inevitably limit its scope to PEPs.[12] Article 28I specifically extends liability to family members of the public official or any other person, presumably referring to close associates of PEPs.

As regards the private sector, Article 46E provides the Court with jurisdiction over legal persons, with the exception of states where, inter alia, 'the victim of the crime is a national of that State' or where the case involves

---

9 See also Article 23 of the UNCAC.

10 Article 28I *Bis* 1(iii).

11 Cf FATF Recommendation 3, which requires countries to apply the crime of money laundering to all serious offences, with a view to including the widest range of predicate offences.

12 For example, the Abacha case discussed in Section 14.7.2 below.

'Extraterritorial acts by non-nationals which threaten a vital interest of that State'.[13] This suggests the possibility of the prosecution of a company (and/or its agents) from within or outside Africa for the bribery of a PEP and/or a money laundering offence. Of course, this is subject to the 'act of corruption' being of a 'serious nature affecting the stability of the State' (Article 28I(1)) as well as threatening 'a vital interest of that State' (Article 46E *Bis*): a perhaps unlikely combination: but see the Thiam case noted below.

14.5 LIMITATIONS ON THE OPERATION OF THE COURT

14.5.1 The 'Serious Nature' Requirement

To engage the jurisdiction of the Court, an act of corruption must be 'of a serious nature affecting the stability of a state, region or the Union'.[14] The use of the word 'serious' is presumably designed to limit cases to those involving PEPs. What triggers such a finding raises numerous issues. Does the phrase require evidence that the corruption-related activity has led to the actual destabilisation (whatever that means) of the state or is it in respect of a *potential threat* to its stability? Certainly corruption by PEPs threatens the political and/or economic stability of a state, a point emphasised in the Preamble to the UNCAC where the States Parties to the Convention express their concern 'about the seriousness of the problems and *threats posed* by corruption to the *stability* and security of societies …' and further express their concern 'about cases of corruption that involve vast quantities of assets, which may constitute a substantial proportion of the resources of States, and that *threaten the political stability* and sustainable development of those States' (emphasis added). In the light of the UNCAC Preamble, it is hoped that the Court will adopt a flexible interpretation of 'stability'. There is a further difficulty as to how the fact of the 'instability' is to be proved. This is presumably a matter for the Court to determine,[15] but once again any case may get bogged down in preliminary arguments over this issue.

The scope of a 'region' is also nowhere explained. Given the positioning of the word after 'state', the drafters presumably meant to refer to a geo-

---

[13] Article 46E *bis* (2)(c) and (d).

[14] Of the fourteen criminal offences listed, only the 'Illicit exploitation of natural resources' includes a similar restriction: see Article 28L *bis*.

[15] The Office of the Prosecutor will also need to make a preliminary decision as to whether there is a reasonable basis to proceed with an investigation: see Article 46G(3).

graphical area that includes multiple jurisdictions.[16] This might cover a case, for example, involving senior military officers who loot vast sums of money allocated for defence equipment required to fight a terrorist group involved in a regional conflict.[17]

14.5.2 The Immunity Clause

Article 46A contains a wide-ranging immunity clause, which provides that:

> No charges shall be commenced or continued before the Court against any serving AU Head of State or government, or anybody acting or entitled to act in such capacity, or other senior state officials based on their functions, during their tenure of office.[18]

This goes far beyond the immunity granted to sitting Heads of State in most constitutions. Further extending the scope to include 'senior state officials based on their functions' is both opaque and unnecessary. As Amnesty International rightly asserts, the immunity provision 'essentially promotes and strengthens the culture of impunity that is already entrenched in most African countries and stands to bring the whole statute into disrepute as it will be portrayed (and may indeed have been intended) as a way to protect senior politicians from accountability for their crimes'.[19]

14.6 INVESTIGATIONS, SENTENCES AND ASSET RECOVERY

Prosecutors will also face a number of challenges as regards effective investigations and successful prosecutions.

---

[16] Although an argument could be mounted that corruption in a particular region within a state could destabilise it: for example, where corruption by leaders in a specific oil producing region of a country diverts revenues from the sale of the oil and gas, which leads to severe economic instability in the entire country.

[17] For example the Boko Haram group which operates in Nigeria, Chad and Cameroon.

[18] Immunity provisions enjoyed by PEPs at the national level are discussed in Section 9.4 above.

[19] Amnesty International, *Malabo Protocol: Legal and Institutional Implications of the Merged and Expended Africa Court*, 2016, at p. 27. See also the Southern African Catholic Bishops' Conference, *The African Court of Justice and Human Rights: Protecting Africans, or Just Africa's Leaders?*, 2014, Briefing Paper 359.

14.6.1 Evidence Gathering

The investigation and prosecution of money laundering and asset recovery almost inevitably involve lengthy and complex financial transnational investigations which are costly in both human and resource terms as well as requiring considerable expertise in a range of disciplines. Whether prosecutors will enjoy the necessary resources and expertise to enable them to carry out their functions effectively is questionable.

In addition, such investigations will almost inevitably require assistance from both the victim state and other states within and outside of Africa. Article 46L(1) requires States Parties to 'co-operate with the Court in the investigation and prosecution of persons accused of committing the crimes defined by this Statute'. In doing so, States Parties are required to comply 'without undue delay with any request for assistance or an order issued by the Court, including but not limited to:

(a) The identification and location of persons;
(b) The taking of testimony and the production of evidence;
(c) The service of documents;
(d) The arrest, detention or extradition of persons;
(e) The surrender or the transfer of the accused to the Court;
(f) The identification, tracing and freezing or seizure of proceeds, property and assets and instrumentalities of crimes for the purpose of eventual forfeiture, without prejudice to the rights of bona fide third parties.'[20]

In doing so, the Court is entitled 'to seek the co-operation or assistance of regional or international courts, non-States Parties or co-operating partners of the AU and may conclude Agreements for that purpose'.[21] This will require multilateral or bilateral agreements or the development of other international co-operation mechanisms.

Given the secrecy surrounding such offences together with the power of PEPs to 'control the controls', evidence gathering within the victim state may be extremely challenging, hence the importance of other countries providing effective co-operation.[22] The lack of clear provisions as to the procedure for obtaining such assistance is a matter of concern. It is essential that investigators have the power to obtain rapidly relevant evidence located in other states (or to

---

[20] Article 46L(2) Malabo Protocol. In the context of corruption and money laundering offences in particular, it is surprising that the provision omits specific reference to the power to require the production of relevant documents and records, including government, bank, financial, corporate or business records.

[21] Article 46L(3).

[22] See generally Chapter 8 above.

prevent its destruction) or to seek the freezing of the proceeds of crime before they are moved to another jurisdiction(s). Whilst the Office of the Prosecutor may seek additional information from states and others,[23] the power to make a formal MLA request is seemingly only available to the Court under Article 46L. Providing the power for the Office of the Prosecutor to obtain MLA from the start of an investigation, particularly as regards maintaining confidentiality of the investigation, is an absolute necessity.[24]

There is clearly much work to be done on addressing the area of MLA. The very detailed provisions on MLA contained in the UNCAC can provide a helpful model here.[25] In addition, the drafters also seem unaware of including alternative means of obtaining information and assistance which by-passes and/or eliminates the need for formal MLA.[26]

The statute makes no mention of whistleblowers. Here the introduction of rules providing for the 'non-disclosure or limitations on the disclosure of information concerning the identity of witnesses' might be considered.[27] This will require the Court to perform a difficult balancing act between admitting potentially vital evidence from anonymous witnesses whilst at the same time protecting the right of accused persons to confront their accusers.[28] Whether the Court will be in a position to offer effective protection to individual whistleblowers is also unclear. The development of 'super-whistleblowers' as epitomised by the leaking of the Panama Papers, and the Luanda Papers may prove to be a more effective source of information and evidence for the Court.

14.6.2 Penalties and Asset Recovery and Enforcement

The judgment of the Court is final. The Court can impose 'prison sentences and/or pecuniary fines'.[29] Given that the object of money laundering is for

---

23 I.e. Organs of the AU or the United Nations, intergovernmental or non-governmental organisations or other reliable sources: see Article 46G(2).

24 An additional point is that MLA requests in sensitive cases will often require strict confidentiality: something that may not be available if an order of the Court is required. Presumably the Office of the Prosecutor will be in a position to obtain the necessary assistance from forensic accountants and other experts in undertaking what will almost inevitably involve complex financial investigations.

25 See Article 46.

26 See Section 8.5 above.

27 See for example, UNCAC Article 32(2). See also the discussion in Section 9.4 above.

28 See Article 46A(4)(e).

29 Article 43A(1) and (2). In imposing sentences and/or penalties, 'the Court should take into account such factors as the gravity of the offence and the individual circumstances of the convicted person'.

PEPs to enjoy the fruits of their criminality, the power to order the forfeiture of proceeds of crime as part of the sentence is attractive and Article 43A(5) provides that the Court may also order 'the forfeiture of any property, proceeds or any asset acquired unlawfully or by criminal conduct, and their return to their rightful owner or to an appropriate Member State'. Article 43A is complemented by Article 45(2), which provides that 'the Court may make an order directly against a convicted person specifying appropriate reparations to, or in respect of, victims including restitution, compensation and rehabilitation'. These provisions reflect the approach in the UNCAC and the AU Convention which have strong provisions requiring States Parties to have in place asset recovery mechanisms, with the return of assets being a fundamental principle of the UNCAC.[30]

A system of conviction-based asset forfeiture is attractive in that offenders are subject to a criminal conviction, face a prison sentence and, as part of their sentence, are also liable to an order for the confiscation of their proceeds of corruption. However, it is premised on a criminal conviction. In practice, this may not be possible. Setting aside the very real challenges of proving the case to the criminal standard, a prosecution will be impossible where the suspect is unavailable or subject to the immunity provision. In addition, enforcing a criminal confiscation order where the assets are located in multiple jurisdictions presents an immense challenge.

Given these realities, limiting the Court to a conviction-based asset recovery mechanism is unnecessary and out-dated and the provisions in the statute are likely to prove of little value in practice. It is disappointing that the Court has no power to make use of non-criminal based asset forfeiture methods.[31]

The Malabo Protocol is silent as to whether a PEP may seek to reach a settlement with the Office of the Prosecutor which involves the return of (at least part of) the proceeds of corruption in exchange for an agreement to defer or withdraw a prosecution. It is an approach which must be introduced if asset recovery is to be effective in practice.

14.7 CASE STUDIES

The Court has jurisdiction only with respect to crimes committed after the entry into force of the Protocol and Statute.[32] Thus it is likely to be some years before it has to consider a case involving money laundering. However, four short case studies involving African PEPs may usefully illustrate the potential

---

[30] Article 51. Chapter V of the Convention is devoted to 'Asset Recovery'.

[31] See Section 10.3 above.

[32] As required under Article 46E(1).

scope and limitations of the Court. The cases are described as if the Court is in operation, the respective states have accepted its jurisdiction and the crimes were committed after the entry in force of the Protocol and Statute.

14.7.1 The Obiang Case

The adoption of the Protocol in Malabo is somewhat ironic given the involvement of Teodorin Obiang Mangue (Obiang), the son of the President of Equatorial Guinea and Vice-President, in corruption and money laundering.[33] Whilst receiving an official government salary of less than US$100,000 he used his position and influence as a government minister to amass more than US$300 million worth of assets through corruption and then laundered them via intermediaries and corporate entities into numerous jurisdictions.[34]

Arguably, the extent of Obiang's criminal activities represents a clear example of corruption of a 'serious nature' and its deleterious impact on the economic well-being of the people of the country arguably affects the 'stability' of Equatorial Guinea. This is the type of case that might come before the Court. However, Obiang's position as Vice-President makes him a 'senior state official' and consequently the immunity provision in Article 46A will apply and no charges of corruption or money laundering can be brought against him during his tenure of office.

14.7.2 The Abacha Case

Sani Abacha seized power in a military coup in Nigeria in 1993 and until his death in 1998 he and his family were involved in the widespread looting of state assets with estimates varying between US$3 billion and US$5 billion. As with the Obiang case, the scale of the grand corruption was arguably enough to satisfy the 'serious nature' requirement of Article 28I.

The untimely death of Abacha would prevent any prosecution of him before the Court. However, his national security adviser and several members of Abacha's family were all involved in laundering his proceeds of corruption around the world.[35] As regards the national security adviser, his immunity from the jurisdiction of the Court ended with his tenure of office, whilst Abacha's

---

33 See the recovery of some of his proceeds of crime discussed in Section 10.3.4.

34 US Department of Justice Press Release, 10 October 2014. Available at https://www.justice.gov/opa/pr/second-vice-president-equatorial-guinea-agrees-relinquish-more-30-million-assets-purchased (accessed 7 June 2020).

35 One such scheme is detailed by Rix, J in *Compagnie Noga et d'Exportation SA v Australia and New Zealand Banking Group*, 2001, unreported, England and Wales High Court, Queen's Bench Division (Comm).

family members did not enjoy any such immunity. Charges of abuse of functions under Article 28I(1)(c) and illicit enrichment under Article 28I(1)(g) (amongst others) and money laundering would be possible against them all. An Indian national, Raj Bhojwani, assisted Abacha with the laundering. He was therefore a close associate and could face money laundering charges before the Court.[36] Convictions would then empower the Court to order the forfeiture and return of the proceeds of crime.

14.7.3 The Chiluba Case

Between 1991 and 2001 Frederick Chiluba was President of Zambia. During his period in office he was involved in the large scale looting of state assets and these were laundered on a global scale. He was assisted by numerous senior public officials, lawyers and corporate entities.[37] Upon leaving office, his successor, Levy Mwanawasa, established a Task Force on Corruption to investigate the case and a prosecution was launched in 2004 with Chiluba being charged with several counts of theft by a public servant. In 2008, Mwanawasa died in office and was succeeded by Rupiah Banda, who was known to be more supportive of Chiluba. In 2009 Chiluba was acquitted in the Lusaka Magistrates' Court on all charges, a verdict that was greeted with much scepticism by CSOs.[38]

As a former Head of State, Chiluba did not enjoy the benefit of the immunity provision in Article 46A and would therefore fall within the jurisdiction of the Court.[39] The Court has a complementary jurisdiction to national courts[40] although any case against Chiluba would be inadmissible 'if it is being investigated or prosecuted by Zambia' or has been investigated and the state has decided not to prosecute 'unless the decision resulted from the unwillingness

[36] In fact in 2010 he was convicted in Jersey of money laundering in connection with the Abacha case and sentenced to six years' imprisonment: see *Attorney-General for Jersey v Bhojwani* [2010] JCA 188 and John Kelleher and Paul Sugden, Money laundering in Jersey: a case analysis: *Att Gen v Bhojwani*, [2011] *Jersey and Guernsey Law Review*. Available at https://www.jerseylaw.je/publications/jglr/Pages/JLR1106_Kelleher.aspx#_ftn6 (accessed 7 June 2020).

[37] The full details by Peter Smith J in *Attorney General for Zambia v Meer Care & Desai* [2007] EWHC 952 (Ch).

[38] For a critique of the decision see 'Press Statement on the Acquittal of Dr. Frederick Chiluba and the General Justice System in Zambia Delivered by 17 Civil Society Organisations on 30th September 2009'. Available at http://gndhlovu.blogspot.co.uk/2009/09/press-statement-on-acquittal-of-dr.html (accessed 7 June 2020).

[39] See Section 14.5.2 above.

[40] Article 46H(1).

or inability of the State to carry out the investigation or prosecution'.[41] In the Chiluba case, the concern focused on possible political pressure that was brought to bear on the trial magistrate.[42] In such circumstances, it is open to the Court to determine that the 'proceedings were … undertaken or the national decision was made for the purpose of shielding the person concerned from criminal responsibility for crimes within the jurisdiction of the court'.[43] How such a situation is to be proved is not explored but it does open up the possibility of the Court having jurisdiction in a Chiluba-type situation.[44]

14.7.4 The Thiam Case

As noted in Section 2.1, Mahmoud Thiam, the Minister of Mines in Guinea, was bribed to award a highly lucrative contract to a Chinese conglomerate, CIF, which also assisted in laundering the proceeds of crime. Assuming that the 'act of corruption' was sufficiently serious, this would provide the Court with jurisdiction not only over Thiam but also the bribe-paying company as the case involved 'Extraterritorial acts by non-nationals which threaten a vital interest of [Guinea]' i.e. its mining sector.[45]

14.8 CONCLUSIONS

Given the challenges in addressing money laundering by PEPs at the national level, the establishment of a pan-African court is a potentially attractive concept. Yet, as this chapter has highlighted, serious doubts remain as to the extent to which, in practice, the Court will be able to undertake this task.

Firstly, linking the money laundering offence to the predicate offence of 'corruption or related offences' significantly and unnecessarily limits the jurisdiction of the Court. This is exacerbated by the requirement that acts of corruption must be of a 'serious nature affecting the stability of a state, region or the Union'. This requirement serves no purpose other than to severely limit the cases which can be heard by the Court. No doubt much time and energy will be wasted on arguments as to the meaning and scope of this obscure phrase.

---

41 Article 46H(2). Article 46H(3) sets out the principles upon which the Court is to determine the matter.

42 The Court may also determine that a case is inadmissible where it is 'not of sufficient gravity to justify further action': Article 46H(2)(d). This is not relevant to corruption cases given the 'serious nature' requirement in Article 28I.

43 Article 46H(3)(a).

44 In fact several senior government officials involved with Chiluba in the corruption were successfully prosecuted in Zambia.

45 Article 46E(2)(d).

Secondly, the immunity clause threatens to undermine the work of the Court. As Amnesty International points out, it 'promotes and strengthens the culture of impunity that is already entrenched in most African countries...'. In essence it protects (at least during their time in office) a very wide range of PEPs from being accountable for their crimes. However, the immunity provision does not offer any protection to the family of PEPs, their close associates nor the bribe-paying companies. Thus the possibility of a successful prosecution for money laundering of those assisting PEPs remains and could provide the 'teeth' that the Court will otherwise lack.

Thirdly, there is the practical problem of obtaining effective international co-operation. The Court will need to establish a procedure for seeking MLA both for the purposes of the trial and for enabling prosecutors at the earliest available opportunity to obtain evidence and to freeze the suspected proceeds of crime no matter where in the world the evidence or proceeds are located.

Fourthly, the asset recovery provisions are too narrowly drawn and there is a need for the Court to enjoy a NCBAF power. In addition, it is important to provide prosecutors with the power to agree settlements with the PEPs (albeit with the approval of the Court) in which the return of the proceeds of corruption to the people of the victim state takes place in exchange for the withdrawal of criminal charges. Similarly, corporate bribe-payers/money launderers may prefer to seek an out-of-court settlement.

Finally, the Malabo Protocol will only come into force after 15 ratifications. By 1 July 2020 only five states had done so. On the face of it, the prospect of reaching the required threshold in the near future is poor. Even if it does come into force, one cannot but agree with the view of Viljoen that without significant amendments, the Court is destined to become an 'empty and ineffectual shell'.[46]

---

[46] Frans Viljoen, A human rights court for Africa and Africans, (2004) 30(1) *Brooklyn Journal of International Law* 1, at 6.

15. Hope for the future: dealing with PEPs: towards enhancing AML strategies in African countries

15.1 INTRODUCTION

The Preface to this book is headed 'Hope for the Future?' I have omitted the question mark now because, as argued in the book, there are real hopes that positive steps are being taken to combat money laundering by PEPs.

The MERs, the reports from the African RBs and those from individual AML agencies on money laundering, especially by PEPs, provide a detailed picture about *how it is done* and *who assists them*. In this there is remarkable consistency throughout Africa. So the question is *how to deal with it?*

The FATF Recommendations provide the basic blueprint for doing so and are of African-wide application. As has been argued, a three prong approach to addressing money laundering by PEPs is required, i.e. at the domestic level, the transnational level and at the corporate level.

15.2 ENHANCING AML STRATEGIES AT THE DOMESTIC LEVEL

15.2.1 PEPs and Leadership: A Fresh Commitment

The quality of life in a country does not depend primarily upon its size or resources but on leadership.[1] Constitutions provide PEPs with the tools and powers for leadership. With these comes the responsibility to use them for the benefit of the people and the development of the country. It is the failure of leadership that has led to the writing of this book. Whilst the AU and many African leaders have identified anti-corruption/AML measures as key priori-

[1] See the very eloquent view of James F Mitchell in *A Season of Light*, Concepts Publishing, 2001, pp. 173 et seq. Mitchell was a former Prime Minister of St Vincent and the Grenadines.

ties and some have developed national AML action plans, the political will to put these into practice remains a challenge.

The 'Fundamental controls over money laundering' enjoyed by PEPs and noted throughout the book will always remain. Some of the case studies have starkly revealed this reality. Yet whilst PEPs enjoy unique money laundering opportunities by virtue of their position, they remain vulnerable if AML safeguards are utilised effectively. This is emphasised in many of the other case studies in the book. It is useful to review them here.

15.2.2 Constitutional Controls

As stressed throughout the book, the national constitution is the supreme law. Its fundamental role is to support just and honest government and 'the articulation of the values binding its people and disciplining its government'.[2] It therefore plays a key AML in respect of PEPs. These include provisions:

- providing for independent AML institutions and agencies;
- requiring PEPs to declare their assets;
- empowering the Auditor General to scrutinise procurement contracts and to oversee their implementation; and
- providing a series of enforceable fundamental rights which can be used as AML tools.

15.2.3 The Role of the Courts

The courts play a key role in enforcing and upholding constitutional rights and protecting the independence of constitutional AML institutions. This requires:

- an independent and courageous judiciary that is prepared to protect the Constitution and constitutional AML institutions from attempts by PEPs to undermine them;
- a flexible approach to *locus standi* that facilitates action by CSOs; and
- a flexible approach to constitutional interpretation.

15.2.4 The 'You Can't Do It Alone' Reality: Public Servants and the Rise of the Whistleblowers

The discussion has emphasised that PEPs 'cannot do it alone'. Money laundering both domestically and transnationally requires the active assistance of

---

2 Per Mohammed JA in *S v Acheson* 1991 (2) SA 805 (Nm) at p. 813 A-B.

a range of PMLs, financial institutions and facilitating states. The Cashgate, Thiam, dos Santos and the EAC pension cases all neatly demonstrate the point.

However, it is also imperative to focus on other public servants who are involved (willingly or otherwise) in assisting PEPs in the laundering activity or have knowledge or at least suspicion of potential illegal activity. They may well face threats from PEPs if they do not co-operate (or at least turn a blind eye) to the on-going criminality: as the Chiluba case highlights. Yet they play a potentially vital role in breaking through the secrecy attaching to money laundering by PEPs. As a starting point, it is crucial that an effective whistle-blowing system is in operation that provides protection for reporting officials and their families. Easier said than done of course, but one that is a worthwhile goal and the implementation of effective whistleblowing laws will help in this respect.

A recent exciting development is the rise of the 'super-whistleblower'. The revelations from the Panama Papers and the Luanda Papers continue to have global repercussions and have exposed for all to see the corruption and money laundering activities of numerous PEPs. Whether the leak comes from an anonymous whistleblower (as in the Panama Papers case) or from a crusading CSO (as in the Luanda Papers case), they highlight a key vulnerability of PEPs.

In the Luanda case, it is also interesting to note the response of those involved in assisting Ms dos Santos create her overseas financial empire. The freezing of assets, the closing of bank accounts and the like are all well and good. Yet the question remains as to why no red flags were seemingly raised about the scale and extent of her financial dealings.

15.2.5 Developing New AML Strategies

African countries must take advantage of the significant international developments discussed below. These include:

- developing new asset recovery techniques including the introduction of unexplained wealth orders;
- taking steps to enhance the transparency in the beneficial ownership of legal persons;
- enhancing the supervision over off-shore banks, companies and trusts; and
- participating in global settlements involving the recovery of the proceeds of crime by PEPs.

15.2.6 The Contribution of CSOs

As demonstrated throughout the book, CSOs continue to make an active contribution to national AML efforts.

Given the availability of information about the AML situation in individual African countries, this work needs to be built upon and enhanced.

There are a number of strategies for doing so:

- *Constitution-watching*: CSOs must play an active oversight role regarding the operation (or otherwise) of the constitutional AML mechanisms. For example, monitoring the office of the Auditor General to ensure that it is carrying out its constitutional mandate and that the legislature is supporting it. Highlighting any failure to do so provides an early warning of potential financial impropriety by PEPs and raises public awareness of the issue.
- *AML-compliance watching*: As the MERs have highlighted, few countries are fully compliant with the FATF standards. Whilst the follow-up process by the African RBs is invaluable, having CSOs highlight these on-going deficiencies and vulnerabilities can create public awareness of the issues and bring pressure to bear for remedial action.
- Working with, and supporting the work of, AML agencies: The vital AML role of FIUs and supervisors, amongst others, is seemingly little known or understood by the public. Similarly the AML vulnerabilities created by the failure of DNFBPs to comply with the reporting obligations seemingly have attracted little, if any, public attention. Working with such agencies to disseminate information about the operation of AML safeguards in practice has great potential in raising public awareness and their consequent strengthening.
- Involvement in any agreement regarding the return of stolen assets as well as an ongoing role in monitoring their effective use for the benefit of the people.
- *Using the Constitution*: Not only are CSOs required to support the Constitution, it is important that they make use of its provisions to challenge attempts by PEPs to weaken AML safeguards. This may involve both invoking fundamental rights provisions as well as bringing judicial review proceedings in appropriate cases. As noted earlier, a flexible approach to *locus standi* by the courts will facilitate such action.

15.3 TRANSNATIONAL LEVEL: STRENGTHENING INTERNATIONAL CO-OPERATION

In the fight against money laundering by PEPs, the earlier chapters have emphasised the vital necessity for effective transnational co-operation between African countries *inter se* and with facilitating and safe haven states. Here there are some positive developments

The exchange of MOUs between numerous African FIUs now facilitates the sharing of financial information on a reciprocal basis without the need for a formal MLA request. This complements the work of the Egmont Group in facilitating the exchange of financial information between FIUs on a global basis.

There is also important work aimed at strengthening international cooperation on tax transparency and addressing illicit financial flows and money laundering. For example, the African Development Bank Group (AfDB) is now providing assistance and advice to African countries on tackling illicit financial flows and money laundering through its 'Strategic Framework and Action Plan for the Prevention of Illicit Financial Flows in Africa (2017–2021)'. This is designed to support the implementation of tax transparency standards by African countries.[3] Similarly, the partnership between the Global Forum on Transparency and Exchange of Information for Tax Purposes and the AU Commission in improving tax co-operation through tax transparency and exchange of information in order to combat corruption and money laundering is producing encouraging results.[4]

Enhancing beneficial ownership transparency is now high on the international agenda. PEPs can no longer rely on all facilitating states maintaining the secrecy that they previously offered. The introduction of public beneficial ownership records is now becoming a global norm. Of course, this is not the final answer, given the issue of ensuring the accuracy of such registers. Even so, it represents another vital move against the laundering of the proceeds of crime by PEPs.

There are also promising new and effective mechanisms for asset recovery. Moving towards a global implementation of NCBAF mechanisms, including unexplained wealth orders, will surely reap rewards and perhaps lead to more 'deals' being made between PEPs and the authorities along the lines of the Obiang case. In the Jammeh case in July 2020, the US Department of Justice sought a NCBAF order against property allegedly acquired with the proceeds of corruption by the former President of Gambia, Yahya Jammeh and his wife, Zineb Jammeh. During his years in power (1994–2017) Jammeh allegedly conspired with family members and close associates to launder the proceeds globally, including through the purchase of the defendant property (including a multi-million dollar mansion) in violation of US and Gambian law.[5] Jammeh also operated over 100 private bank accounts directly or through companies

---

[3] The AfDB is also currently developing a 'Strategy for Economic Governance in Africa' which will emphasise further support to African countries on developing tax transparency.

[4] See Global Forum on Transparency and Exchange of Information for Tax Purposes *Tax Transparency in Africa 2020*, p. 58.

[5] *United States v Real property located in Potomac, Maryland, commonly known as 9908 Bentcross Drive, Potomac, Md 20854 and all appurtenances, improvements,*

or foundations. As 'property constituting, derived from, or traceable to the proceeds of "specified unlawful activity," as that term is defined in 18 U.S.C. §1956(c)(7), or a conspiracy to commit "specified unlawful activity," and as property involved in money laundering violations of 18 U.S.C. §§1956 and 1957,' the plaintiff (the United States) sought the forfeiture of the property under 18 USC §981(a)(1)(A) and (a)(1)(C). It remains to be seen whether Jammeh will seek to make a 'deal' with the authorities or whether the property will be subject to a NCBAF order.

Above all, there is evidence that there is a growing political commitment on the part of facilitating and safe haven states to take active steps to tackle PEPs and their laundered proceeds of crime. The 'no hiding place' for PEPs is still some way off but it is a goal worth aspiring to.

15.4 ADDRESSING THE PRIVATE SECTOR

The techniques designed to persuade the bribe-paying companies to 'reveal all' provide another promising approach towards revealing details of the corrupt deals with PEPs and the laundering of the proceeds of crime. As the Alstom and Airbus cases highlight, even the most powerful private legal entities cannot disregard the threat of debarment and the potential dire economic consequences.

In addition, the hope is that use of joint investigation teams from the 'home' countries of the bribe-paying companies will provide a further incentive towards the 'reveal all' approach. The Airbus case is a truly remarkable example of the effectiveness of such a strategy.

It is vital that the victim African countries benefit from these developments. In particular:

- to obtain full information from the bribe-payers identifying the domestic PEPs in receipt of the bribe payments and the method(s) of laundering them;
- to obtain full international co-operation through the provision of evidence and other material for use in domestic prosecutions of PEPs and their associates;
- to ensure that each African victim country is a party to any global settlement and can therefore obtain compensation and redress from the bribe-payers; and

---

and attachments located thereon, and any property traceable thereto, [1-3 and 28] Case 8:20-cv-02071, 15 July 2020.

- where this is not forthcoming, the prosecution of the bribe-paying company should be considered accompanied with the threat of debarment following any successful prosecution.

These developments provide African victim states with a unique opportunity to break through the secrecy associated with corruption and money laundering by their PEPs.

15.5 A FINAL REFLECTION

The economic and developmental problems in African countries caused by money laundering by PEPs remain acute. The Thiam case is indeed a classic case that encapsulates all the key challenges discussed in this book:

- the bribery of a foreign PEP by a company intending to obtain or retain business;
- the PEP using their position and influence to ensure that the company obtains the contract;
- there are no effective safeguards built into the procurement process;
- the resultant contract is highly disadvantageous to the country;
- the proceeds of crime are laundered through the global financial system;
- financial institutions fail to undertake effective AML checks;
- off-shore companies are created in a variety of jurisdictions with the beneficial ownership by the PEP hidden;
- the companies are used to purchase valuable real estate and other property in a 'safe haven' state;
- the importance of providing effective mechanisms for the return of the proceeds of crime to the victim country.

Such situations are exacerbated by the failure of so many African countries to comply fully with their AML obligations or to develop national AML plans and/or to implement them in an effective manner.

Yet as the book has demonstrated, there are real grounds for optimism. We have come a long way in a relatively short space of time. There are new and exciting AML strategies. There is a growing global political commitment to tackle money laundering by African PEPs.

PEPs may still seek to use their political influence domestically to 'control the controls' but even here the book has highlighted strategies for addressing these effectively. PEPs enjoy no such control globally and this constitutes their greatest vulnerability. The development of the political will, especially on the part of facilitating and safe haven states, to take active AML steps is a key development. In essence it is a combination of this global political will coupled with economic threats against those paying and laundering the bribes that is making the difference.

Of course, much work is still needed and it is idealistic to expect that the problems of PEPs and money laundering will rapidly become a thing of the past. Yet it is right to feel optimistic that things are moving in the right direction and that Thiam-type cases can be addressed. After all, this is what African countries and their people demand and deserve. Perhaps the present position is best described in the words of Winston Churchill: 'Now this is not the end. It is not even the beginning of the end, but it is, perhaps, the end of the beginning.'

Bibliography

Adangor, Z, The Presidential Pardon granted to Chief DSP Alamieyeseigha, (2015) 39 *Journal of Law, Policy and Globalization* 178.

African Union Advisory Board on Corruption, *Concept note on the 3rd Edition of the African Anti-Corruption Dialogue on the theme 'Towards a Common African Position on Asset Recovery'*, Arusha, 2019.

Akech, Migai, Abuse of power and corruption in Kenya, (2011) 18(1) *Indiana Journal of Global Legal Issues* 342.

Amnesty International, *Malabo Protocol: Legal and Institutional Implications of the Merged and Expended Africa Court*, 2016.

Amundsen, Inge, *Political Corruption in Africa: Extraction and Power Preservation*, Edward Elgar, 2019.

Bacarese, Alan, 'Malawi's Cashgate Crisis: An African Corruption Metaphor or a Sign of Hope?' Basel Institute on Governance, 2015.

Banco, Sarah, et al. Anti-Corruption Initiatives in Africa, in Marc Hammerson and John C LaMaster (eds), *Oil and Gas in Africa: A Legal and Commercial Analysis of the Upstream Industry*, Globe Law and Business, 2015, pp. 157–63.

Bank of Ghana/Financial Intelligence Centre, *AML/CFT&P Guidelines for Banks and Non-Bank Financial Institutions*, issued in January 2018.

Birt, Michael, The power of the UK to legislate for the Crown Dependencies without consent: Fact or fiction? (2017) 21(2) *Jersey and Guernsey Law Review* 152.

Boutros, Andrew S and T Markus Frank, 'Carbon Copy' prosecutions: a growing anti-corruption phenomenon in a shrinking world, [2012] *U Chicago Legal Forum* 259.

Bruinsma, G, and W Bernasco, Criminal groups and transnational illegal markets, [2004] *Crime, Law and Social Change*, 79–94.

Burgess, Tom, *The Looting Machine*, 2015, William Collins.

Carter, Brett L, The rise of kleptocracy: autocrats versus activists in Africa, (2018) 29(1) *Journal of Democracy* 54.

Chioma, Unini, Recent decision in *Barr Ikenga Imo v The President* and the constitutionality of Order 6 of 2018, (18 October 2018) *The Nigerian Lawyer.*

Chipkin, Ivor and Swilling, Mark, *Shadow State: The Politics of State Capture*, Wits University Press, 2018.

Chu, Vivian, 'The President's Pardon and Legal Effect on Collateral Consequences', 26 July 2016. Available at https://www.everycrsreport.com/reports/R44571.html (accessed 7 June 2020).

Clark, Naeemah, The impact of mass communications in America, (1968) *Annals* 68.

Colangelo, Anthony J, Double jeopardy and multiple sovereigns: a jurisdictional theory, (2009) 86 *Washington University Law Review* 769.

Commission for Africa, *Our Common Interest*, 2005.

Commonwealth Secretariat, *Commonwealth (Latimer House) Principles on the Accountability of and Relationship between the Three Branches of Government.*

Davis, Joanne *Parliamentarians and Corruption in Africa: The Challenge of Leadership and the Practice of Politics*, Ottawa, The Parliamentary Centre, 2009.

Demone, Bradley, LGBT rights in Malawi: one step back, two steps forward? The case of *R v Steven Monjeza Soko and Tiwonge Chimbalanga Kachepa*, (2016) 60(3) *Journal of African Law* 365.

Duker, William F, The President's power to pardon: a constitutional history, (1977) 18 *William and Mary Law Review* 475.

Enweremadu, David U, Nigeria's quest to recover looted assets: The Abacha Affair, (2013) 48(2) *Africa Spectrum* 51.

ESAAMLG (Eastern and Southern Africa Anti-Money Laundering Group), *20 Years: From Arusha to Ezulwini: Looking Back and Looking Ahead* Dar es Salaam, 2019.

ESAAMLG, *Annual Report 2016–2017*, Dar es Salaam, 2017.

ESAAMLG, *Botswana: Mutual Evaluation Report*, 2017.

ESAAMLG, *First Round Mutual Evaluations: Post Evaluation Progress Report of Mozambique on AML/CFT Measures*, 2018 (the ESAAMLG Mozambique report).

ESAAMLG, *First Round Mutual Evaluation – Post Evaluation Progress Report of Rwanda*, 2017.

ESAAMLG, *Malawi: Mutual Evaluation Report*, 2019.

ESAAMLG, *Mauritius: Mutual Evaluation Report*, 2018.

ESAAMLG, *Memorandum of Understanding among Member Countries of the Eastern and, Southern Africa Anti-Money Laundering Group.*

ESAAMLG, *Mutual Evaluation Procedures*, 2008.

ESAAMLG, *Mutual Evaluation Report of Mauritius*, 2016.

ESAAMLG, *Post Evaluation Progress Report of Mozambique on AML/CFT Measures*, 2018.

ESAAMLG, *Procurement Corruption in the Public Sector and Associated Money Laundering in the ESAAMLG Region*, 2019.

ESAAMLG, *Seychelles Mutual Evaluation Report*, 2018.

ESAAMLG, *Survey Report on De-risking in the ESAAMLG Region*, 2016.

ESAAMLG, *Uganda Mutual Evaluation Report*, 2016.

ESAAMLG, *Uganda: Second Follow-Up Report*, 2018.

EY 14th Global Fraud Survey, *Corporate Misconduct: Individual Consequences*, 2016.

FATF (Financial Action Task Force), *Best Practices Paper: The Use of the FATF Recommendations to Combat Corruption*, Paris, 2013.

FATF, *Concealment of Beneficial Ownership*, Paris, 2018.

FATF, *Guidance: Politically Exposed Persons*, Paris, 2013.

FATF, *Guidance for a Risk-Based Approach: Virtual Assets and Virtual Asset Service Providers*, 2019.

FATF, *Guidance on Transparency and Beneficial Ownership*, 2014.

FATF, *Laundering the Proceeds of Corruption*, Paris, 2011.

FATF, *Money Laundering and Terrorist Financing Vulnerabilities of Legal Professionals*, Paris, 2013.

FATF, *Professional Money Laundering*, Paris, 2018.

FATF, *Report to G20 Finance Ministers and Central Bank Governors*, Paris, 2018.

Findlay, Michael, Daniel Neilson and Jason Sharman, 'Global Shell Games: Testing Money Launderers' and Terrorist Financiers' Access to Shell Companies', Centre for Governance and Public Policy, 2012.

Fombad, Charles, and Nico Steytler (eds), *Corruption and Constitutionalism in Africa: Revisiting Control Measures and Strategies*, Oxford University Press, 2020.

Forsyth, Miranda, 'Fourteen Jailed: Politics and Justice in Vanuatu', ANU Briefing Paper, 2015/65.
G20, *High-Level Principles on Beneficial Transparency Ownership*, 2014.
Ghana, Republic of, *National Anti-Money Laundering and Countering the Financing of Terrorism (AML/CFT) Risk Assessment of Ghana*, Accra, 2018.
GIABA (Inter Governmental Action Group against Money Laundering in West Africa), *Annual Report*, 2017.
GIABA, *Anti-money laundering and counter-terrorist financing measures – Cabo Verde, Second Round Mutual Evaluation Report*, 2019.
GIABA, *Corruption – Money Laundering nexus: An analysis of risks and control measures in West Africa*, 2010.
GIABA, *Ghana: First Enhanced Follow-Up Report and Technical Compliance Re-Rating*, 2018.
GIABA, *Money laundering relating to fraud in public procurement in West Africa: A case study of Nigeria*, 2014.
GIABA, *Money Laundering and Terrorist Financing Linked to the Extractive Industry/ Mining Sector in West Africa*, 2019.
GIABA, 'Mutual Evaluation Implementation Action Plan' drawn up for Senegal in 2011.
GIABA, *Process and Procedures: Mutual Evaluations*, 2014.
GIABA, *Report of the GIABA Seminar on Transparency of Beneficial Ownership for Francophone African Countries*, 2018, GIABA *Annual Report 2018*.
GIABA, *The vulnerabilities of designated non-financial businesses and professions to money laundering and terrorist financing and the adequacy of control measures in West Africa*, Dakar, 2015.
GIABA Research Report, *The Vulnerabilities of Designated Non-Financial Businesses and Professions to Money Laundering and Terrorist Financing and the Adequacy of Control Measures in West Africa*, 2015.
Gikonyo, Constance, The legal profession in Kenya and its anti-money laundering obligations or lack thereof, (2019) 22(2) *JMLC* 247.
Gilmore, William, *Dirty Money: The Evolution of Money Laundering Countermeasures*, 2nd edn., Council of Europe Publishing, 1999.
Global Financial Integrity, *Illicit Financial Flows to and from 148 Developing Countries: 2006–2015*, 2019.
Global Forum on Transparency and Exchange of Information for Tax Purposes, *Tax Transparency in Africa 2020*, 2020.
Global Initiative 'Fighting corruption during the coronavirus pandemic', 2020.
Global Witness, *In Pursuit of Hidden Owners Behind Companies*, London, 2018.
Goredema, Charles and Jackson Madzima, 'An assessment of the links between corruption and the implementation of anti-money laundering strategies and measures in the ESAAMLG region', Report for the ESAAMLG, 2009.
Haldevang, Max de, 'How Africa's richest woman bought her way out of scrutiny from Western banks', QuartzAfrica, 2020.
Hall, M, and T Young, Recent constitutional developments in Mozambique, (1991) 35(1) *Journal of African Law* 102.
Hamman, A, and R Koen, *Cave Pecuniam*: lawyers as launderers, [2012] *PER* 49.
Hammerson, Marc, LaMaster, John C, (eds), *Oil and Gas in Africa: A Legal and Commercial Analysis of the Upstream Industry*, Globe Law and Business, 2015.
Hatchard, John, *Combating Corruption: Legal Approaches to Supporting Good Governance and Integrity in Africa*, Edward Elgar, 2014.

Hatchard, John, Legal practitioners as potential money launderers: Beneficial ownership transparency and PEPs: *Solicitors Regulation Authority v Sharif*, (2019) 31(1) *Denning Law Journal* 189–97.

Hatchard, John, Presidential removal: Unzipping the Constitutional Provisions, (2000) 44 *Journal of African Law* 1.

Hatchard, John, Recent developments in combating the bribery of foreign public officials: a cause for optimism? (2007) 85 *University of Detroit-Mercy Law Review* 1.

Hatchard John, The role, independence and accountability of the Auditor General: A comparative analysis, (2018) 30(2) *Denning Law Journal* 51.

High Level Panel, *Illicit Financial Flows: Report of the High Level Panel on Illicit Financial Flows from Africa*, 2015.

Holtmeier, Jay, Cross-border corruption enforcement: a case for measured coordination among multiple enforcement authorities, (2015) 84 *Fordham LR* 493.

International Monetary Fund (IMF), *Fiscal Monitoring: Curbing Corruption*, 2019.

International Monetary Fund (IMF), *Republic of Mozambique: Diagnostic Report on Transparency, Governance and Corruption*, 2019.

Irwin, A, J Slay, J Choo, and L Lui, Money laundering and terrorist financing in virtual environments: a feasible study, (2014) 17(1) *JMLC* 50–77.

Jalloh, Charles, A classification of the crimes in the Malabo Protocol, in Jalloh Charles, Clarke Kamari and Nmehielle Vincent (eds), *The African Court of Justice and Human and Peoples' Rights in Context: Development and Challenges*, Cambridge University Press, 2019.

Kehinde, S, The immunity clause under the Nigerian 1999 Constitution, (2016) *The Lawyers Chronicle.*

Kelleher, John, and Paul Sugden, Money laundering in Jersey: a case analysis: *Att Gen v Bhojwani*, [2011] *Jersey and Guernsey Law Review.*

Kenya, Republic of *Report of the Judicial Commission of Enquiry in the Goldenberg Affair*, Nairobi, 2005.

Klug, Heinz, Accountability and the role of independent constitutional institutions in South Africa's post-apartheid constitutions, (2015–2016) 60 *New York Law School Law Review* 153.

Knobel, Andres, 'The Achilles heel of effective beneficial ownership registration: Why is everyone fixed on 25%?', Tax Justice Network, 2017.

Knobel, Andres, Moran Harari and Markus Meinzer, 'The state of play of beneficial ownership registration: A visual overview', Tax Justice Network, 2018.

KPMG, *Anti-Bribery and Corruption: Rising to the Challenge in the Age of Globalization*, 2015.

Kreutner, Martin, 10 guiding principles and parameters on the nation of anti-corruption bodies, in Martin Kreutner (ed.), *Practice Meets Science, Contemporary Anti-Corruption Dialogue*, Vienna, IACSS, 2010.

Larranga, Lucio Fabiani, 'Double Jeopardy? Siemens Defendant Loses Argentina Dismissal Motion', The FCPA blog, 21 July 2015.

MENAFATF (Middle East & North Africa Financial Action Task Force), *Islamic Republic of Mauritania: Mutual Evaluation Report*, Manama, 2018.

MENAFATF, *Money Laundering and Terrorist Financing Trends and Indicators in the Middle East and North Africa Region-Update*, 2013.

MENAFATF, *Politically Exposed Persons in Relation to AML/CFT*, 2008.

MENAFATF, *Typologies Report on Money Laundering and Corruption*, 2017.

Mitchell, James F, *A Season of Light*, Concepts Publishing, 2001.

Mniwasa, Eugene, The financial intelligence unit and money laundering control in Tanzania, (2019) 22(3) *JMLC* 543–62.
Muhia, Jane, 'Key Legal Provisions in the Exercise of the Presidential Power of Mercy in Kenya', Nairobi, 2016.
Murungu, C Bhoke, Towards a criminal chamber in the African Court of Justice and Human Rights, (2011) 9(5) *Journal of International Criminal Justice* 1067.
Mwinga, Katai, 'The process of removing the immunity of a former President: The Zambian experience', Inter-Parliamentary Union, 2014.
National Crime Authority, *Taken to the Cleaners: Money Laundering in Australia*, Canberra, 1991.
Nesti, Lorenzo, The 2010 'Agreement on Mutual Enforcement of Debarment Decisions' and its impact for the fight against fraud and corruption in public procurement, (2014) 14(1) *Journal of Public Procurement* 62–95.
Nicholls, Colin, Tim Daniel, Alan Bacarese, James Maton and John Hatchard, *Corruption and Misuse of Public Office*, 2nd edn., Oxford University Press, 2011.
Nicholls, Colin, Tim Daniel, Alan Bacarese, James Maton and John Hatchard, *Corruption and Misuse of Public Office*, 3rd edn., Oxford University Press, 2017.
Noseda, Fillipo, Too much information: When the UK gets it wrong, (2017) 21(2) *Jersey and Guernsey Law Review* 182.
Novak, Andrew, *Comparative Executive Clemency: The Constitutional Pardon Power and the Prerogative of Mercy in Global Perspective*, Routledge, 2016.
Obermeyer, Bastien, and Frederik Obermaier, *The Panama Papers*, OneWorld, London, 2016.
OECD (Organisation for Economic Cooperation and Development), *Behind the Corporate Veil: Using Corporate Entities for Illicit Purposes*, Paris, 2001.
OECD, *Foreign Bribery Report: An Analysis of the Crime of Bribery of Foreign Public Officials*, 2014.
OECD, *Working Group on Bribery Annual Report*, Paris, 2011.
Olivier, Piet, 'Crime and Punishment (and Presidential Pardons): Does the Constitution Permit the Pardoning of the Corrupt?', Helen Suzman Foundation. 2016.
Pieth, Mark, Lucinda Low and Nicola Bonucci, *The OECD Convention on Bribery: A Commentary*, 2nd edn., Cambridge University Press, 2014.
Pinard, Michael, Collateral consequences of criminal convictions: Confronting issues of race and dignity, (2010) 85 *New York University Law Journal* 457.
Rai, J P, Exercise of the pardoning power in India: emerging challenges, (2014) XII(2) *NEHU Journal* 1–26.
Report of Nigeria National Risk Assessment on Money Laundering and Terrorism Financing 2016, Abuja, 2016.
Revenue Watch Institute/Transparency International, *Promoting Revenue Transparency: 2011 Report on Oil and Gas Companies*, 2011.
Roberts-Wray, Sir Kenneth, *Commonwealth and Colonial Law*, Sweet & Maxwell, 1966.
Rose, Cecily, Money laundering and the African Court of Justice and Human and Peoples' Rights, in Jalloh Charles, Clarke Kamari and Nmehielle Vincent (eds), *The African Court of Justice and Human and Peoples' Rights in Context: Development and Challenges*, Cambridge University Press, 2019, p. 505.
Sackett, Lee-Anne, Vanuatu Constitutional Cases Nos 6 and 7 of 2015: Article 38 Pardons and Multilingual Legal Interpretation Principles, [2015] (2) *Journal of South Pacific Law* 1.

Sebba, Leslie, The pardoning power: a world survey, (1977) 68 *Journal of Criminal Law and Criminology* 83.

Simwayi, Musonda and Muhammed Haseed, The role of Financial Intelligence Units in combating money laundering: A comparative analysis of Zambia, Zimbabwe and Malawi, (2012) 15(1) *JMLC* 112–34.

Sirleaf, M, The African Justice Cascade and the Malabo Protocol, (2019) 11(1) *International Journal of Transitional Justice* 71.

Soopramanien, Shalini, Explaining the unexplained wealth orders: (Mauritius) Good Governance and Integrity Reporting Act 2015, (2018) 39(1) *Statute Law Review* 46.

Southern African Catholic Bishops' Conference, *The African Court of Justice and Human Rights: Protecting Africans, or Just Africa's Leaders?* 2014.

StAR (Stolen Assets Recovery) Initiative, *Politically Exposed Persons: Preventive Measures for the Banking Sector*, Washington DC, 2012.

StAR (Stolen Assets Recovery) Initiative, *The Puppet Masters: How the Corrupt Use Legal Structures to Hide Stolen Assets and What to Do About It*, Washington DC, 2011.

Tax Justice Network, *Financial Secrecy Index: Key Financial Secrecy Indicator 2: Trust and Foundation Register*, 2020.

Thompson II, Richard M, 'The President's Pardon Power and Legal Effects on Collateral Consequences', Congressional Research Service, 2016.

Transparency International, *Corruption on Your Doorstep: How Corrupt Capital is Used to Buy Property in the UK*, London, 2016.

Transparency International, *Corruption Perceptions Index 2019*, London, 2019.

Transparency International, *Exporting Corruption: Progress Report 2018*, London, 2018.

Transparency International (UK), *Out of the Shadows: Promoting Openness and Accountability in the Global Defence Industry*, London, 2016.

United States, Department of Justice, *FCPA: A Resource Guide to the US Foreign Corrupt Practices Act*, DoJ, Washington DC, 2015.

United States, Department of State, *International Narcotics Control Strategy Report*, 2018.

United States, Senate Permanent Subcommittee on Investigations Committee on Homeland Security and Governmental Affairs *Keeping Foreign Corruption Out of the United States: Four Case Histories*, 2010.

Viljoen, Frans, A human rights court for Africa and Africans, (2004) 30(1) *Brooklyn Journal of International Law* 1.

Whisker, James and Mark Lokanan, *Anti-money laundering and counter-terrorist threats posed by mobile money*, (2019) 22(1) *JMLC* 158–72.

World Bank Group, *Guidelines: Procurement of Goods, Works, and Non-Consulting Services under IBRD Loans and IDA Credits & Grants by World Bank Borrowers*, 2011, updated 2014.

Yilmaz, Serder and Yakub Beris, Good governance and the emergence of a new accountability agenda, in Gabor Peteri (ed.), *Finding the Money: Public Accountability and Service Efficiency through Fiscal Transparency*, Open Society Initiative, 2008.

Young, Simon N M, Why civil actions against corruption? (2009) *Journal of Financial Crime* 144.

Zambia Financial Intelligence Centre, *5th Money Laundering and Terrorist Financing Trends Report 2018*, Lusaka, 2018.

Index